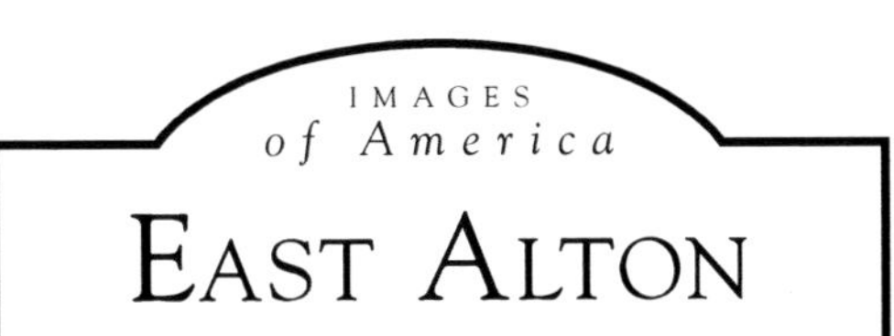
IMAGES
of America
EAST ALTON

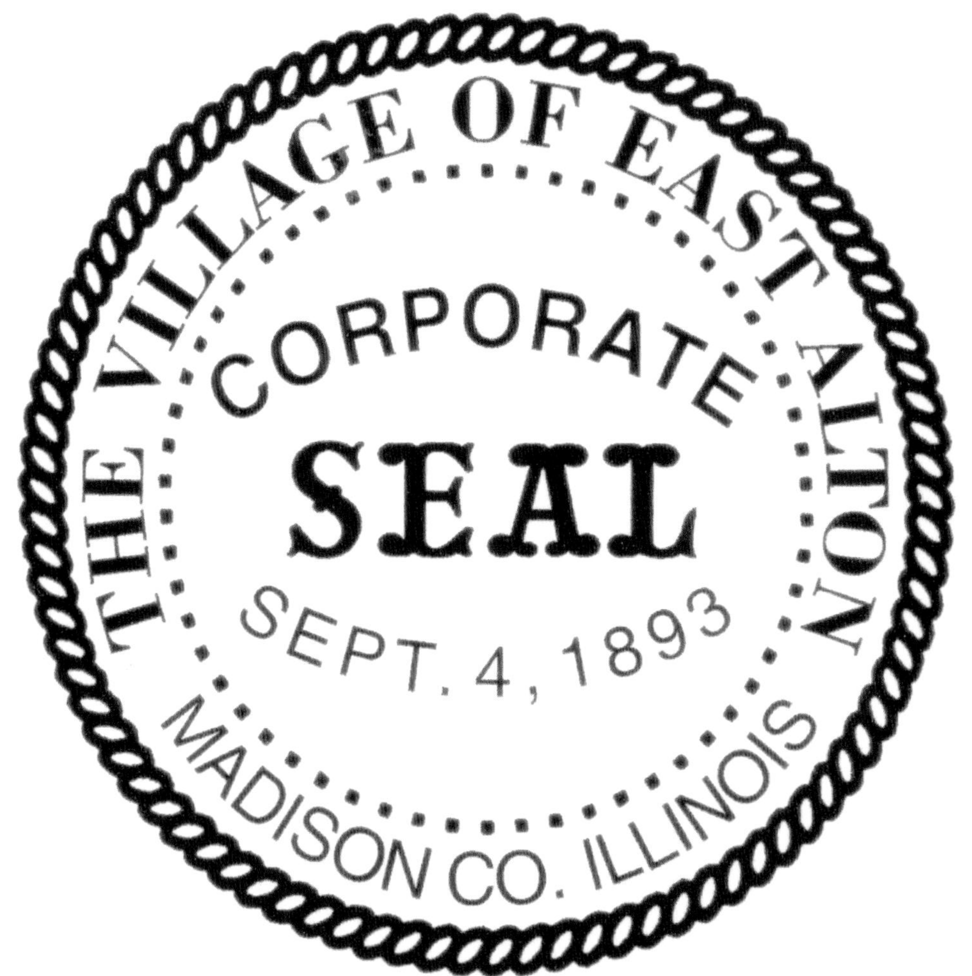

The city seal was designed by the president and board of trustees in September 1893. The ordinance adopting the seal was signed by the first president (mayor), David G. Tomlinson. (Courtesy of East Alton Historical Museum.)

On the Cover: This viaduct is the second at this location on West St. Louis Avenue. It was installed in the 1920s, serving until it was replaced by the present viaduct in 1990. This viaduct caused many problems due to flooding from large rains and to 18-wheel semi-trucks getting stuck under it. (Courtesy of East Alton Historical Museum.)

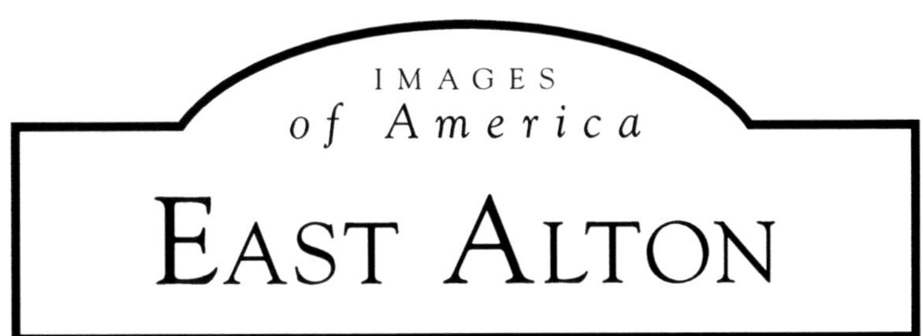

Jason D. Bricker and Judith M. Richie

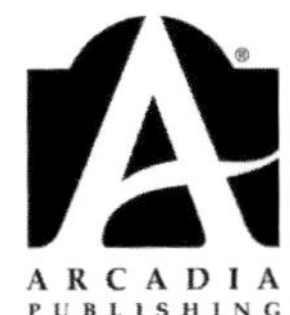

ISBN 978-1-4671-2573-4

Published by Arcadia Publishing
Charleston, South Carolina

Printed in the United States of America

Library of Congress Control Number: 2016960214

For all general information, please contact Arcadia Publishing:
Telephone 843-853-2070
Fax 843-853-0044
E-mail sales@arcadiapublishing.com
For customer service and orders:
Toll-Free 1-888-313-2665

Visit us on the Internet at www.arcadiapublishing.com

This book is dedicated to Merrill Rosenthal, who taught generations of students at East Alton Junior High and preserved the rich history of East Alton.

Contents

Foreword

One of the many joys about living in a small town is listening to the old-timers tell the stories of days gone by. The conversation would usually end with comments about the need to preserve our history. Then life went on as everyone remained busy with their day-to-day obligations. As the day approached that I would become mayor of East Alton, I remembered the many conversations I heard about the history of our village. It occurred to me that this was an opportunity to appoint the History Committee to work on preserving East Alton history. I knew there was a small, core group of residents that were eager to save our history. What I was amazed by was the number of residents who immediately expressed interest in the History Committee. These residents included current citizens of East Alton and some who have since moved out of town but still have a love for the village. It only took a few months to realize that this committee would be able to gather enough history to open a museum. I thought this was fantastic but quickly learned that there was more to come.

As the committee quickly grew in size and enthusiasm, I was pleasantly surprised that committee members Judy Richie and Jason Bricker decided to explore authoring this book. A simple picture from the past can start a discussion that will last as long as at least two people make the time. The cliché that every picture tells a thousand words is so true when looking at historical pictures. This is a book that can be read individually or looked at by several people at once. Depending on who you are, when looking at the book each picture will tell different and numerous stories. I am excited about this village of East Alton history book—every page will be an opportunity for the readers to reflect on their version of time that the photograph reflects. The young reader will have a unique opportunity to explore the history of our community, whether they live here or are just passing through.

Incorporated on September 4, 1893, the village of East Alton has a proud history. I am glad that you have taken some time to reflect on the past as it guides us into the future.

—Joe Silkwood
Mayor

ACKNOWLEDGMENTS

This book is a photographic journey through the village of East Alton's history, from the early 1800s through the present. It tells the stories of many of the people, businesses, schools, churches, homes, organizations, and events that shaped the village. It makes every attempt to recount the information relayed to the authors from citizens, newspapers, and research as accurately as possible. This publication does not intend to omit important events but can only preserve information made known to the authors. For the best possible historical credibility, the information in the book has been reviewed by multiple sources.

This book could not be written without the numerous contributions from residents and nonresidents interested in preserving East Alton history. Mayor Joe Silkwood, a lifelong resident, realized a need to preserve East Alton history and encouraged the beginning of a history museum. Through the beginning of the museum, photographs, memorabilia, newspaper articles, stories, and research into those items sparked the interest in writing this book.

We want to thank numerous individuals who have contributed photographs, newspaper articles, diaries, and information for this project, which will be added to the East Alton Historical Museum. We also want to thank the director of East Alton Public Library, Richard Chartrand, for his guidance during this project; Lacy McDonald, history manager at Hayner Public Library, for her research and expertise on setting up the new museum; Beverly Bauser at Madison County Genealogy for her valuable research; Alton History Museum; and Graveman Photography for developing glass-plate negatives from the late 1800 and early 1900s and transforming small or unclear photographs into usable images.

We must thank Kathleen Robison and Loretta Haydon Silkwood for technical support; volunteers for proofreading and research; and Janice Carver and Tim Ross for the sketches. All the photographs and research information will be added to the East Alton Historical Museum.

Unless otherwise credited, the photographs in this book are from the archives of the East Alton Historical Museum.

INTRODUCTION

Settlements of pioneers from Virginia and the Carolinas occurred here during the earliest days of Madison County, which was formed in 1812. Though no precise date exists for the settlement of what now lies slightly west of the old heart of East Alton, it was in 1808 that two men laid out a one-half square mile parcel of land in Section 17 of Wood River Township, then called Upper Alton Township. Walter Seely and John Wallace called the town Milton. In Milton, below the forks of the Wood River, the ancestors of many of East Alton's citizens began their fight for survival in Illinois. Milton contained two sawmills, a grist (flour) mill, a distillery, a tavern, a blacksmith shop, and a store. Milton had a population of about 50 people. A dam was built across the river to run the sawmills, which were located on opposite sides of the river.

Reverend Thomas and Henrietta Lippencott were early settlers in Milton. In 1819, she was instrumental in organizing the first Sunday school in Illinois with 20 children. The passing of Milton appears to have been caused mainly by illness, which was blamed on the pestilential air. The dam that provided water to run the mills caused stagnant water, which probably attracted a large number of mosquitoes. The disease, called milk sickness, came from the milk of cows and claimed Henrietta as one of its first victims. The year 1820 was very hot in the summer and very cold in the winter, which heightened the illnesses. Many who survived the illness moved on to other lands—some only as far as the sandy bottom lands, known as the American Bottoms, on the other side of the river, settling in what is now East Alton. After the death of Henrietta, Thomas moved the family to St. Louis. Not much was known about the settlement after that.

At the beginning of the War of 1812, the settlers built a blockhouse for protection. Beeman's Fort was in Section 21, about a mile south of Milton. The most remembered event of this early settlement was the Wood River Massacre, which occurred on July 10, 1814, when Rachel Reagan, her two children, two children of Abel Moore, and two children of William Moore were massacred by hostile Indians.

In 1853, George A. Smith, George W. Carr, and George Smith purchased what is the original plot of what is now known as East Alton for $2,450, approximately $15.31 per acre. On October 26, 1854, George and Sally Smith sold their interest to George A. Smith and George W. Carr. On June 27, 1859, George A. Smith, George W. Carr, and Clara Carr, known as G.W. Carr and Company, sold lots 13 to 20 to John Delno. On March 23, 1860, Jeremiah Danaan purchased lots 11 and 12 in the town of Emerald. This is the first permanent settlement of the village.

The railroads had a great influence on the settling of East Alton. In the late 1830s, the Alton & Shawneetown Railroad and the Illinois & St. Louis Railroad were started and used Alton Junction as a transfer and stock feed point. The Irish came with the railroad boom, settling in the area. They gave the area its first name of Emerald and named the main street Shamrock. The railroad people, not being local, referred to the town as Alton Junction because of the junction or cut-off to Alton between St. Louis and Chicago, New York, and other points east. Early atlases identified the area by both names.

From 1837 to 1854, the Chicago & Alton, the Indianapolis & St. Louis, and the Terre Haute & St. Louis Railroads combined and were known as the "Bee Line." In 1868, the Cincinnati, Cleveland, Chicago & St Louis Railroad, the Big Four, became known with through trains from St. Louis to New York. More familiar to locals was a train between Alton and East Alton that made travel easier than the roads of the day. The locals called this train the "Plug." It continued until March 3, 1939.

The worst train wreck in Illinois, the Wann Disaster, occurred on January 21, 1893, at the Alton Junction. The *Southwestern Limited* 109 was running late going into Wann (another local name for the junction) and came upon an open switch. The train crashed into a freight train with oil cars, causing a huge explosion. Residents tried to help rescue the people on the train, but 41 lost their lives and at least 75 were injured, many of them seriously.

While religious groups flourished in Madison County, the first church to be organized was First Baptist Church, named Wann Baptist, on July 2, 1891. Prior to its organization, prayer and worship services were held in homes or the one-room school of Blackjack, also known as Emerald.

As early as 1878, pioneers recognized the business potential of the Alton Junction/Emerald area, which was rich in natural resources. The Stoneware Pipe Company was one of the earliest manufacturing concerns. In the 1870s, Zephaniah B. Job built a driving park (similar to harness races of today). In 1892, Franklin W. Olin purchased land from Z.B. Job and built the Western Cartridge Company. By 1893, the plant was operational. In 1904, Beal Brothers established the Beal Tool plant.

By August 1893, Alton Junction had outgrown its unorganized days, and the leaders of the community voted for incorporation. There were 43 votes cast, 41 to incorporate, one against, and one defective ballot. The new village was to be known as East Alton.

On April 2, 1900, a fire started in the store and dwelling of J.B. VanPreter, spreading to the store and dwelling of William Clarke. The fire continued to spread to other buildings and businesses, destroying most of downtown. The Wood River had flooded, leaving a large pool of water when the flood subsided. Buckets of water were taken from the pool to extinguish the fire. After the fire, business owners rebuilt the business district. Flooding has always been a problem for the village. In 1902, Wood River flooded, covering approximately 10,000 acres, again damaging downtown businesses and washing away farm buildings.

Women played an important part in East Alton's growth. In 1906, Thomas and Elizabeth VanPreter established a general merchandise store with Elizabeth a common figure in her wagon, peddling goods. Florence Day came to East Alton after her husband's death in 1903. She was a teacher and principal until her retirement. She was responsible for starting the Parent Teacher Association, Mother's Club, and hot lunches at schools. Alice Job, daughter of Z.B. Job, went to Paris to study art and traveled extensively, becoming a renowned artist.

World War I was a booming time in East Alton. In January 1914, H.J. Bowman Jr. signed a contract with the French and British governments to provide horses for the war. A stockyard was established on the old Job Ranch with approximately 250,000 horses shipped overseas.

With the vision of the founding fathers, East Alton has continued to grow from incorporation through the 1990s, adding businesses, schools, police and fire departments, a new village hall, a library, a bank, and a post office.

One

It Takes a Village

The first settlement in the vicinity of East Alton that was known by name was the town of Milton. The exact date of its settlement is not definitely known but is believed to be around 1808. John Wallace and Walter Seeley laid out the town, which consisted of two sawmills, a gristmill, a distillery, a tavern, and a store, with a population of 50 people. A dam was built across the Wood River to provide water to run the mills.

At the beginning of the War of 1812, the settlers built Beeman's Fort for their protection. Because Indians had not been sighted, the six or eight families residing at the forks of Wood River moved back to their farms. On July 10, 1814, Rachel Reagan, her two children, two children of Abel Moore, and two children of William Moore were massacred by hostile Indians. After the Wood River Massacre, life settled down.

Rev. Thomas and Henrietta Lippincott were early settlers in Milton. In 1819, she was instrumental in organizing the first Sunday school in the state. Milk sickness took Henrietta, and the year of sickness was the beginning of the end of Milton. By 1820, the town was abandoned.

Not much is known about the settlement until in 1853. Far-sighted George A. Smith, George W. Carr, and George Smith realized the settlement was there to stay. They platted a tract of land containing 180 acres in the east half of Section 16. This is the first permanent settlement of the village.

As early as 1878, businessmen recognized the potential of the Alton Junction/Emerald area. The Stoneware Pipe Company was one of the earliest manufacturing concerns. In 1892, Franklin W. Olin purchased land from Z.B. Job to build the Western Cartridge Company.

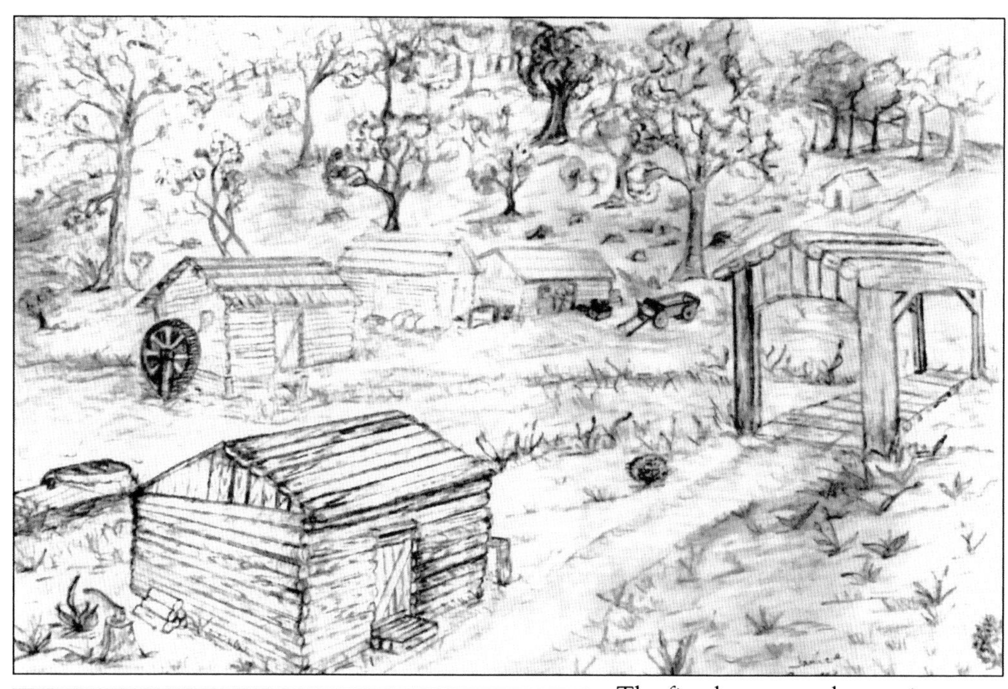

The first known settlement in the vicinity of East Alton was Milton, situated below the forks of the Wood River. The exact date of the settlement is not known, but it is believed to be 1808 or 1809. This partial sketch by Janice Carver depicts the Milton settlement in 1808.

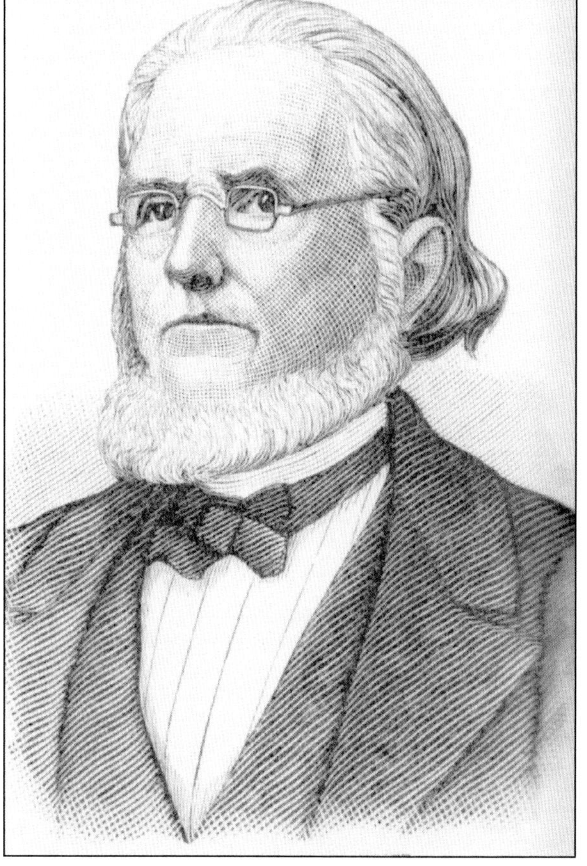

Pictured around 1809, Rev. Thomas Lippincott, an early member of the Milton settlement, was later an apostle of freedom. He worked with Gov. Edward Coles in resisting the attempt to make Illinois a slave state. He also owned a store at Milton under the name of Lippincott and Company.

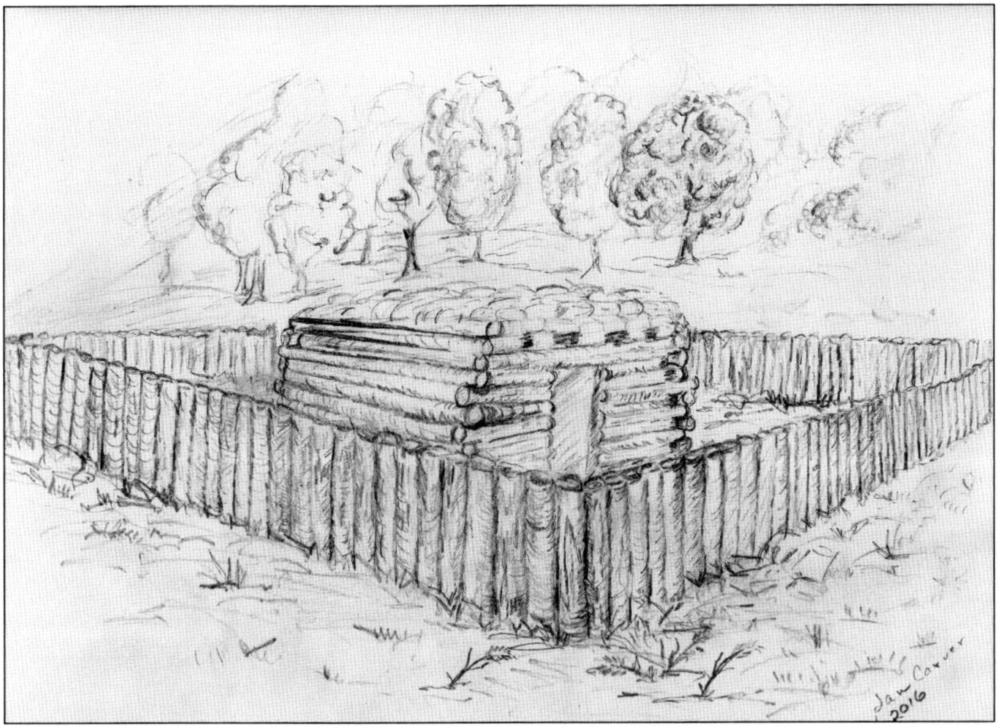

A civilian fortress was built by James Beeman in 1811. The fort was in Section 21, about one mile south of the old town of Milton. During the War of 1812, the fort was used for protection from hostile Indians. The Wood River Massacre claimed seven victims in July 1814. The fort was used from June 20, 1811, to July 10, 1814. This sketch by Janice Carver depicts the Beeman Fort in 1811.

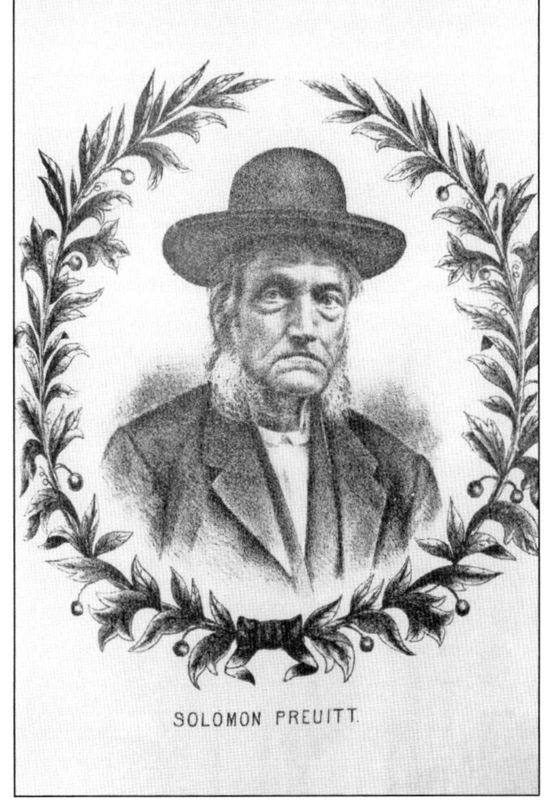

Maj. Solomon Preuitt (also spelled Prewitt or Pruitt), born in 1790, was one of the earliest settlers of Madison County. Older abstracts show that the land on which the village stands was given to Preuitt in a land grant by Pres. James Monroe, who held office from 1817 to 1825. Preuitt was a military man, volunteering in 1813 to fight against Great Britain and again in 1831 and 1832 in the Black Hawk War.

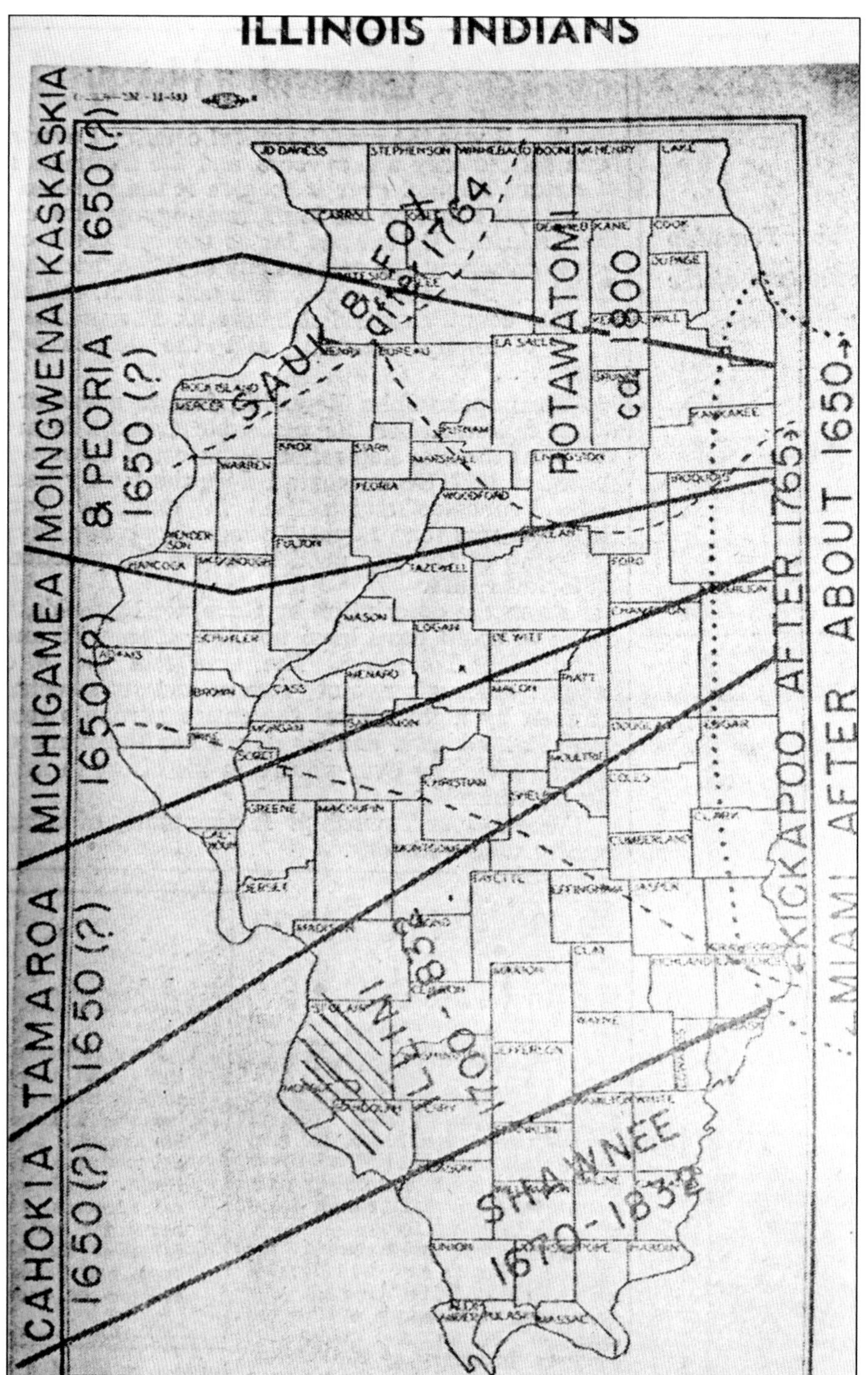

This map indicates the location of Indian tribes in Illinois from the 1650s to the 1800s. The way of life of the Indians was dictated by the natural raw materials available in the area. These resources provided the food, clothing, and houses of the Indians.

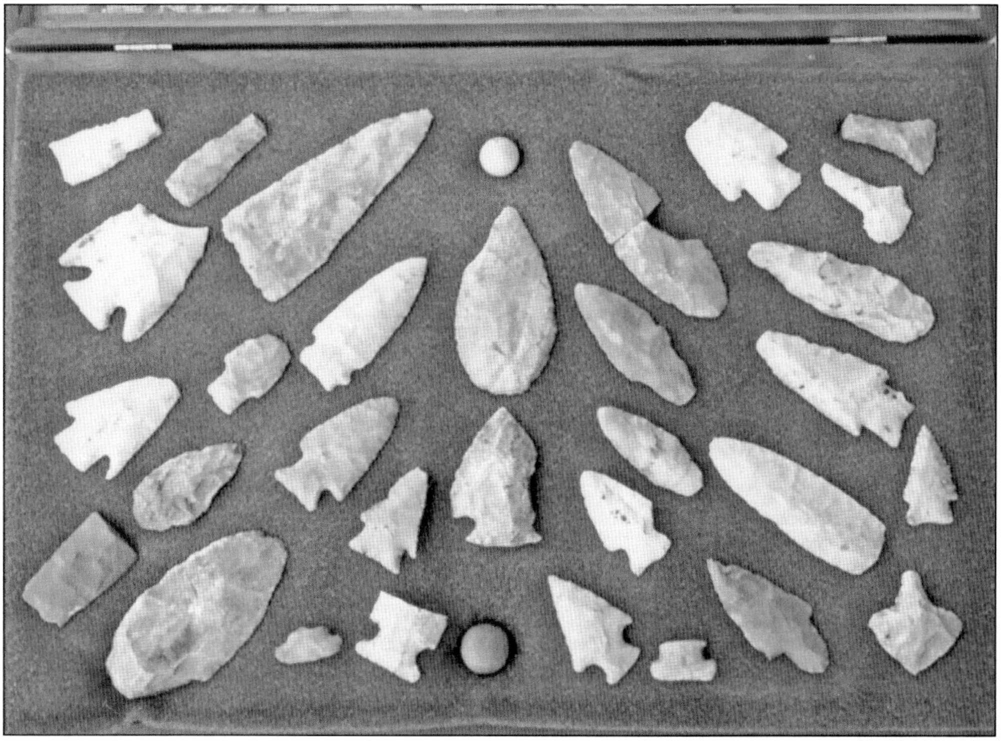

These arrowheads (above) and Indian artifacts (below) were found along the Wood River. The Indians who lived in the area led a Stone Age lifestyle. They had stone tools and weapons made from resources available. (Both, courtesy of Woodrow Peterson.)

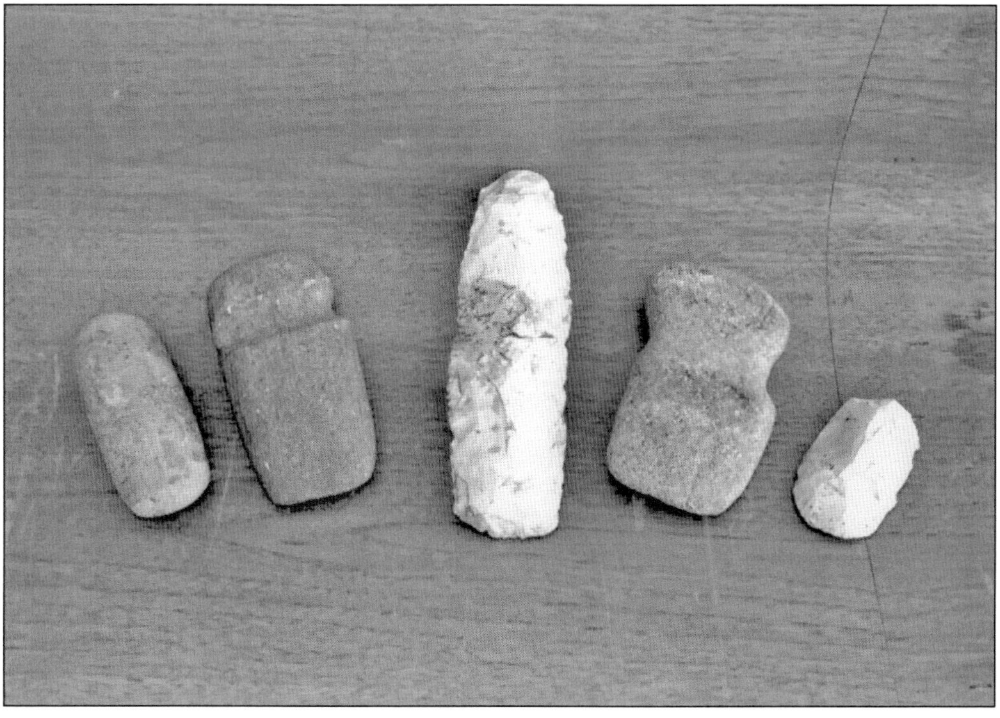

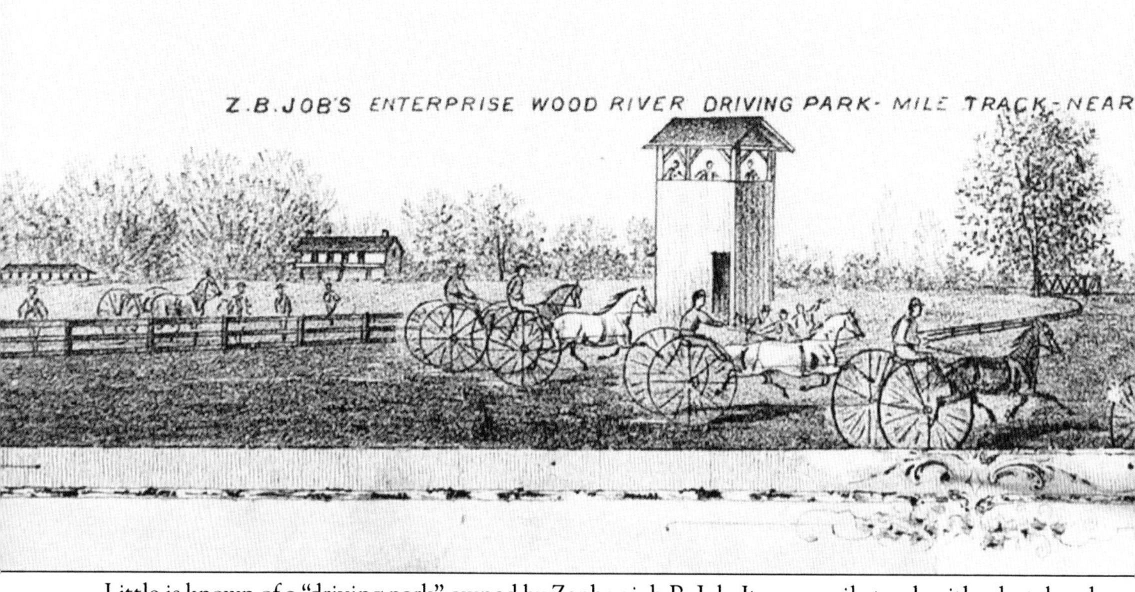

Little is known of a "driving park" owned by Zephaniah B. Job. It was a mile track with a hotel and grandstand and was located on the east side of West St. Louis Avenue between the viaduct and the Wood River, where the present Illinois state offices are located. The races were similar to the

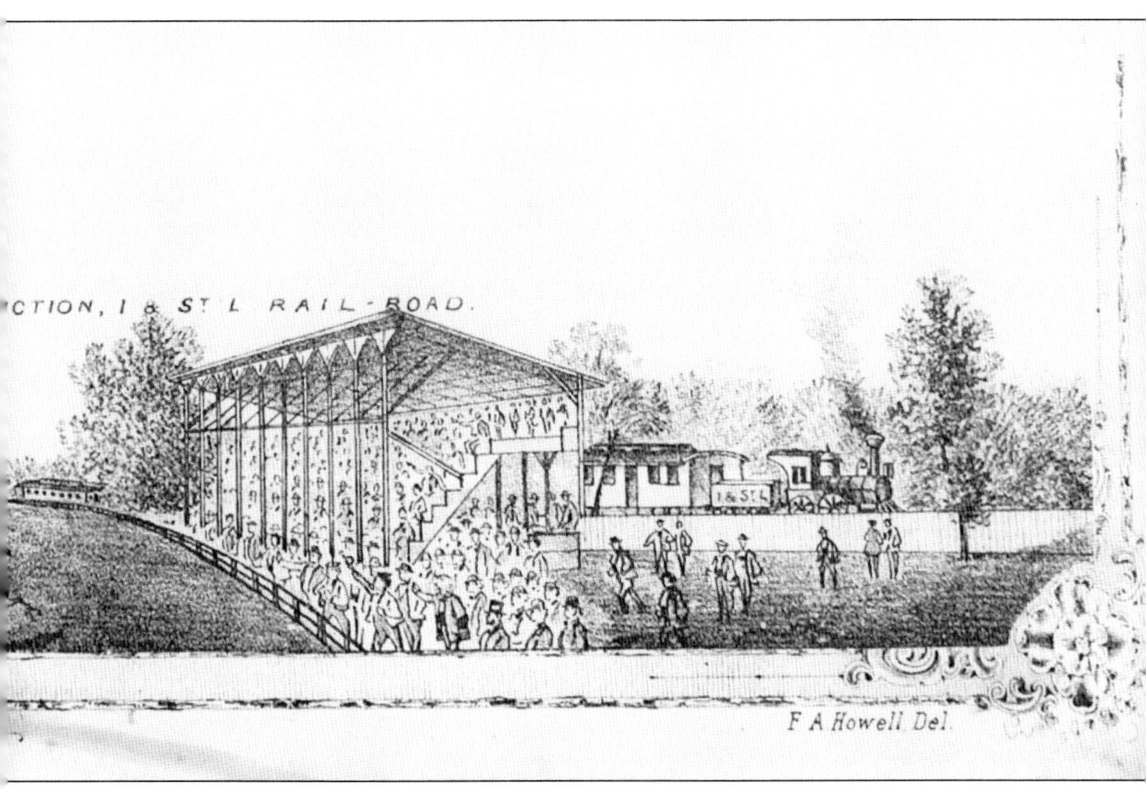

harness races of today. The driving park was in operation in the 1870s. This was the first driving park in Madison County. (Drawings from *History of Madison County, Illinois with Illustrations*, published by Brink, McCormack & Co.)

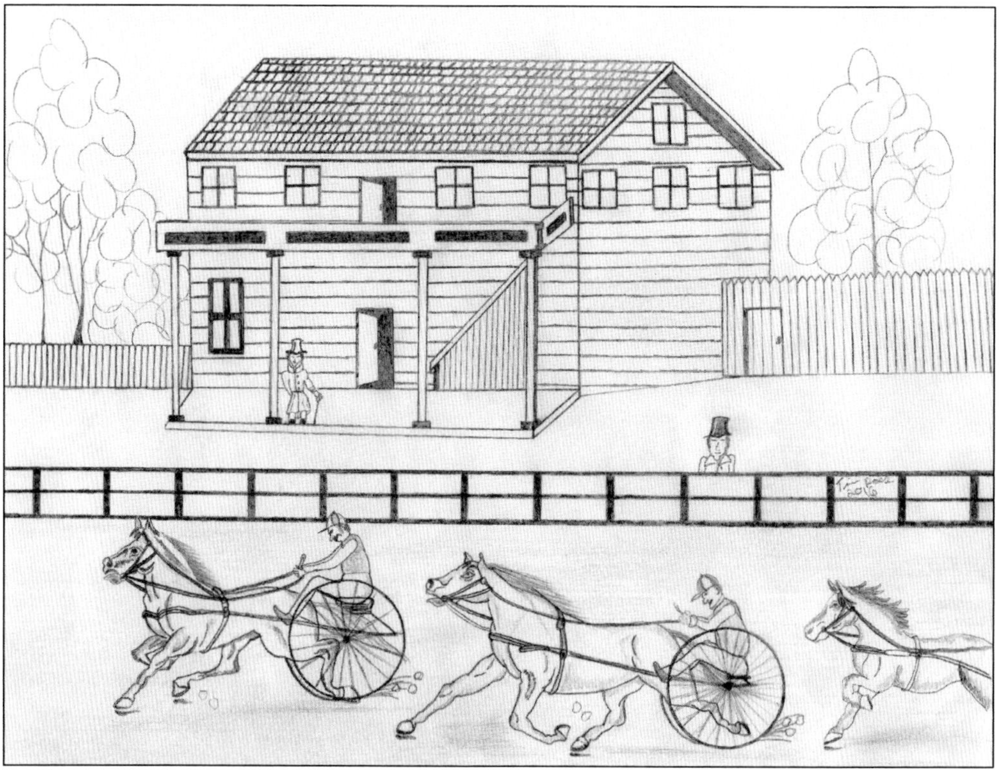

The Driving Park Hotel, owned by Zephaniah B. Job, was located near the driving park between the current viaduct and the Wood River. The hotel was burned down on May 4, 1874, by James Smith and William Clayton. The two men were also charged with attempting to burn the residence of Jacob Koch. It was believed the men were connected to several mysterious fires in the same vicinity. This sketch by Tim Ross depicts the Driving Park Hotel of 1870.

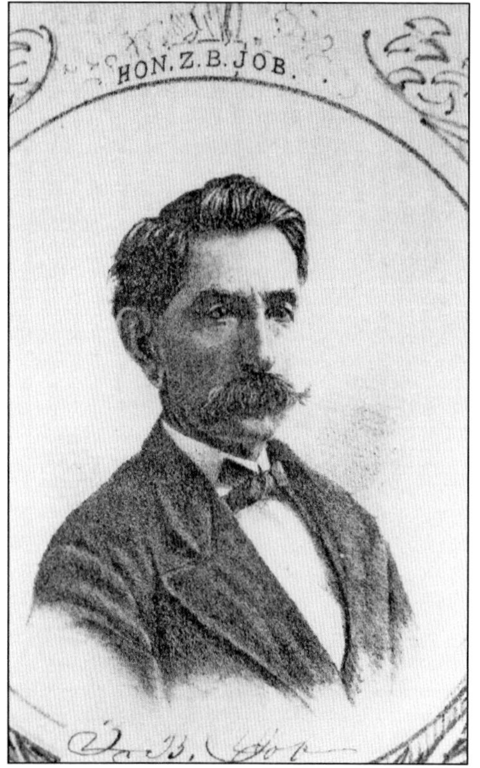

The land east of the Big Four Railroad, where most of the village now lies, was deeded by the government to Zephaniah B. Job in 1856. Job was one of the largest local landholders (with about 900 acres) and played an important part in the village's growth. On July 9, 1892, he sold land to Franklin Olin, who built the Equitable Powder Manufacturing Company on the Wood River. He donated the site for the first church, the First Baptist Church, which was erected on Church Street and completed in 1893. (Courtesy of Hayner Public Library.)

At a time when most women married and stayed home to care for the family, Alice E. Job, daughter of Z.B. Job, struck out for Europe after graduating from Lindenwood College to further her study of painting at the Julian Studio in Paris. She returned to the United States in 1892. In 1895, she went abroad again to paint cherry blossoms in Japan and landscapes in China. Her paintings were displayed in the Fifth Avenue studio of Macbeth Gallery in New York. She again traveled through China, India, and Burma and had the distinction of being the first white woman to make a trip through Tibet with a coolie train.

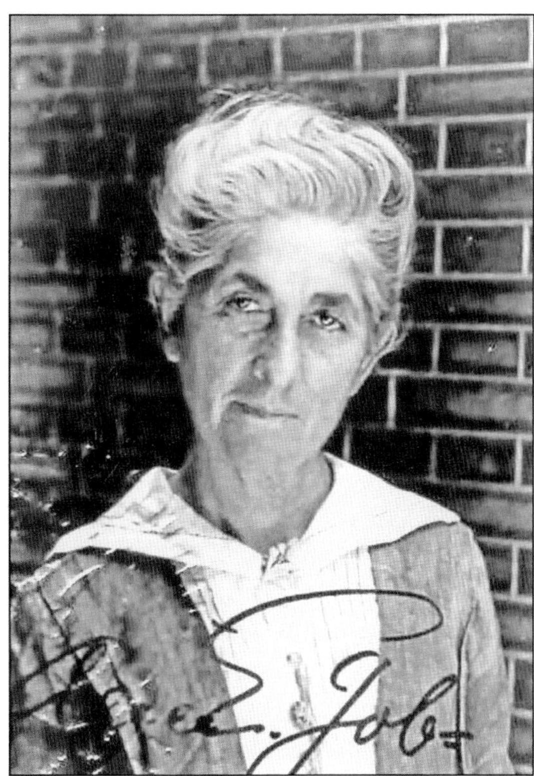

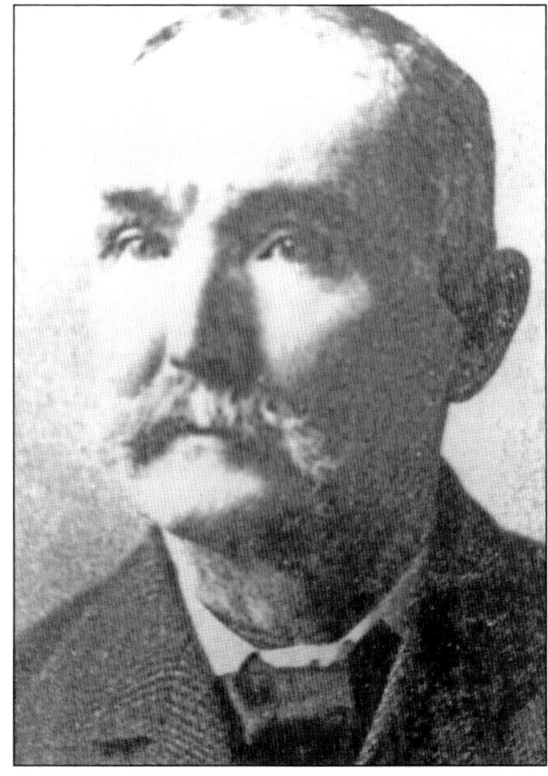

Z.B. Job's nephew Zephaniah B. Silver purchased land from him in 1866. The land lay between the railroad and the present Bowman Avenue and was known as Silver Ridge. Silver donated land for the first school with the provision that it be used for educational purposes. The school eventually served as a community building, church, and voting place. When the village was incorporated in 1893, Silver was elected as a trustee.

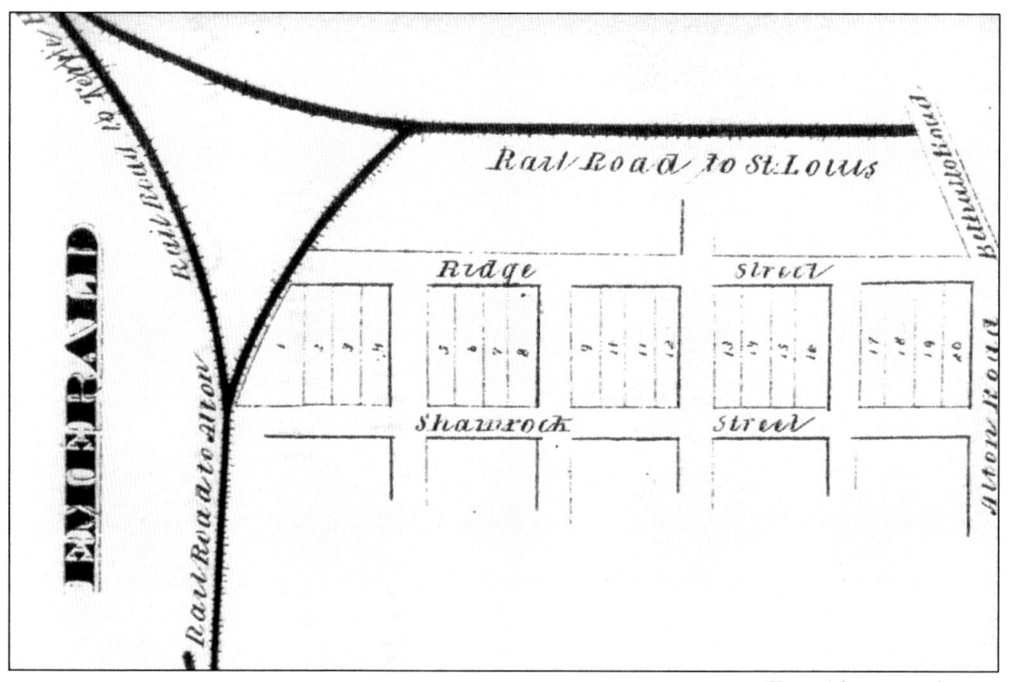

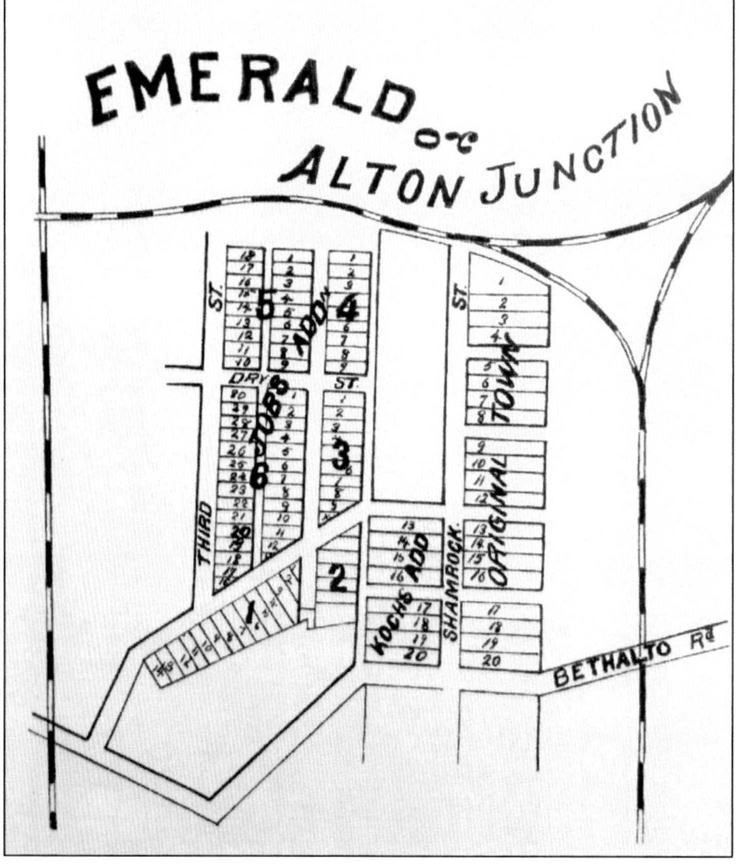

East Alton was first platted with the name of Emerald sometime in the late 1850s or early 1860s. The original town lay between what are now Shamrock and Church Streets east of the Wood River. This is the first known map of Emerald, dated 1873.

In 1865, the village was called Emerald by the locals and Alton Junction by the railroaders. This 1892 map shows the growth of the village with the railroad boom.

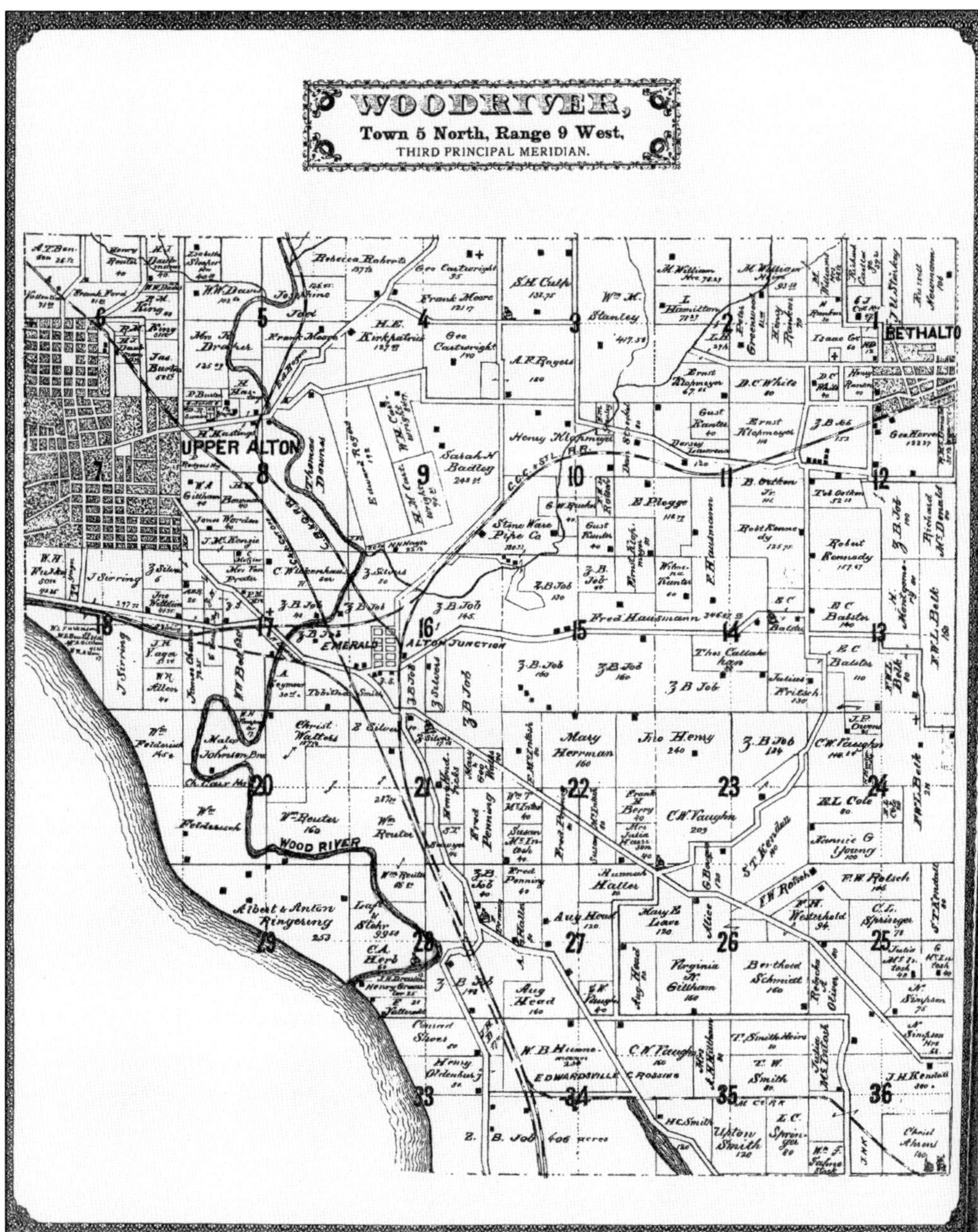

What is now called Wood River Creek was once Wood River. The river could be navigated by boat in the 1800s. This 1892 map shows the path Wood River followed near what was called Niagara. The map also indicates the plats and their owners.

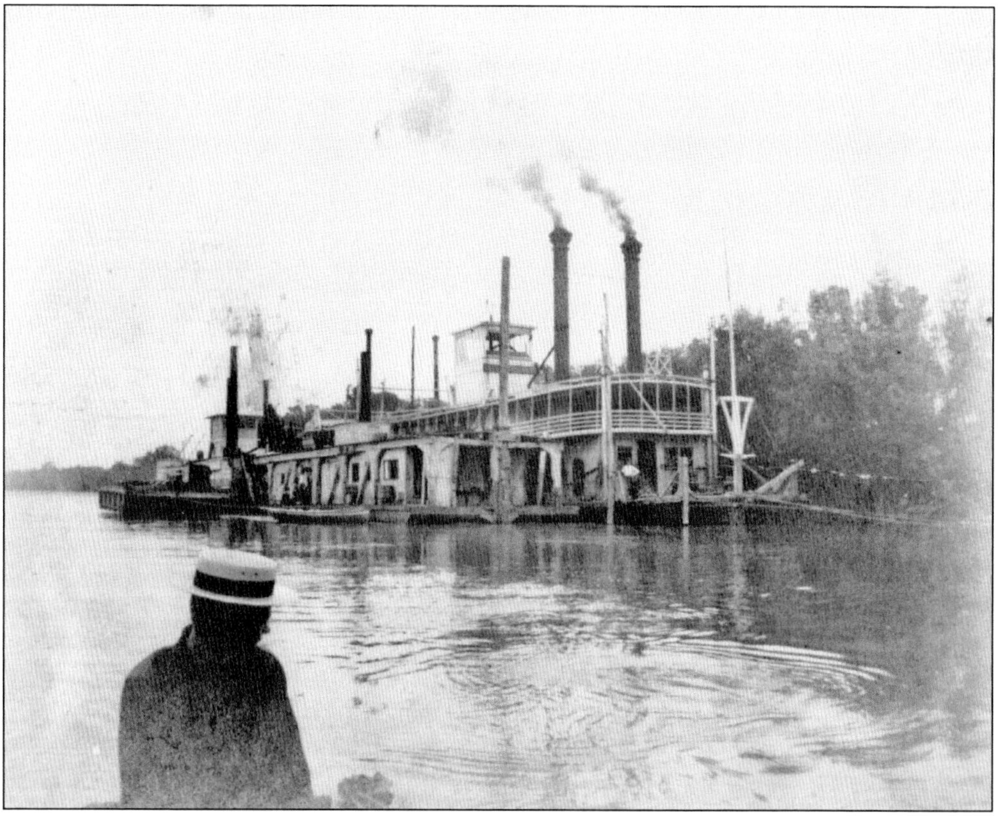

In the late 1800s, steamboats would dock on the Mississippi River near the mouth of the Wood River. A small boat would be attached to the side of the steamboat to offload cargo for delivery to the locals. The small boat would navigate the Wood River to settlements along the river. The people in the picture are unidentified. (Photograph by George H. Ringering, courtesy of the Ringering family.)

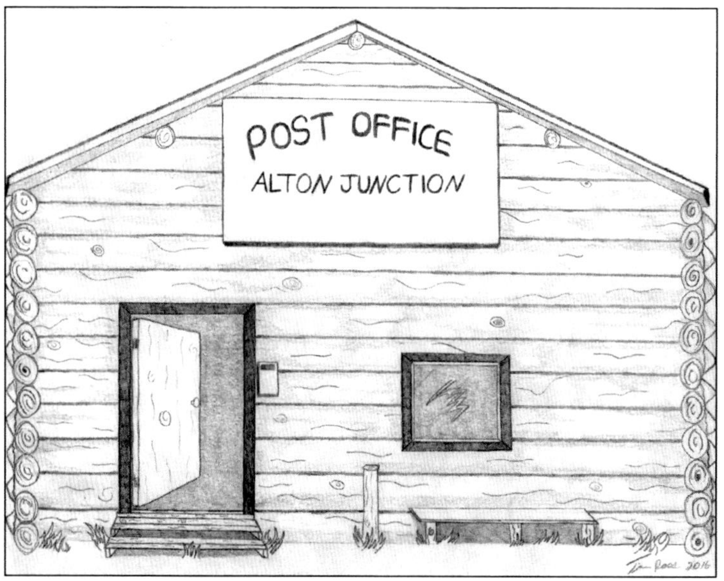

Prior to the first official post office, mail was picked up at the Four Mile House, a tavern located on West St. Louis Avenue where the Ritz Theatre was later housed. On August 17, 1868, a post office was established in Alton Junction. John Koch was the first postmaster and served for eight years. In 1886, Alton Junction had a population of 13. This sketch by Tim Ross depicts the first official post office.

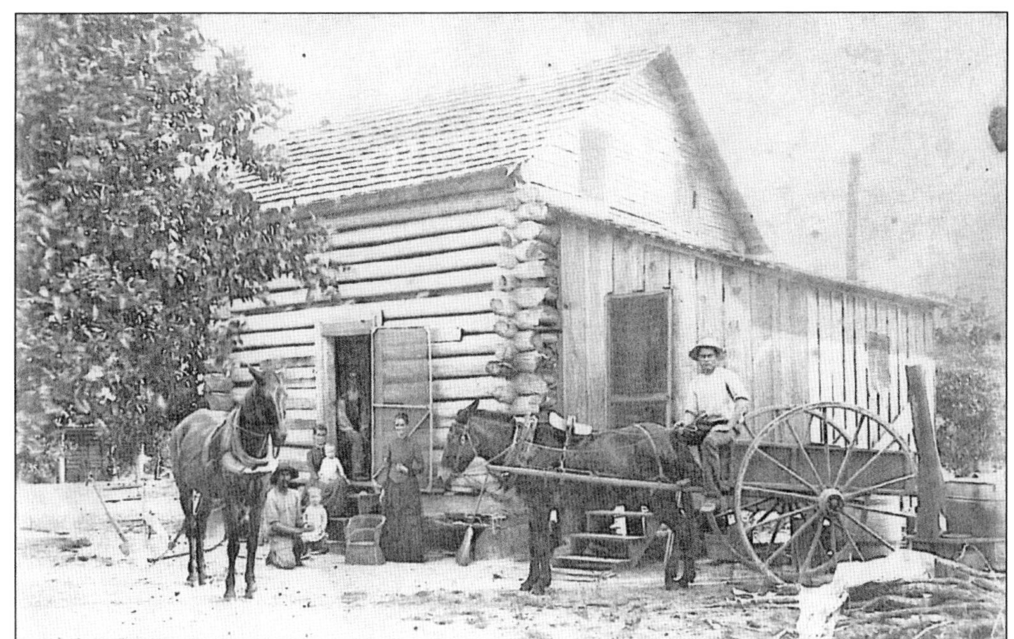

Although travel was difficult, James Weiss, on the left holding the child, and his family traveled to Florida to pick oranges in the 1890s. They returned to East Alton after the crops were picked. On July 6, 1898, he became the first East Alton police officer to lose his life in the line of duty. (Courtesy of Darren Carlton.)

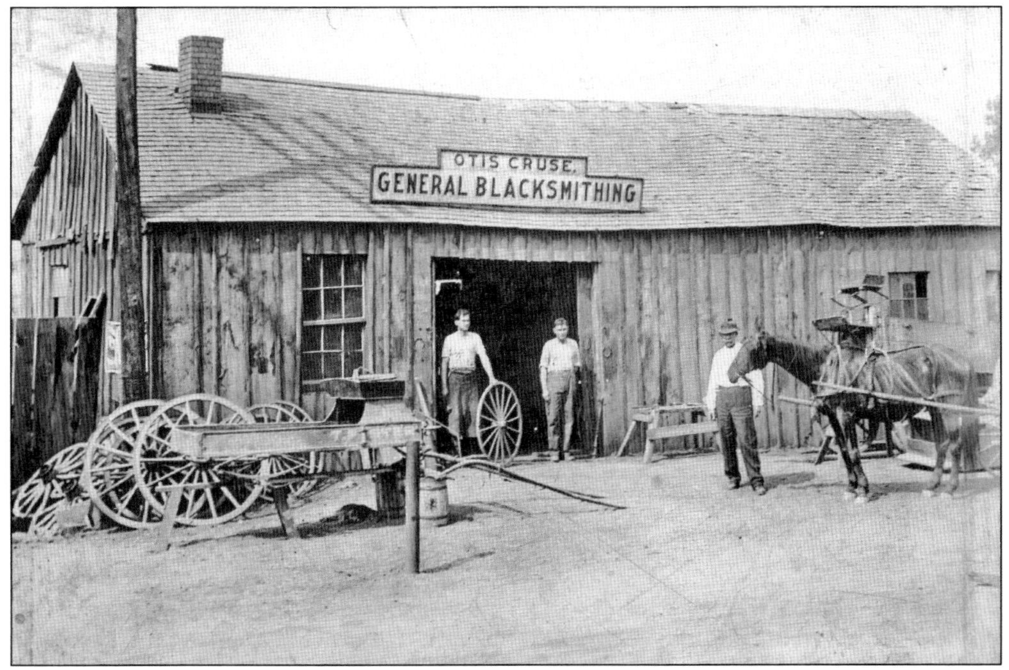

Otis Cruse General Blacksmithing Shop opened in 1882 on the corner of Goulding and West St. Louis Avenues. Pictured are blacksmith Otis Cruse (with his hand on the wheel), helper Frank Ellis, and a client standing by the horse. Due to the changing economy, the shop closed in the 1900s. (Courtesy of Melvin and Shirley McCann, granddaughter of Otis Cruse.)

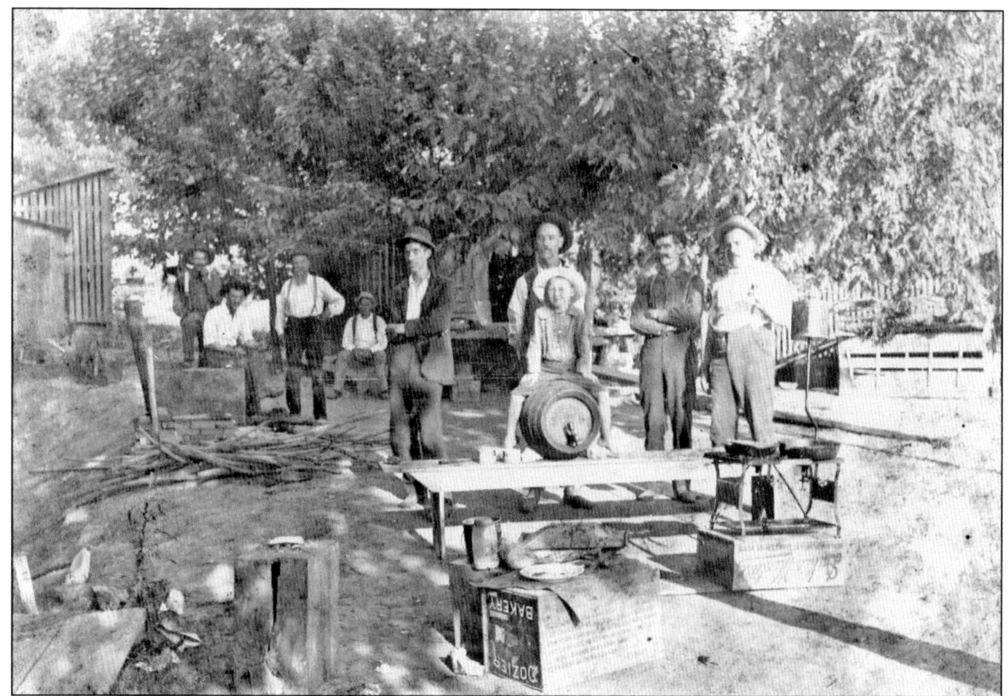

Founding fathers picnic near the close of the century. From left to right are unidentified, George Smith Sr., Henry Neidekorn, Leonard Elble, Edmund Pearce, William Cobb (standing behind the barrel), George Smith Jr. (on the barrel), John Pearce, and Dr. Charles N. Pence. Pence, Cobb, and Smith Sr. were, at separate times, mayors between 1898 and 1907. (Photograph by George H. Ringering, courtesy of the Ringering family.)

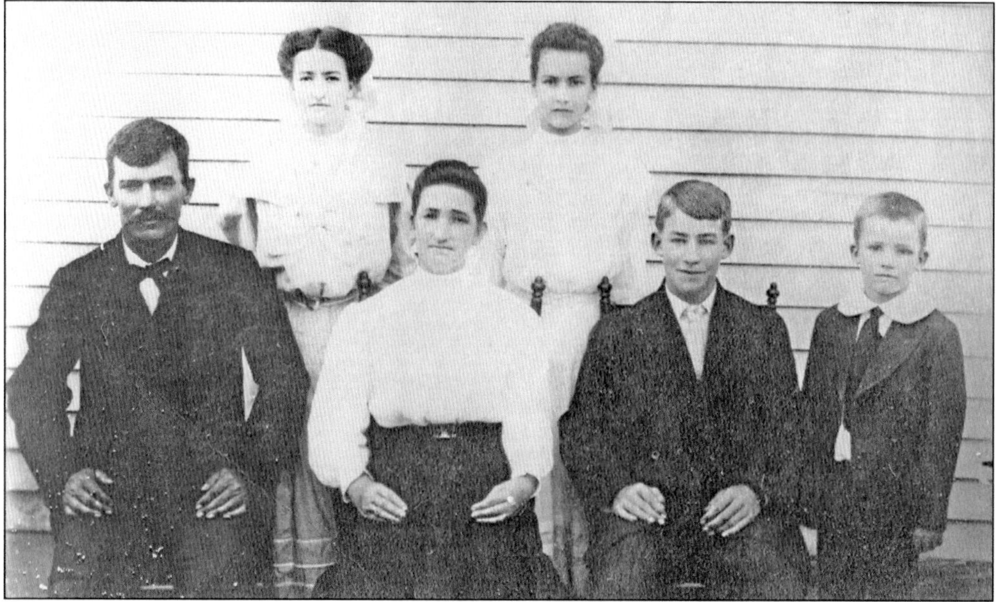

The Smith family is pictured on their farm on Airline Drive around 1903–1904. From left to right are (first row) George Sr., Tena (wife), George Jr., and Charlie; (second row) Edna and Daisy. George Sr. started the First Federal Savings and Loan in 1907. (Courtesy of Sheryl Smith Ferry.)

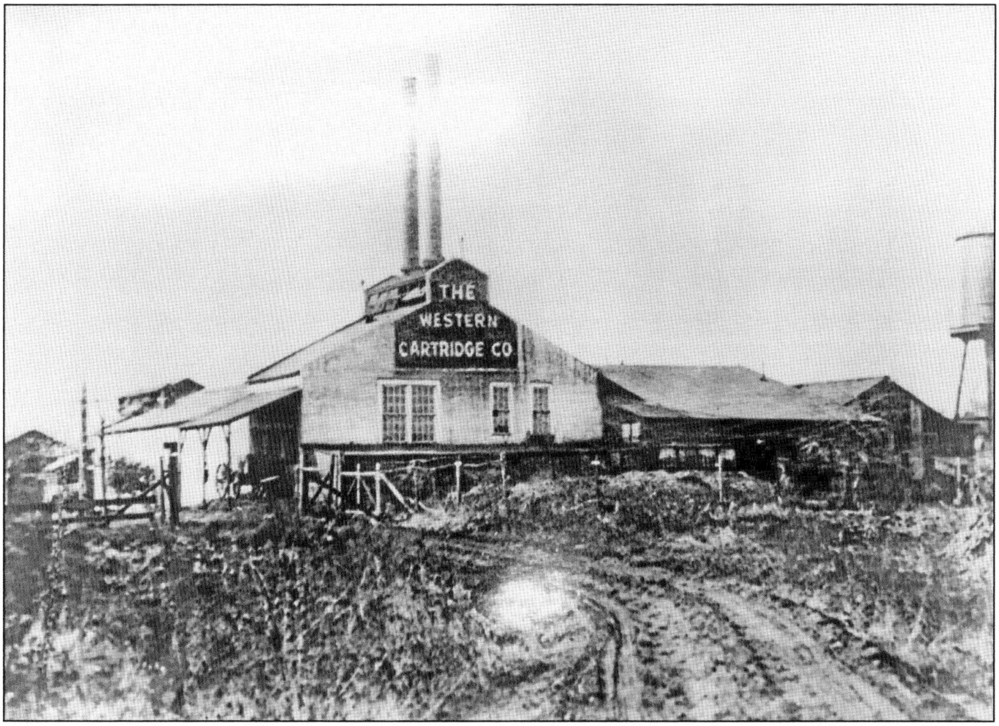

Franklin W. Olin established a plant to produce blasting powder, used in the mining industry. By February 1893, the plant was in operation under the name of the Equitable Powder Manufacturing Company. The company produced blasting and rifle powder and later, as the Western Cartridge Company, firearms and ammunition. The Western Cartridge Company purchased this building, located on the south bank of the Wood River, from Union Cap and Chemical Company in 1907.

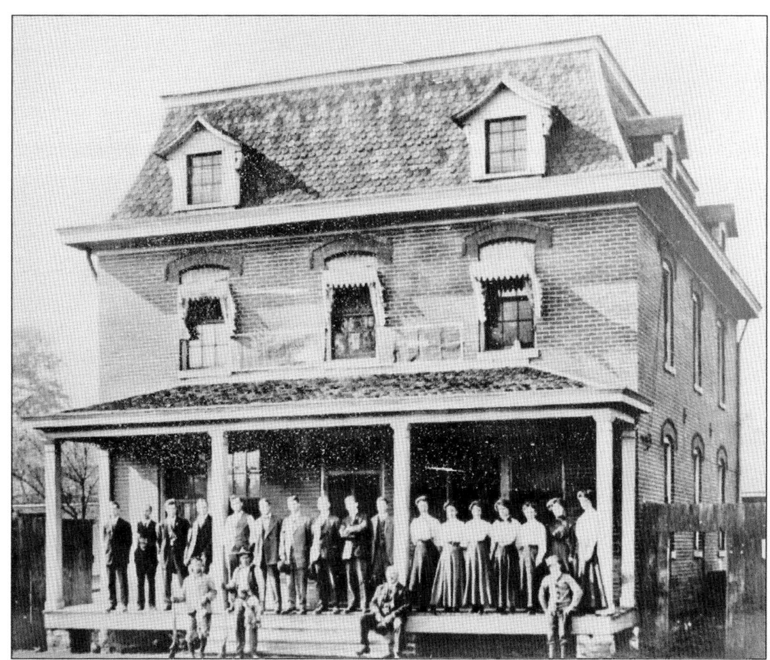

The original office building of the Equitable Powder Manufacturing Company and the Western Cartridge Company, located on Powder Mill Road, was used until around 1916. Seated on the steps is Franklin W. Olin. The rest of the people are unidentified but are believed to be the executive office staff.

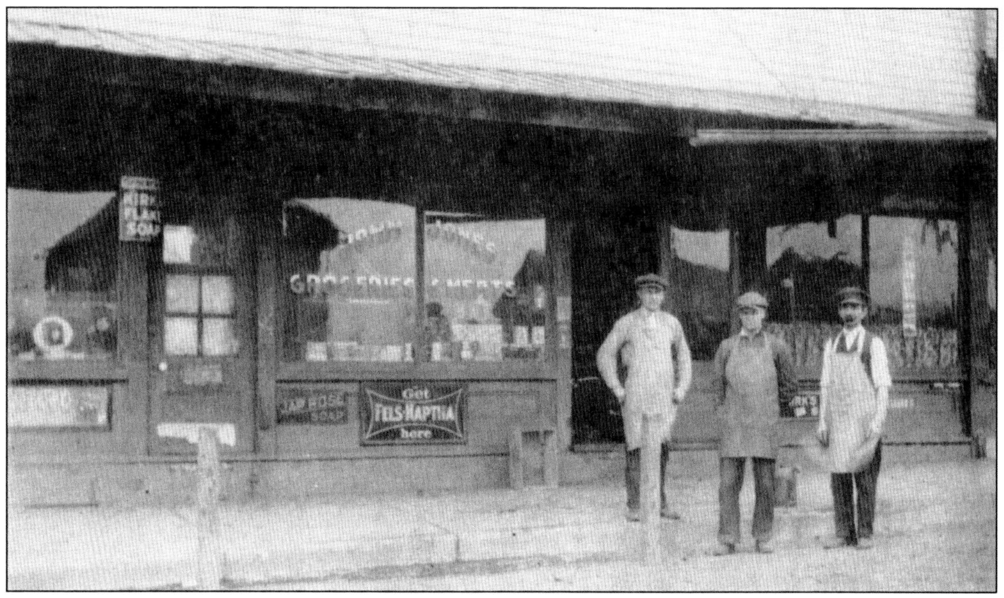

The John Jones Grocery located at the corner of Smith Street and St. Louis Road (now West St. Louis Avenue) was a busy store in 1914. It was operated by John Jones and his nephew Earl Jones. Pictured from left to right are Fred Rampenthal, Earl Jones, and Joseph Rowson. This corner has been the site of many business operations since 1914, including the Illinois State Bank.

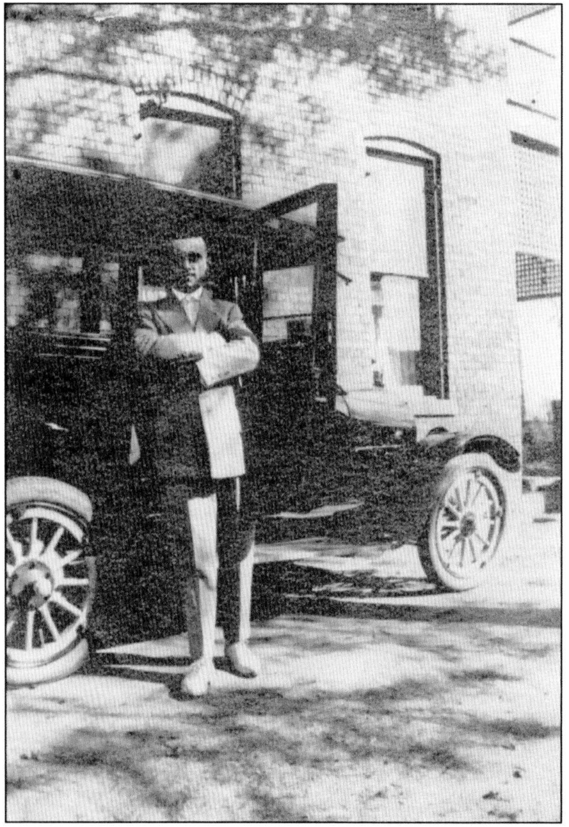

Leo J. Pavish Sr., born in 1886, came to the United States from Croatia at the age of 18 and to East Alton in his 30s. He is pictured here with his Stanley Steamer car. The popular Stanley Steamer is a nostalgic passion for present-day classic car enthusiasts. (Courtesy of Dolly Pavish Diaguid.)

Two

Stepping-Stones to Growth

The railroads had a great influence on the settling of East Alton. In the late 1830s, the Alton & Shawneetown Railroad and the Illinois & St. Louis Railroad started using Alton Junction as a transfer and stock feed point. The Irish settled in the area, which they called Emerald, with the railroad boom. The railroad people referred to the town as Alton Junction because of the junction or cut-off to Alton between St. Louis and Chicago.

From 1837 to 1868, additional railroads used East Alton as a cut-off to points north and east, creating the Big Four Railroad. The most familiar train to locals ran between Alton and East Alton until 1939. The local people called this train the "Plug." At its height, the Plug ran six passenger trains and made 17 runs per day.

The Wann Disaster, named after the water tower located at Alton Junction, was the worst train wreck in Illinois. On January 21, 1893, the *Southwestern Limited* 109 was running late going into Wann and came upon an open switch. The train crashed into a freight train with oil cars, causing a huge explosion. Other tank cars, freight cars, and flatcars were set aflame by the burning oil. A total of 18 train cars and two houses were burnt to ashes. Residents tried to help rescue the people on the train, but 41 lost their lives and at least 75 were injured, many of them seriously. The only medicine for burns at the time was raw linseed oil. William Henry gave two barrels of linseed oil, some of which was taken to the scene of the crash. The second floor of his grocery store was pressed into service as an aid station where people were attended to until they could be transferred to St. Joseph Hospital. The property loss was placed at $100,000.

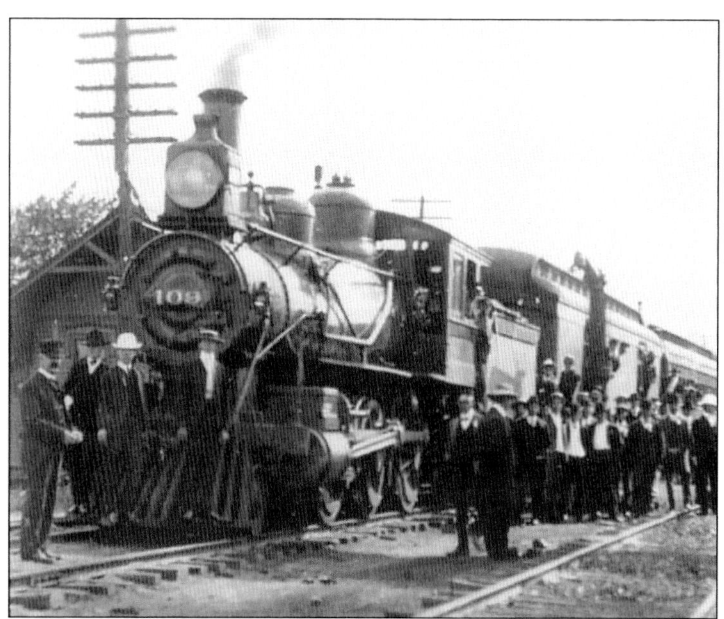

The Southwestern Limited 109 was running late going into the Alton Junction and came upon an open switch. The train crashed into a freight train with oil cars, causing a huge explosion. Forty-one residents lost their lives, and at least 75 were seriously injured trying to rescue people on the train. The train wreck is referred to as the Wann Disaster. This photograph was taken around 1893. (Courtesy of Woodrow Peterson.)

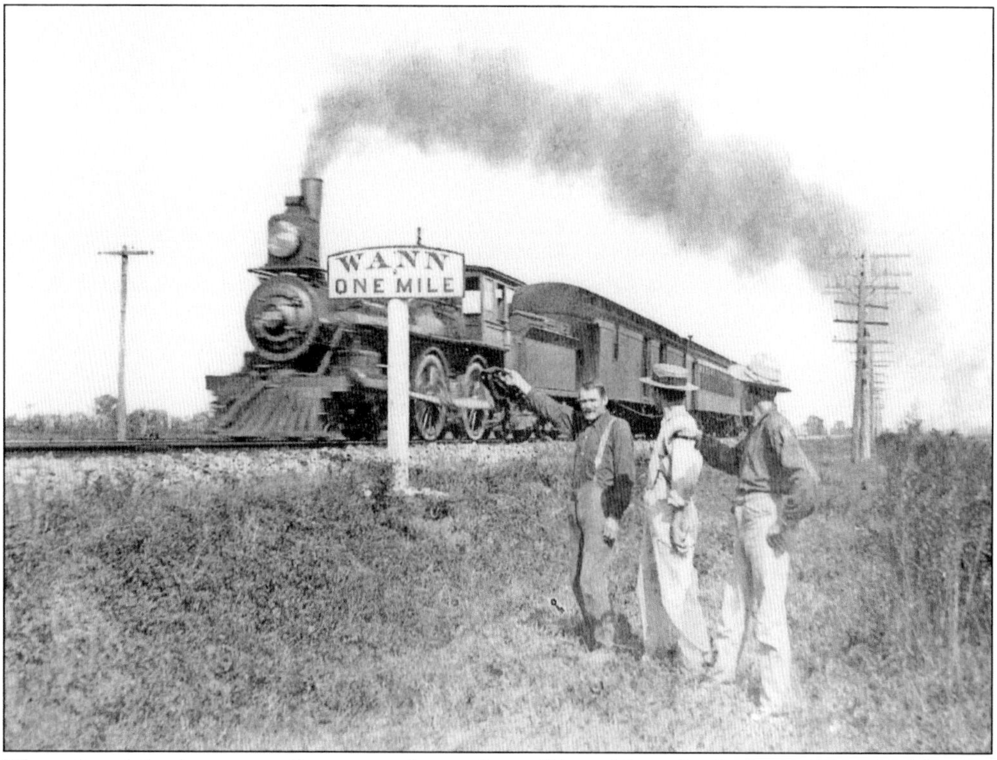

The railroads had a great influence on the settling of East Alton. In the late 1830s, the Alton & Shawneetown Railroad and the Illinois & St. Louis Railroad were formed. Due to the number of Irish who came with the railroad boom, East Alton was called Emerald. Locals referred to the junction as Wann, derived from the railroad tower of that name located south of the village. (Photograph by George H. Ringering, courtesy of the Ringering family.)

Henry Wiegand, of the Wann Baptist Church, lost his life helping rescue people burned in the Wann Disaster on January 21, 1893. A memorial to him is still at the First Baptist Church on Bowman Avenue. The bell was purchased out of dollar donations from every member of the church. Engraved on the bell is "1893 Henry Wiegand, January 21, Memorial Explosion Dedication 1894."

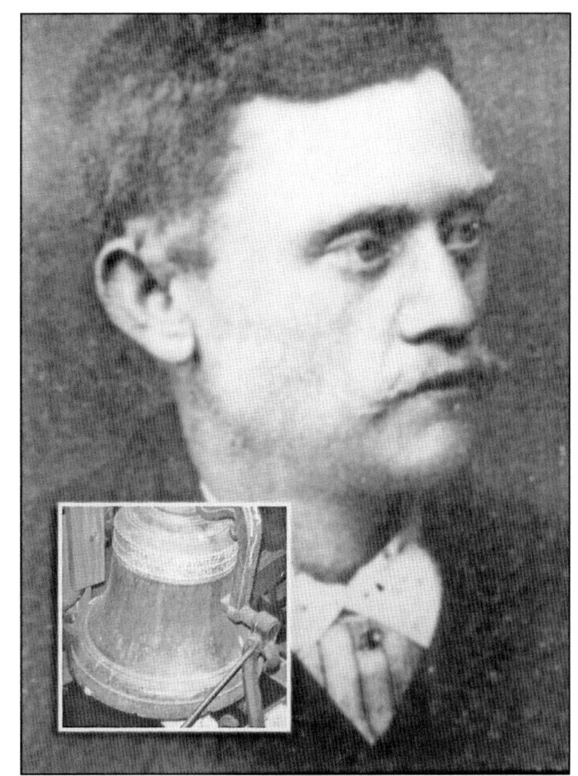

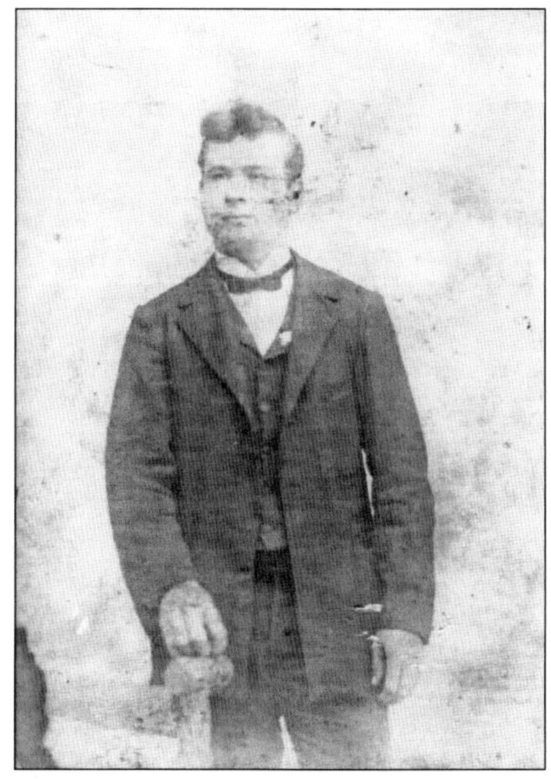

Frank A. Miller was a survivor of the Wann Disaster on January 21, 1893. Frank's father, William, and brothers Edward, Julius, and William Jr. all went to assist those involved in the accident. At the time of the explosion, all of them were near and consequently received injuries. Frank's father and brother Edward received fatal injuries. A double funeral took place from their home. (Courtesy of Jason Parker, great-grandson of Frank Miller.)

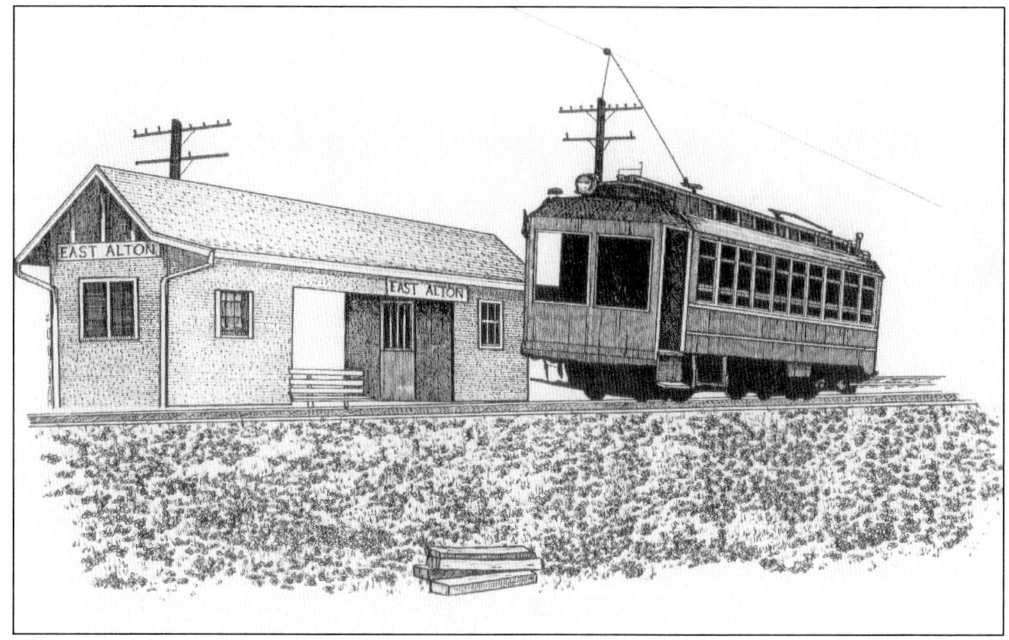

This streetcar depot was at the rear of Romero's Restaurant just south of the viaduct. The streetcar, "Old Yellowhammer," furnished rapid transportation from Alton to St. Louis in the 1930s. In the early 1920s, a baseball diamond was located north of the depot. This area was a favorite camping ground for bands of Gypsies.

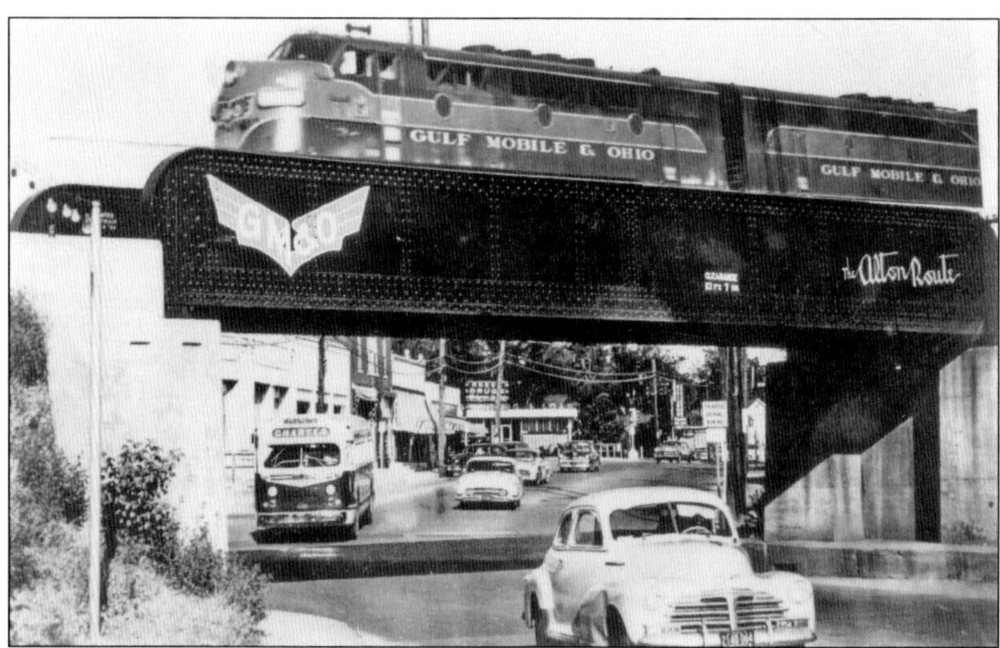

This viaduct is the second at this location on West St. Louis Avenue. It was installed in the 1920s, serving until it was replaced by the present viaduct in 1990. This viaduct suffered flooding from large rains, and 18-wheel semi-trucks frequently got stuck under it.

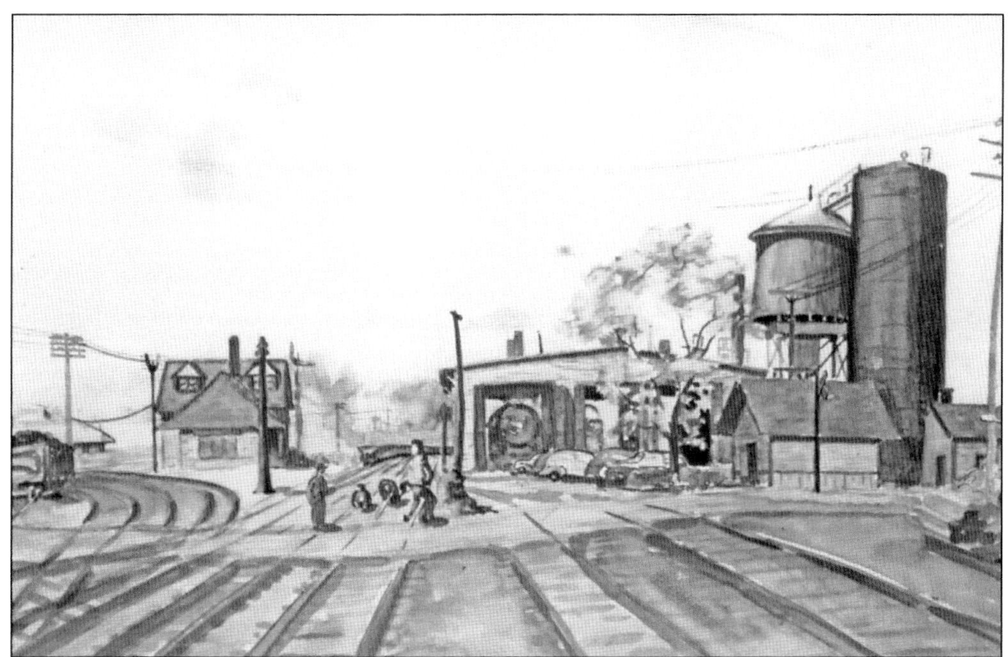

Between 1851 and 1857, the Indianapolis & St. Louis Railroad and the St. Louis & Alton passed through East Alton. The early trains ran on steam, which made it necessary to have water towers located along the route. A water tower was located north of Job's stockyard where trains stopped to take on water. This picture is of the old roundhouse, water tower, and buildings as they looked in 1945. The oil painting was by S. Traband in 1945.

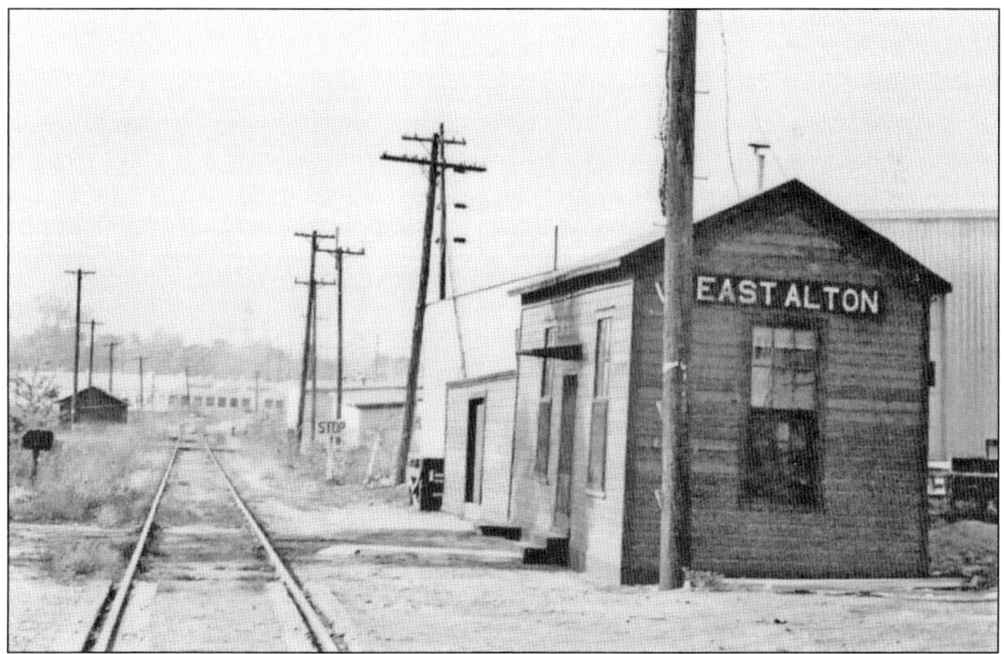

Burlington placed the East Alton train order office on the line to Beardstown. It was near the stop boards of the New York Central's branch to downtown Alton. This track ran behind the main Winchester plant.

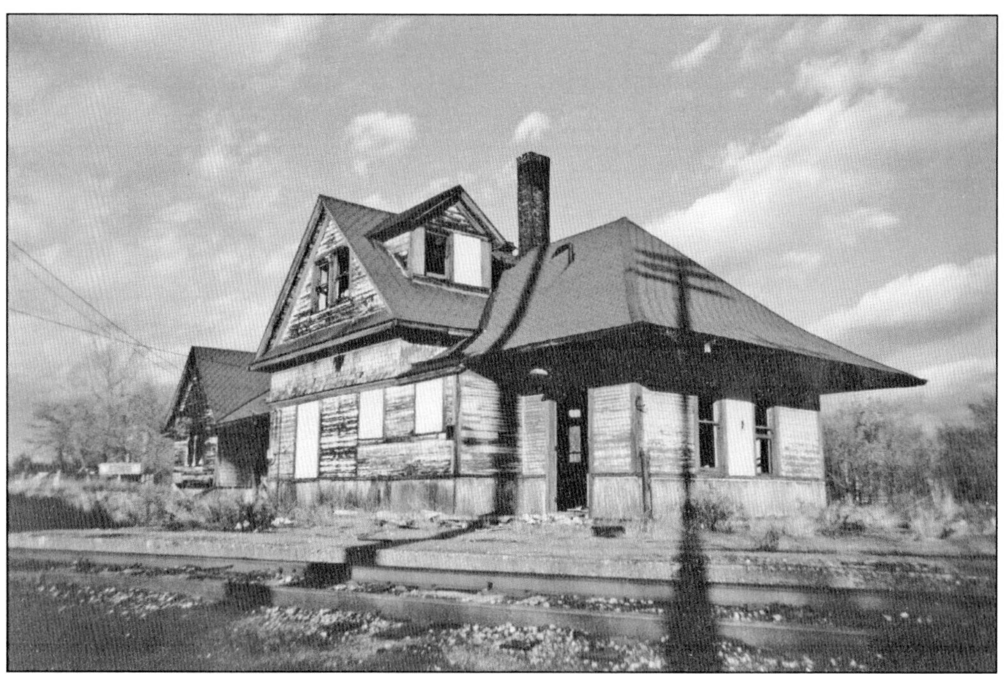

The New York Central's East Alton station was located were the Wann Disaster occurred in January 1893 and was part of the Big Four route. The original station was destroyed by fire in 1901 and was rebuilt in 1902. This station was destroyed by fire in 1977. (Courtesy of Shirley Ringering McCann.)

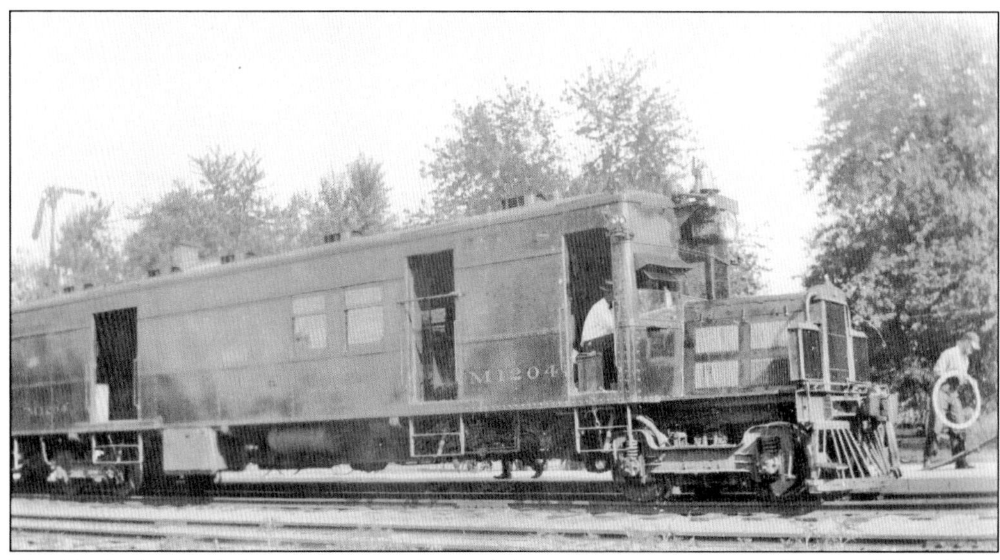

The Plug had a diesel-electric engine and provided transportation between Alton and East Alton in the 1930s, which made travel easier than the roads of the day. The engineer received his orders from a person outside the train who would hand him a piece of paper on the end of a long stick. (Photograph by George H. Ringering, courtesy of the Ringering family.)

Three

The Village Becomes a Reality

By August 1893, Alton Junction/Emerald had outgrown its unorganized days, and the leaders of the community voted for incorporation. The new village was named East Alton.

The first official business was to discuss the need for a jail. By 1895, the town hall was completed with a jail being added to the building. A post office was built on the corner of Shamrock and West Main Streets. In 1895, oil lamps, which had to be lit by hand, were available to residents, with the village providing oil for one year. By 1897, roads were being constructed to connect with other villages, and that same year, Central Union Telephone Company stretched wire within the village for telephone service. By 1900, brick sidewalks were replacing plank sidewalks.

On April 2, 1900, a fire started in the store and dwelling of J.B. VanPreter, spreading to the store and dwelling of William Clarke, two dwellings in the rear owned by A.E. Benbow, and from there across the road to William Henry's saloon, a barbershop, and a shed where farm machinery was kept. All of these buildings were destroyed, and only the heroic efforts of the East Alton people saved the building of William Henry, from which the fire could easily have spread and destroyed the entire village. After the fire, business owners rebuilt the business district. In 1902, Wood River flooded, covering approximately 10,000 acres, again damaging downtown and washing away farm buildings.

It was a common sight to see store owners delivering food and necessities by horse and wagon to residents in the early 1900s. The Illinois State Bank was organized in 1904, giving the residents modern banking services. In 1909, the first automobile owned within the city limits made an appearance, going a speedy 15 miles per hour. By 1913, electric lights were replacing the oil lamps, and in the 1920s central water, gas, and sewer service made their separate ways into the village. The early doctors to serve the community were Dr. Charles N. Pence, who was the first, Dr. Guy L. McKinney, and Dr. Charles A. Moore.

Jas Mullane
Pat O'Mara
L.G. Tomlinson
Marion Shryock
Thomas Roberson
John Winzele
Frank A. Neukam
G. W. Walls
Gus H Patterson
Charles C Parks
Jacob Baum
A. Seymour
Elijah Lindley
John L. Ray
L. A. Patterson
Jesse Jones
Frank Devaney
Benjman Padock
John Paddock
M. McInerny
Ahart Bar
John Crawford
Isaac Steel
Allen Paddock
Chas. C Richards
W. A. Lindley
Thomas Philbert
Frank Teipel
Jas Miller
O. M. Emory
Louis Sturkey
Albert Jones
T. D. Walling

J. N. Luddeke
J. F. Teipel
Chas Hermann
Adolph Wolf
Charles F Kangebrauck
Geo. L. Smith
Wm Bennett
Wm St. Henry

These are the signatures of citizens who signed the papers for incorporation in 1893.

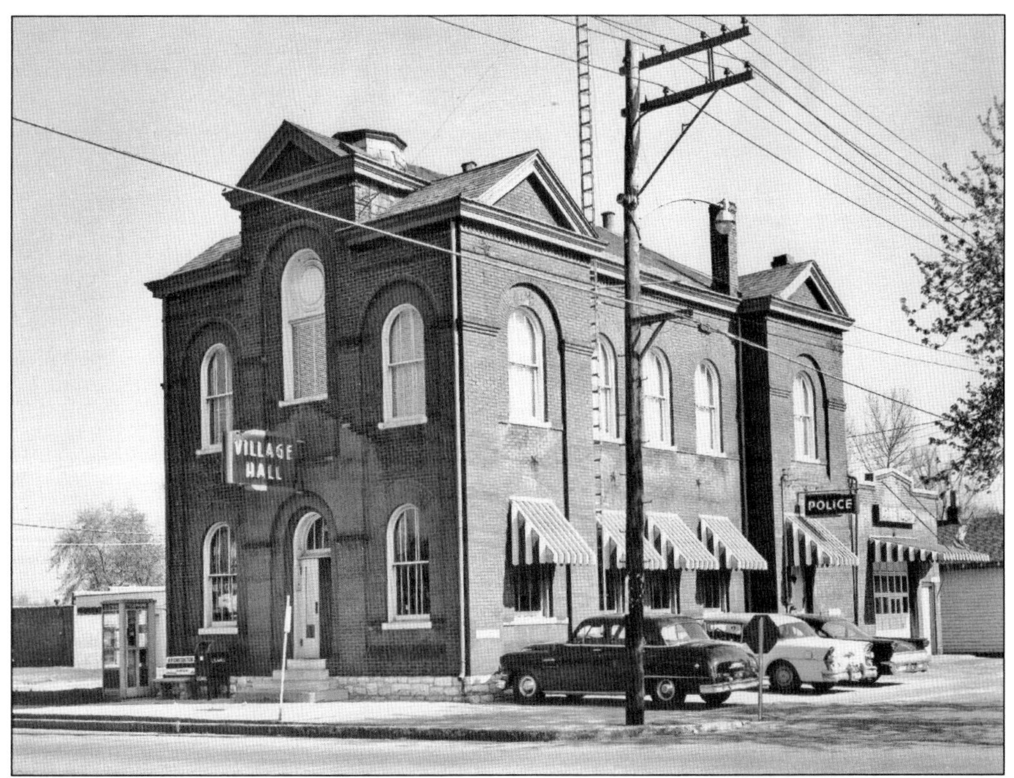

The East Alton City Hall was completed and dedicated in 1898. Z.B. Job was the guest speaker for the dedication. A flagpole was placed on top of the cupola (not shown). The fire station was built in 1927 to the rear of the hall. This building was razed in 1969.

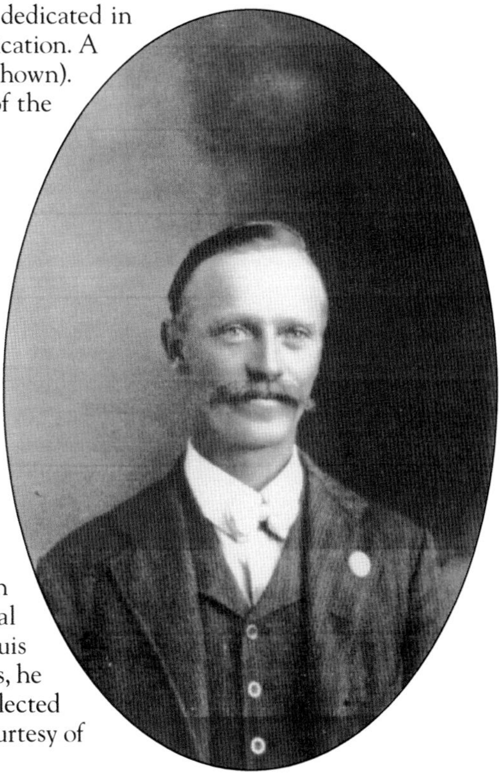

George H. Ringering moved to East Alton in 1897. He worked as a carpenter and built several homes from lumber purchased when the St. Louis World Fair was razed in 1904. Along with homes, he built a number of boats for river use. He was elected township assessor from 1914 through 1918. (Courtesy of the Ringering family.)

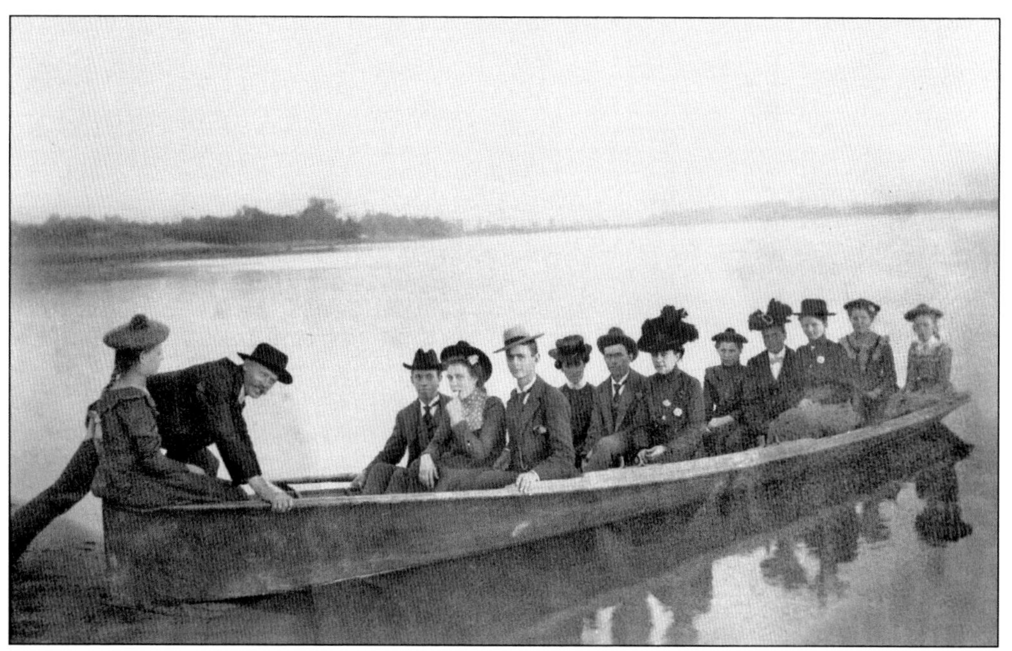

In the early 1900s, after attending church, the Ringering family would load into the boat George built and cruise the Mississippi River. From the boat, they could see the clock on St. Mary's Church in Alton and St. Charles, Missouri. Pictured from front to back and left to right are Yetrude Olson, George Ringering, Johnny Ringering, Nettie Ford, William Klopmeier, Gesina Ringering, Herman Ringering, Mary Fisher, unidentified, Henry Ringering, Martha Fischer, Fannie Ringering, and unidentified. (Courtesy of the Ringering family.)

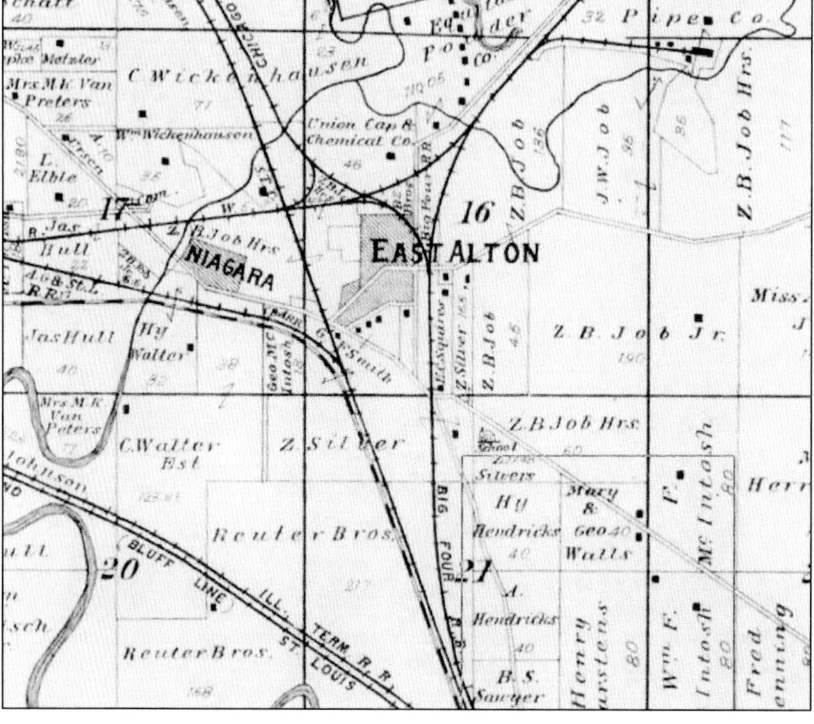

This map shows the location of the town of Niagara, which was founded by H.J. Bowman and platted in 1904. It was named after Niagara Falls and the small falls along the Wood River where Niagara was located. This map also shows the plats in the area.

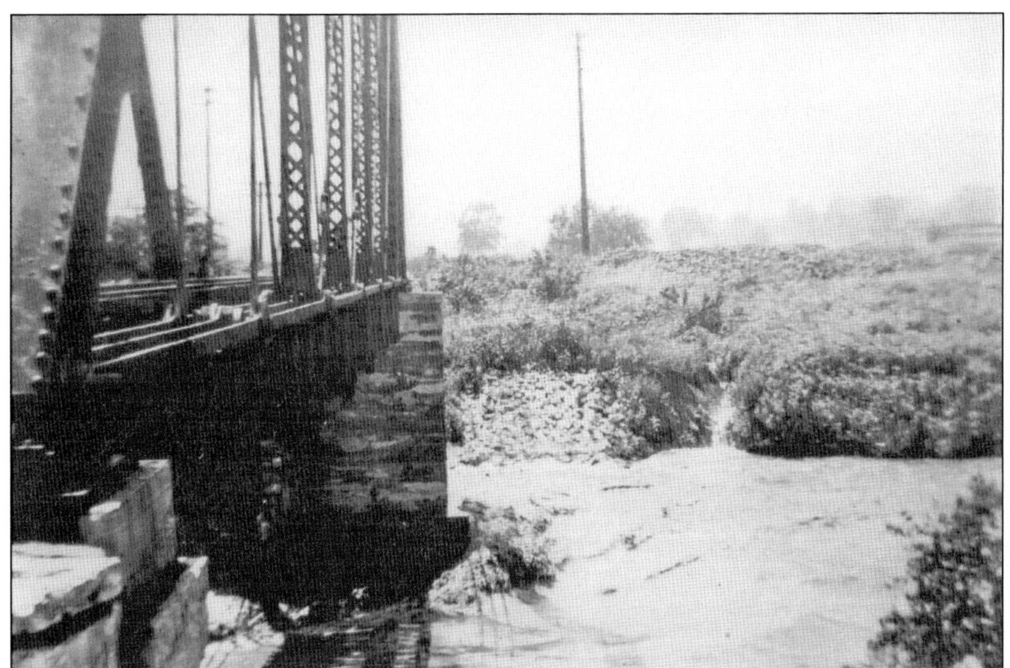

This bridge was constructed over the Wood River near where the Milton Settlement is believed to have been located. A spring fed into the river, causing a small waterfall. This location was originally named Niagara because of the falls. The building in the background on the right is believed to be a barn on the Wickenhauser farm. (Photograph by George H. Ringering; courtesy of Mae Landreth.)

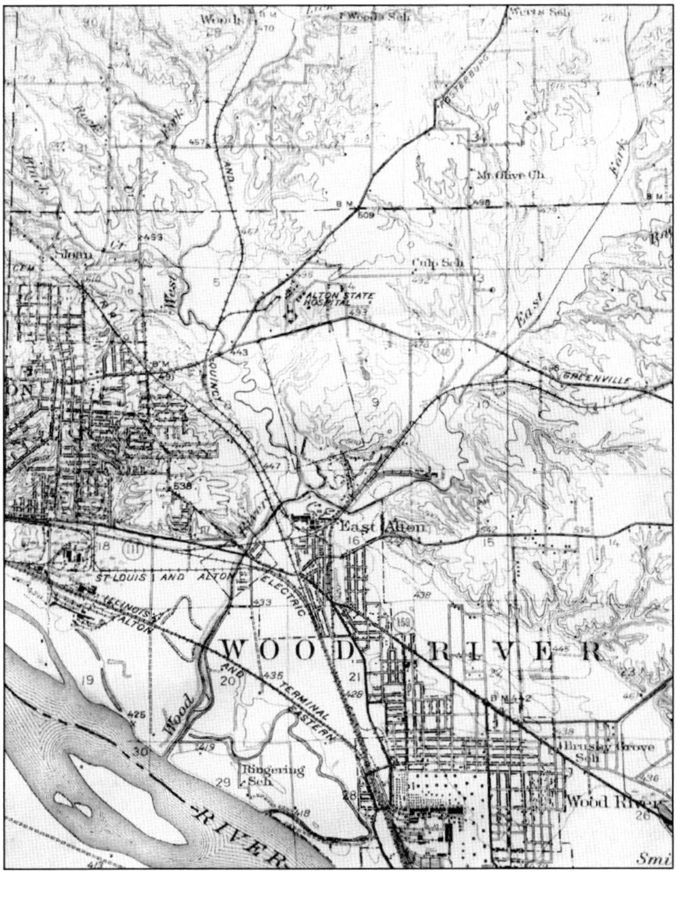

Through the years, flooding has been a major issue for the village. This map, dated 1922 and updated in 1944, shows the proximity of East Alton to the Wood and Mississippi Rivers.

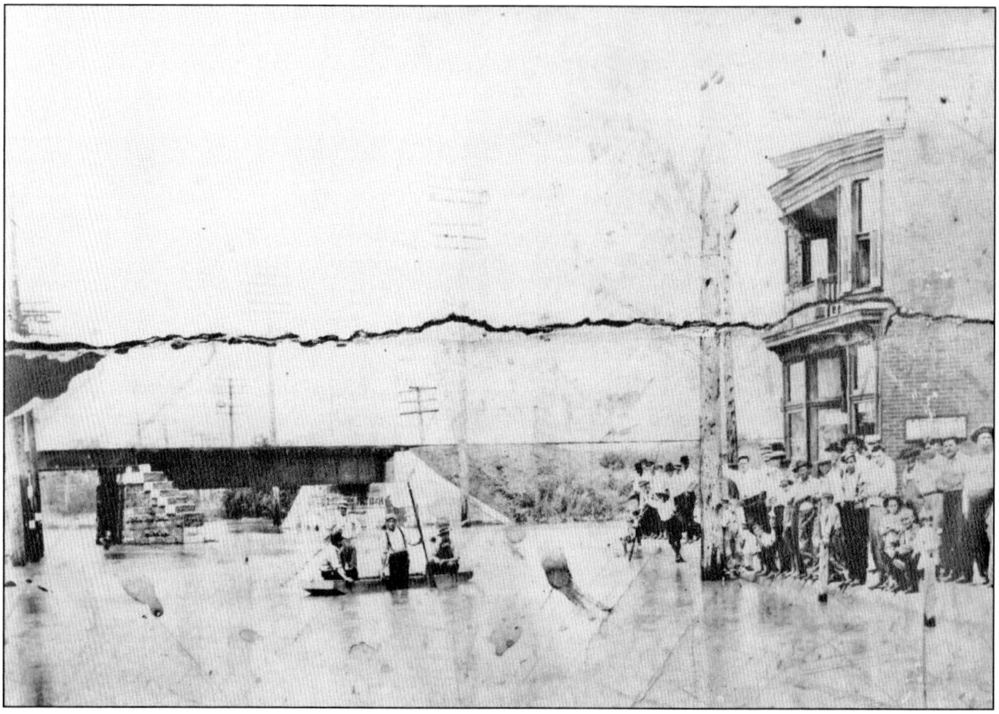

High water is seen in East Alton on July 14, 1912. The building is the Bill Clark building, where John Jones ran a grocery store. Some of the people in the picture are Earl Ballard, his daughter Lillian, Bill Busse, and Sam Hawkins, the town marshal. The bridge is the Baltimore & Ohio Railroad bridge, then called the Chicago & Alton Railroad.

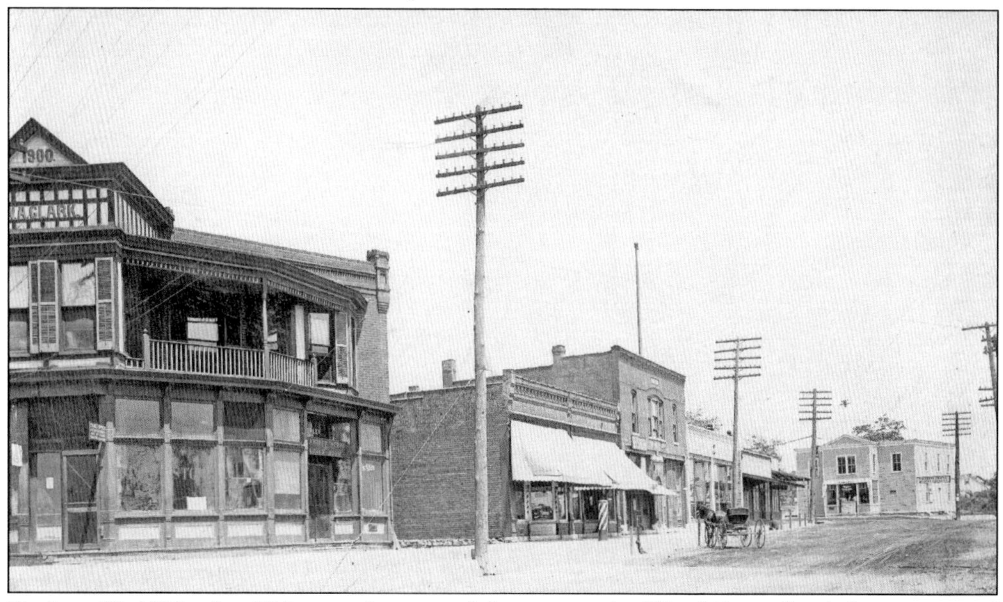

On June 29, 1902, after 36 hours of continual downpour, the Wood River flooded an estimated 10,000 acres of land on both sides of the river. Water stood on East Alton Avenue (now West St. Louis Avenue) 18 inches deeper than ever before, and three feet of sand was deposited on the main street by the flood. Downtown East Alton was also called the Levee District.

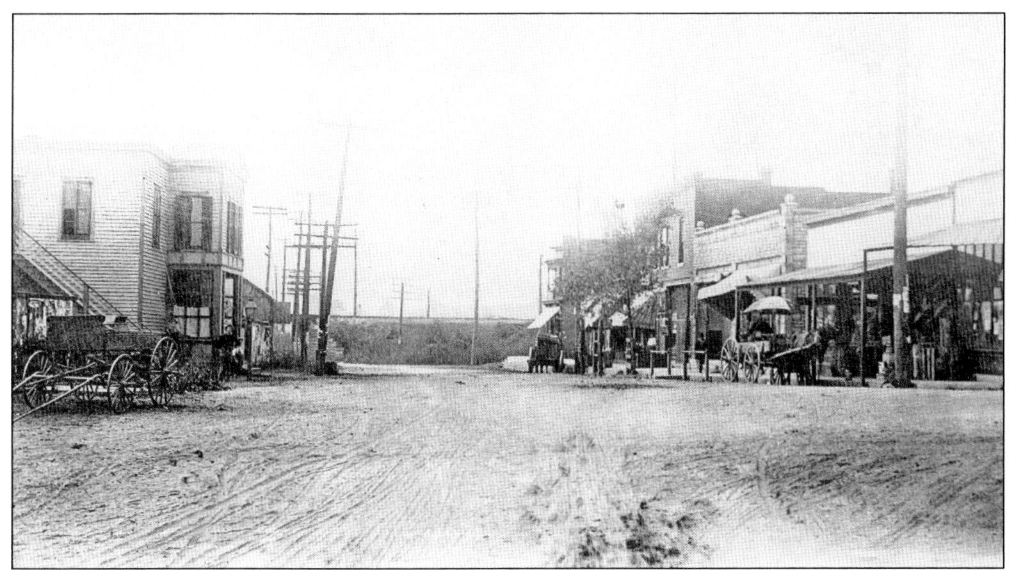

In 1893, downtown East Alton consisted of Shamrock Street (quite narrow and rough), Smithey Avenue (later changed to Smith Street), Church Street, and Main Street. On the hill at the end of the street is a train track that is still used today, and on the right, the last store is VanPreter's store. (Courtesy of Mae Lambert.)

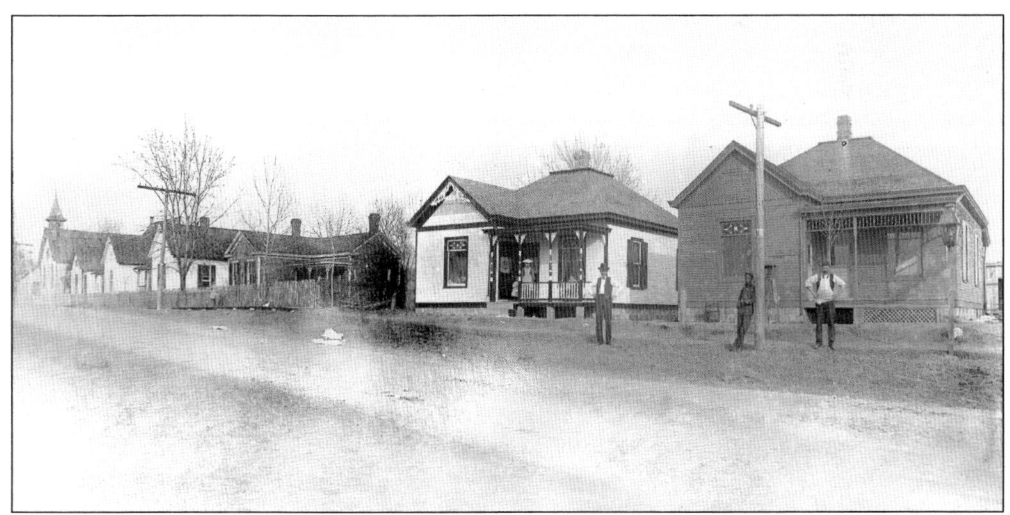

West Main Street is pictured in the 1920s or 1930s. Note the lamppost, which had to be lit by hand, and the electricity or telephone post. During the late 1890s and early 1900s, both electricity and telephones were finding their way into the village. On the far left is the First Methodist Church, which was later the Assembly of God Church. (Courtesy of the Ringering family.)

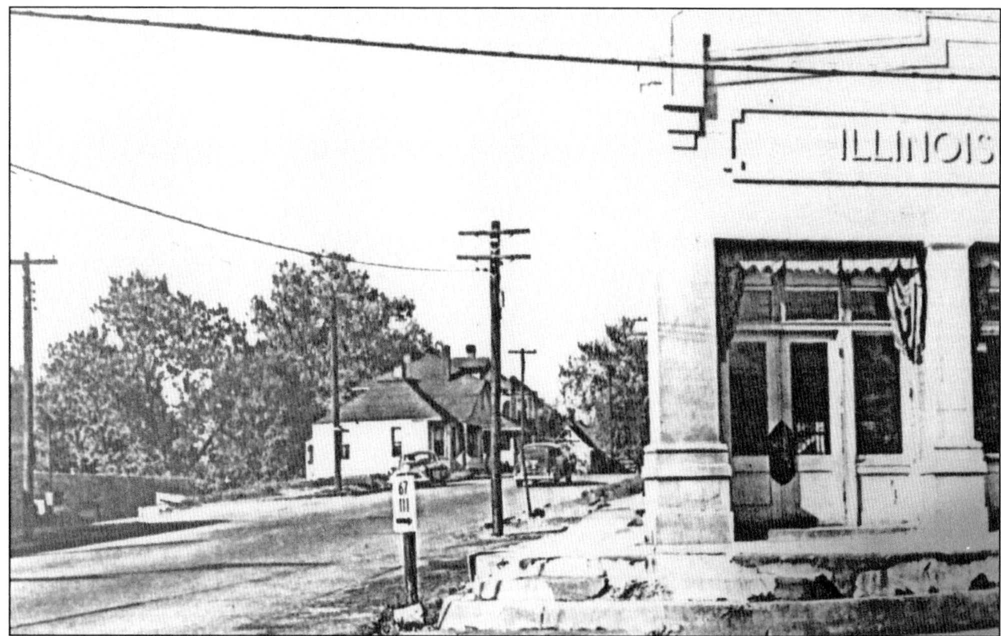

The Illinois State Bank was established in 1904, doing business on West St. Louis Avenue. This location was successfully robbed on two occasions during the Roaring Twenties. The bank was moved to West St. Louis Avenue and West Main Street in the 1920s, replacing the store owned by John Jones, whose building was partially swept away in the flood of 1906.

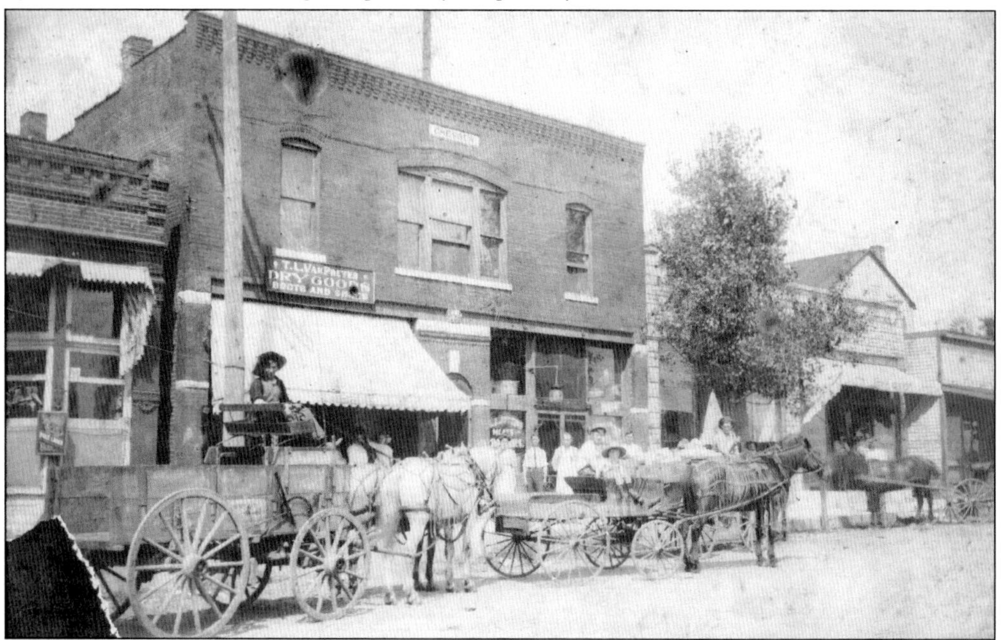

The VanPreter Dry Goods Store and Jutting Store were located in downtown East Alton on West St. Louis Avenue. Before supermarkets, most families bought their groceries and dry goods from small neighborhood stores that delivered the staples by horse and wagon. On the wagon seat on the left is Oscar Hand, in the smaller delivery wagon are Earl Robinson (left) and Vernon Jutting (right), and in the loaded wagon is Shorty Barnhorn. The picture was taken in 1910.

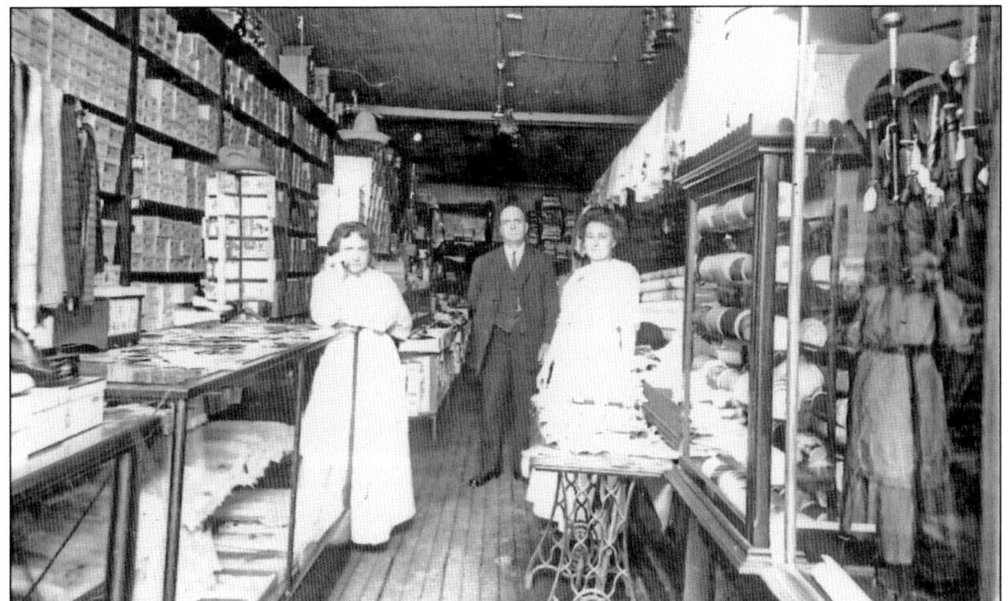

This early-1900s photograph was taken inside the VanPreter store with Elizabeth VanPreter (right) and Lottie Cooper (left); the gentleman is unidentified. VanPreter bet people she had anything they wanted in her store, which boasted over 1,000 items. She enjoyed people and business. She continued the business after her husband died in 1942. Her theory was "if you treat people right, then you will get treated right." (Courtesy of Deb Pruitt, granddaughter of Margaret Pruitt.)

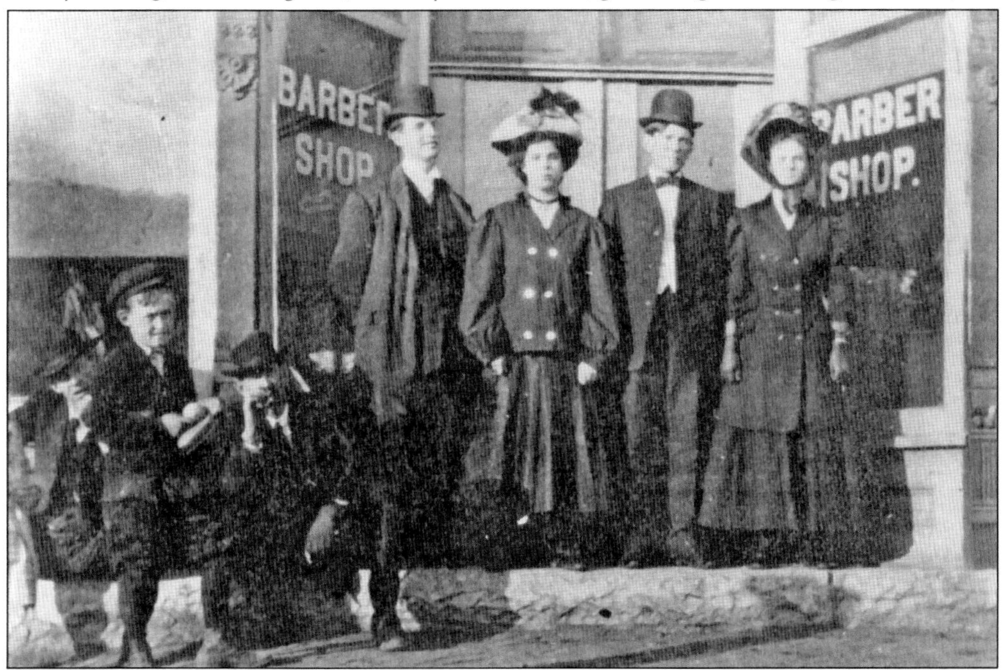

Pictured on a Sunday afternoon standing in front of a barbershop in downtown East Alton are, from left to right, T.L. VanPreter, Charles A. VanPreter, J.B. VanPreter, Edward Franklin, Sara Desilvey Ford, Clarence Hale, and Mae Bright Smith. Local businessman Lawrence Hale took the picture.

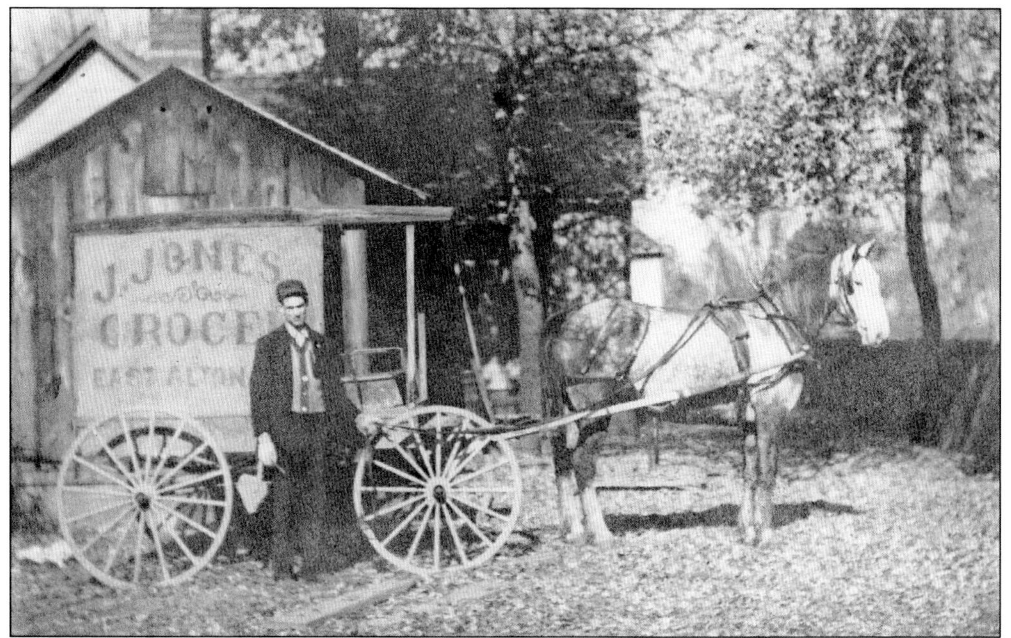

This photograph was taken around 1895. John Jones, a local store owner, delivered groceries and dry goods by horse and wagon to customers. His store was located on West Main Street and West St. Louis Avenue and was partially swept away in the 1906 flood. (Courtesy of David and Robert Sever.)

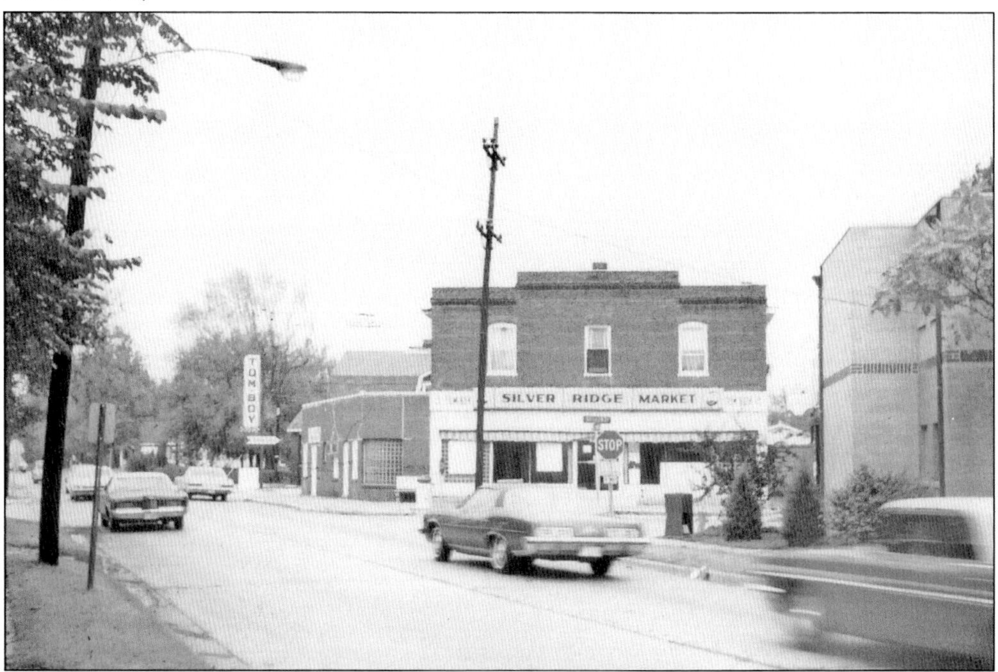

The Silver Ridge Market was one of the oldest grocery stores in East Alton. H. Frank Yoder Sr. owned several grocery stores starting in 1899. As the business grew, he moved to new locations, the last being 636 Broadway, where Silver Ridge was located. Yoder Jr. became associated with Silver Ridge Market in 1919. In August 1949, Robert and Eileen Dunn purchased the business.

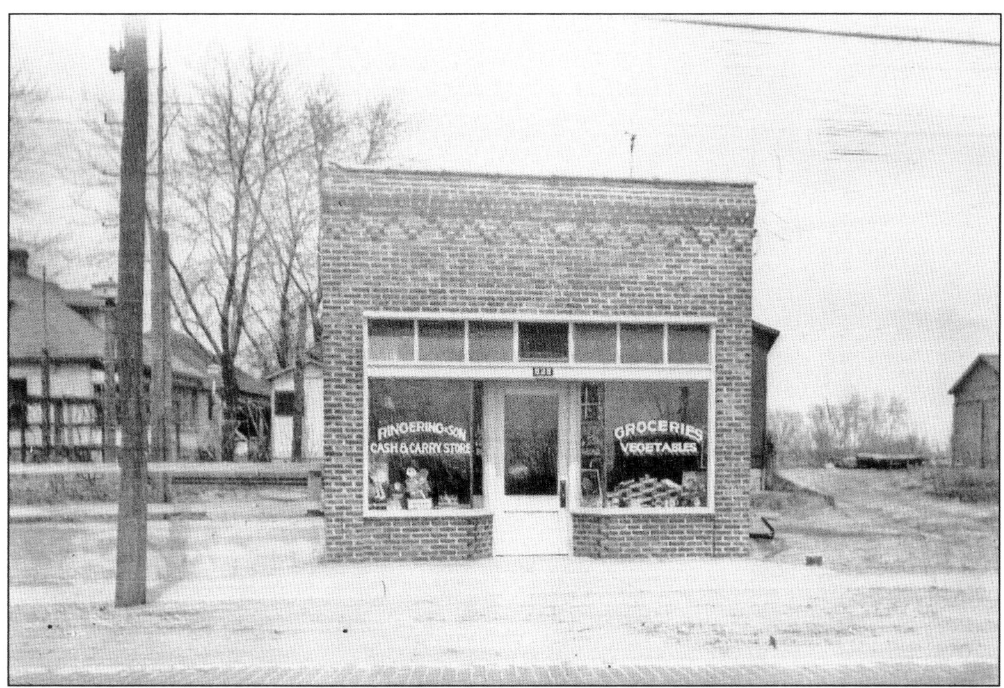

Ringering Grocery Store was built by George H. Ringering in 1920 on his property at 628 West St. Louis Avenue. The grocery store was run by Ringering and his son Carl. The store was sold to Emma Underbrink in the 1930s. (Courtesy of the Ringering family.)

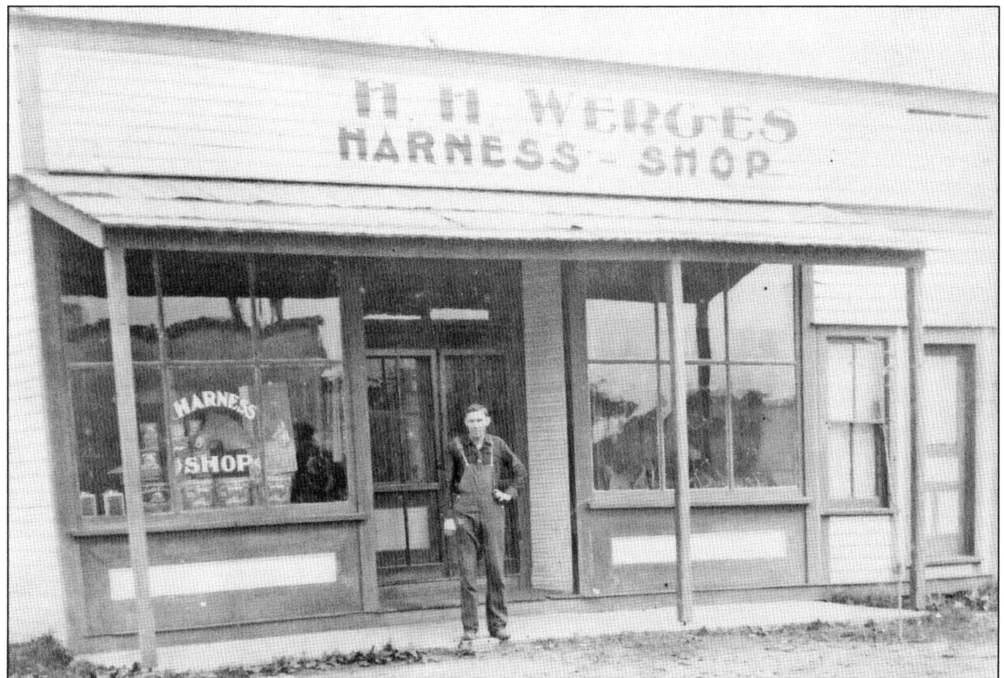

Herman W. Werges is standing in front of his harness shop on the corner of West St. Louis Avenue and Smith Street around 1900. The adjoining building belonged to W.F. Busse, who operated a drugstore.

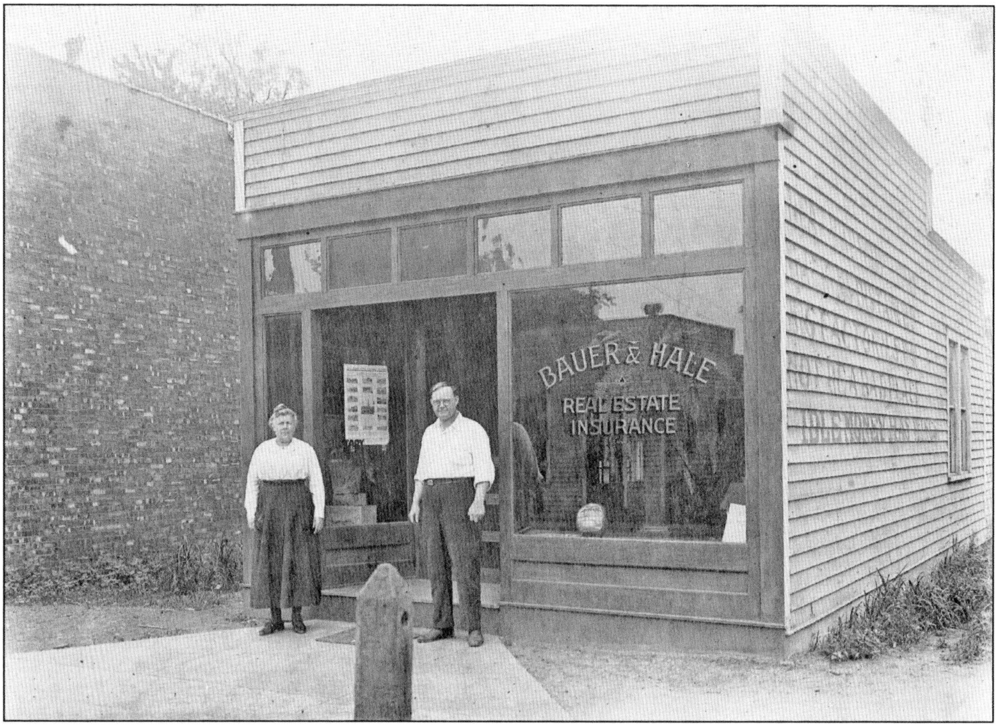

Bauer and Hale were in a partnership from 1918 until early 1920s. Henry Bauer was an insurance broker, Nora Bauer was the office manager, and Walter Hale Sr. was both an insurance and a real estate broker. Nora Bauer and Walter Hale Sr. are pictured. (Courtesy of Allen Hale.)

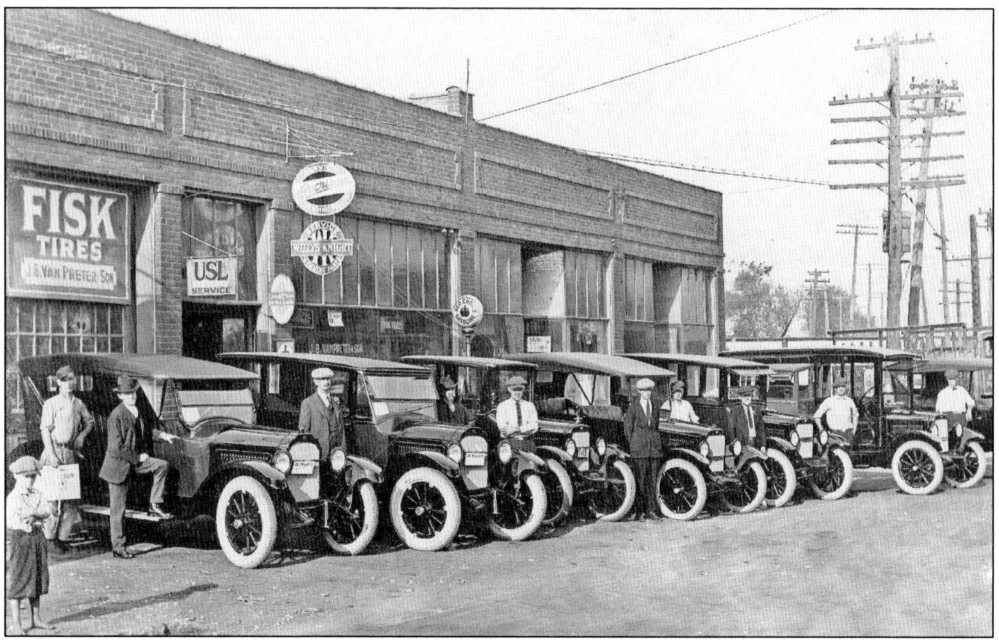

The J.B. VanPreter and Son Automobile Dealership was established in 1917, handling Willys-Knight and Overland cars. The gentleman directly beneath the overhanging sign is J.B. VanPreter. The dealership was located on West St. Louis Avenue.

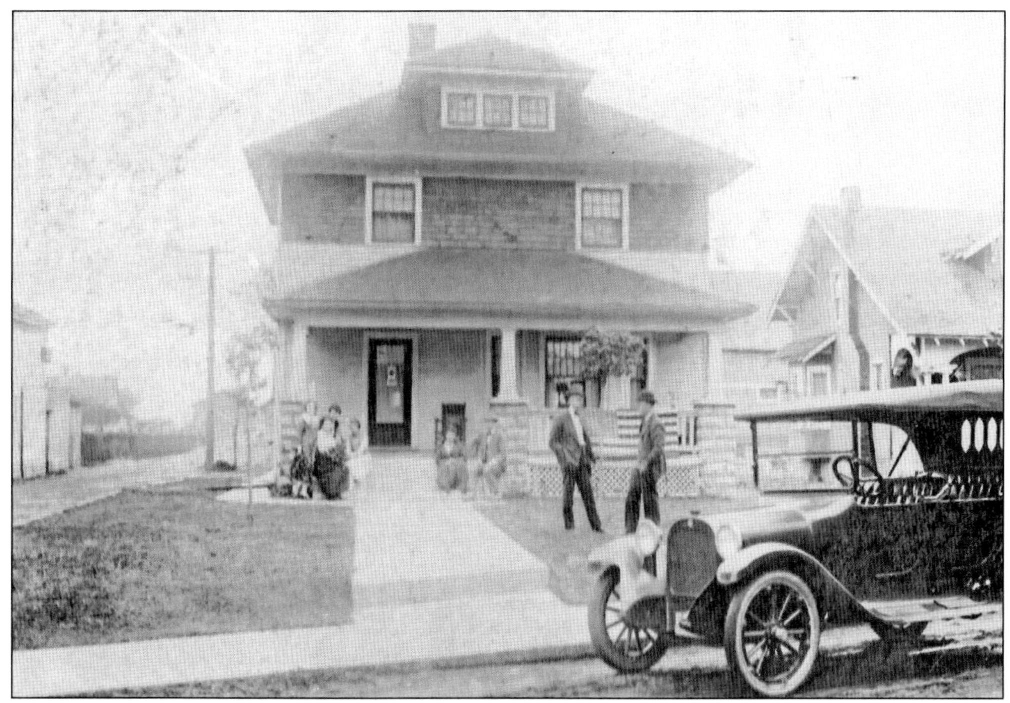

The VanPreter family home on Smith Street is pictured around 1919. On the left in the black skirt and white blouse is Elizabeth VanPreter. To the right of her is her daughter Margaret, and standing on the lawn with the white shirt is Thomas VanPreter. The other people in the photograph are unidentified. (Courtesy of Deb Pruitt, granddaughter of Margaret Pruitt.)

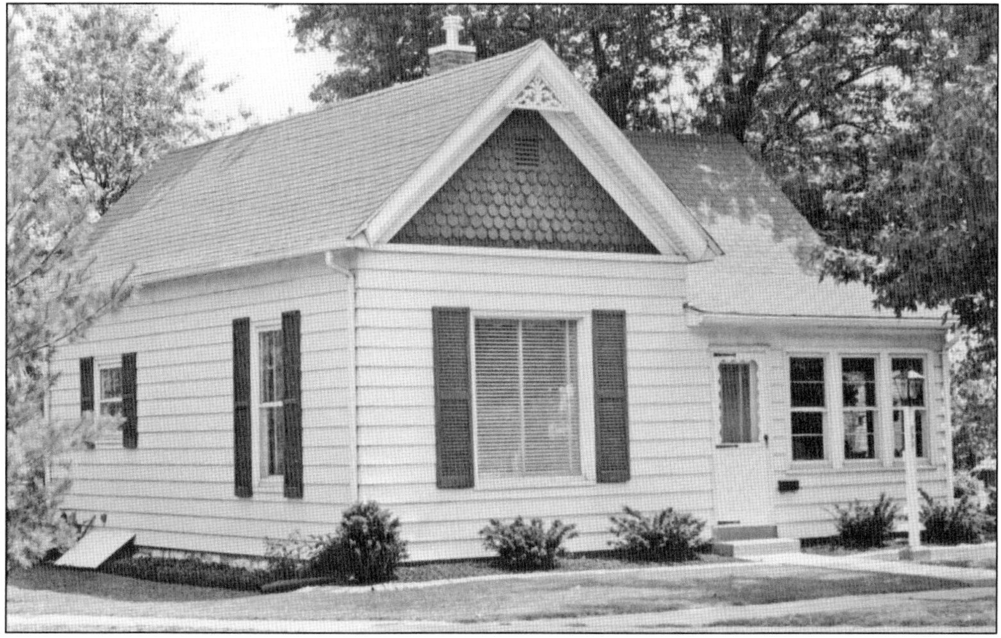

This house at 232 Church Street, the former home of Margaret VanPreter Pruitt, was built in 1892 and had been in the VanPreter family since 1932. The property was originally part of Z.B. Job's estate. This house is still in use today.

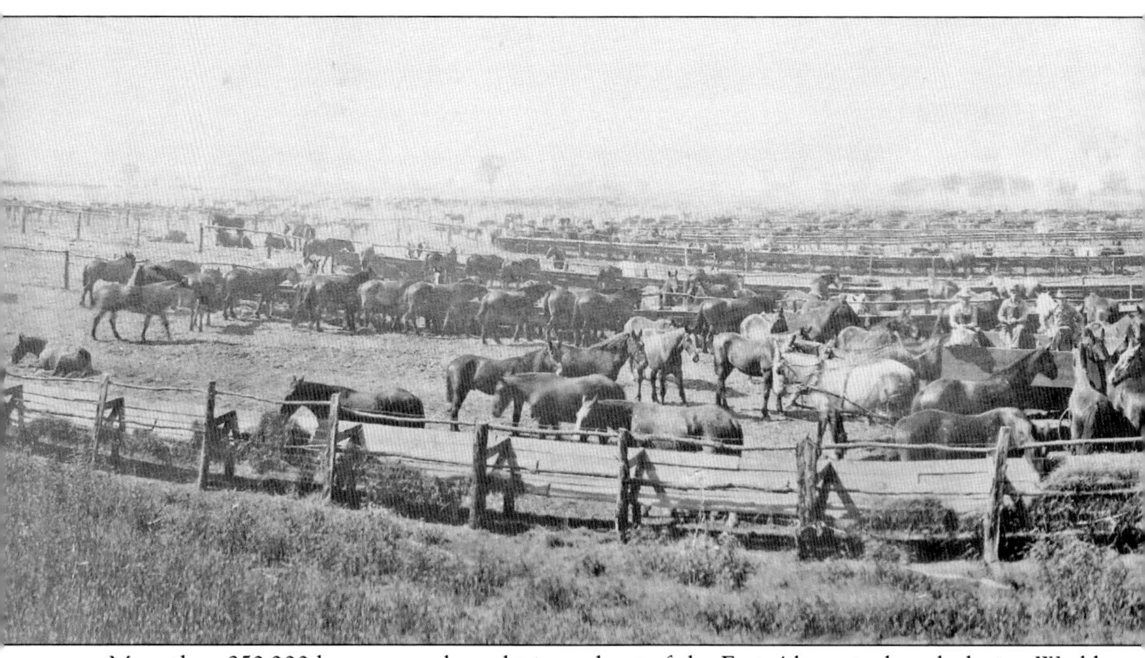

More than 250,000 horses were brought in and out of the East Alton stockyards during World War I. The horses were shipped overseas to the British, French, and Belgian governments for use in the war in Europe. The buying of horses for use in the military was a big enterprise that brought millions of dollars to horse owners. The horses served during battle and were subjected

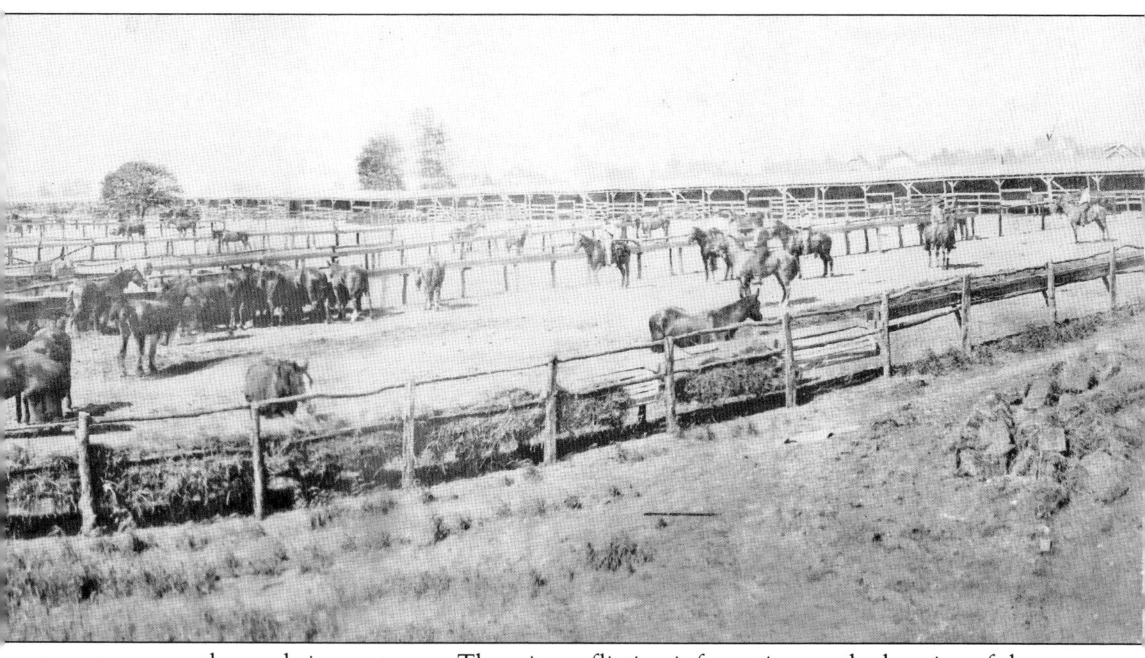

to extreme weather and circumstances. There is conflicting information on the location of the stockyards. They are believed to have been located between the Big Four Railroad on Shamrock Street, St. Louis Avenue, and the Washington School to Third Street near the recreation center. (Courtesy of Dan Merritt.)

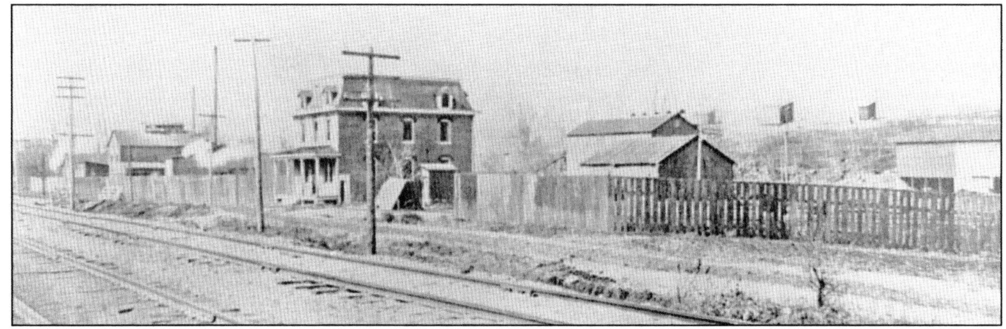

Between the buildings and the railroad tracks is Powder Mill Road around 1916. The railroad tracks in the foreground are the Big Four Railroad's main line. The Equitable Powder Manufacturing Company built part of its plant in this area due to the location of the railroad.

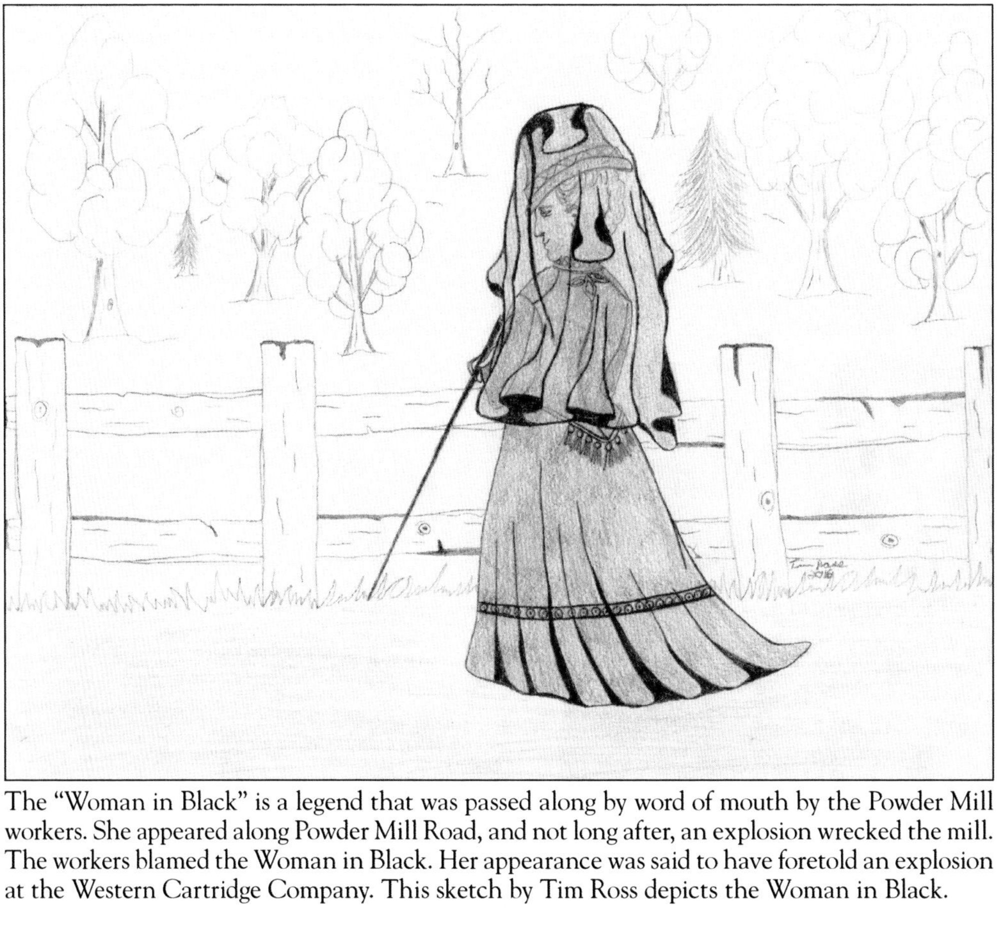

The "Woman in Black" is a legend that was passed along by word of mouth by the Powder Mill workers. She appeared along Powder Mill Road, and not long after, an explosion wrecked the mill. The workers blamed the Woman in Black. Her appearance was said to have foretold an explosion at the Western Cartridge Company. This sketch by Tim Ross depicts the Woman in Black.

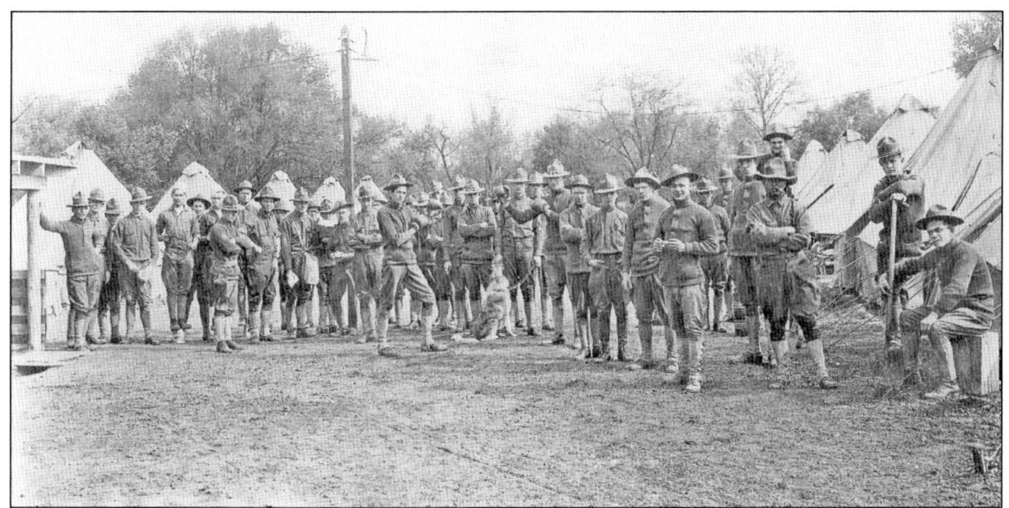

The 5th Infantry National Guard troop was stationed in East Alton from March until September 1918 to keep watch over the Western Cartridge Company. The Western Cartridge Company had obtained several US government contracts for ammunition for World War I. The troop was reassigned to Springfield and marched from East Alton to Springfield, covering approximately 30 miles per day.

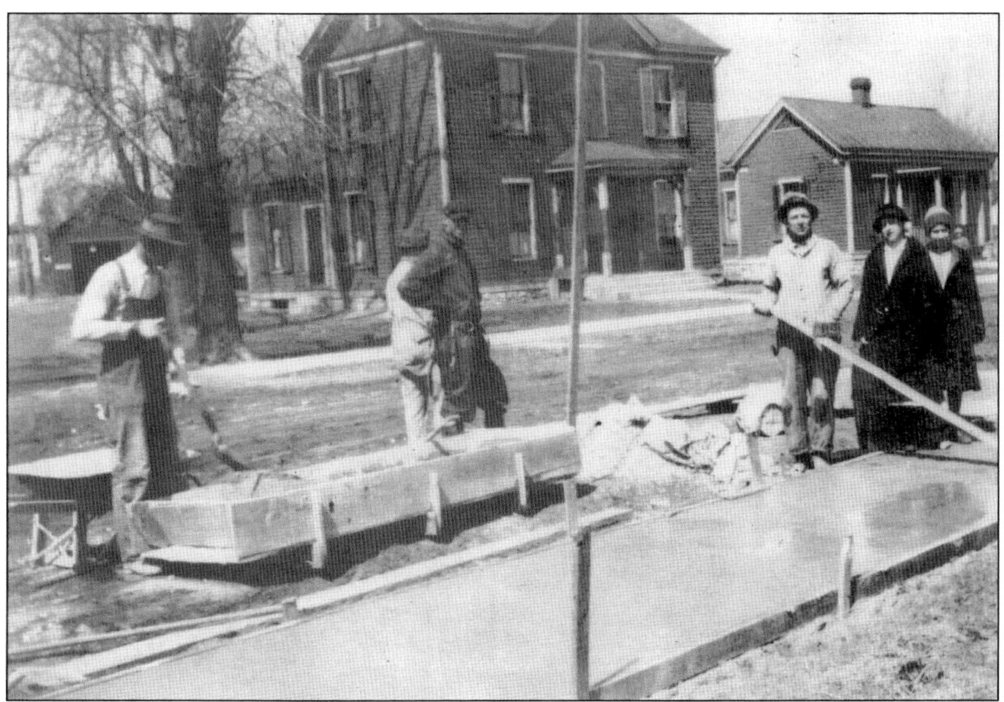

The first concrete sidewalk is East Alton was poured on Smith Street in the 1920s. Prior to concrete sidewalks, brick or board planks were laid for sidewalks.

George F. Smith Jr. was president and chairman of the board of First Federal Savings and Loan from 1934 to the time of his death in 1985. His father, George Sr., started the business in 1907. Prior to going into the savings and loan business, George Jr. was in farming, homebuilding, and the material and lumber businesses. (Courtesy of Sheryl Smith Ferry.)

Pictured are the Smith farmhouses at 410 West Airline Drive, which is at the top of Job's Hill. The house in the foreground was built in 1915 and was the original George F. Smith Sr. house. The house in the background was built by Charles N. Smith in 1925. (Courtesy of Kelly Slayden and Spencer Smith.)

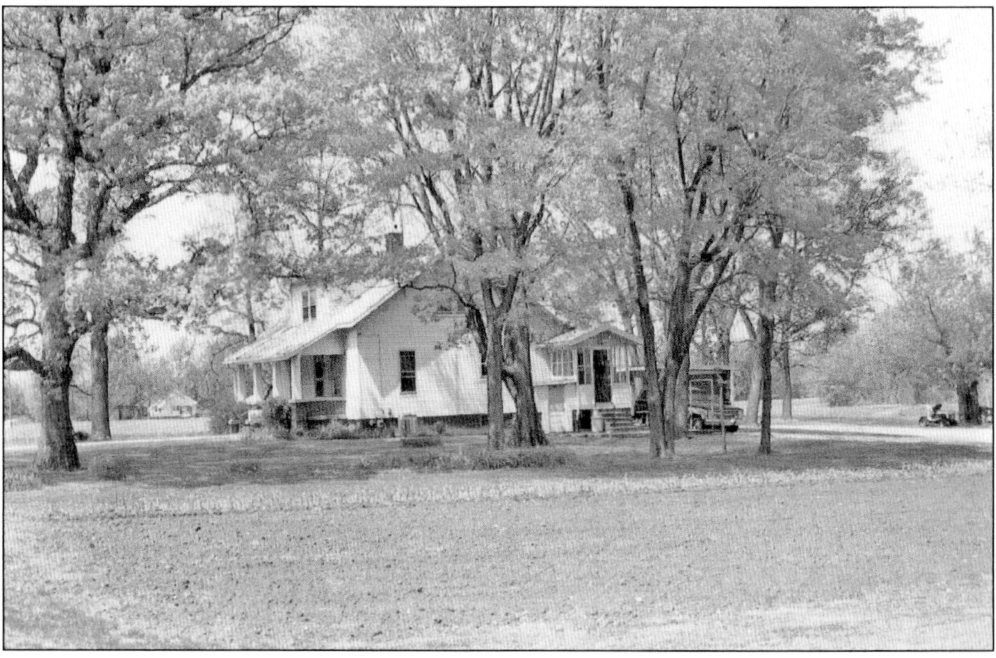

This barn was built in 1915 at the Smith farm on West Airline Drive, with the silo added in 1939. The Smiths started putting a Christmas tree on top of the silo in 1952. The barn and silo are still standing. (Courtesy of Kelly Slayden and Spencer Smith.)

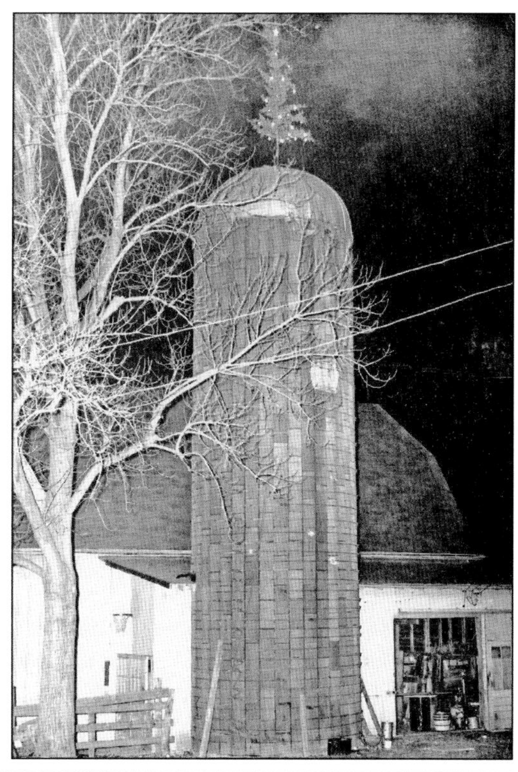

This house at 106 East Main Street belonged to Jack Hawk (pictured), who drove a horse-drawn powder wagon for the Western Cartridge Company. There is a hitching post out front, and Main Street was a dirt road at that time. This house was built in 1919. (Courtesy of Martha Campbell.)

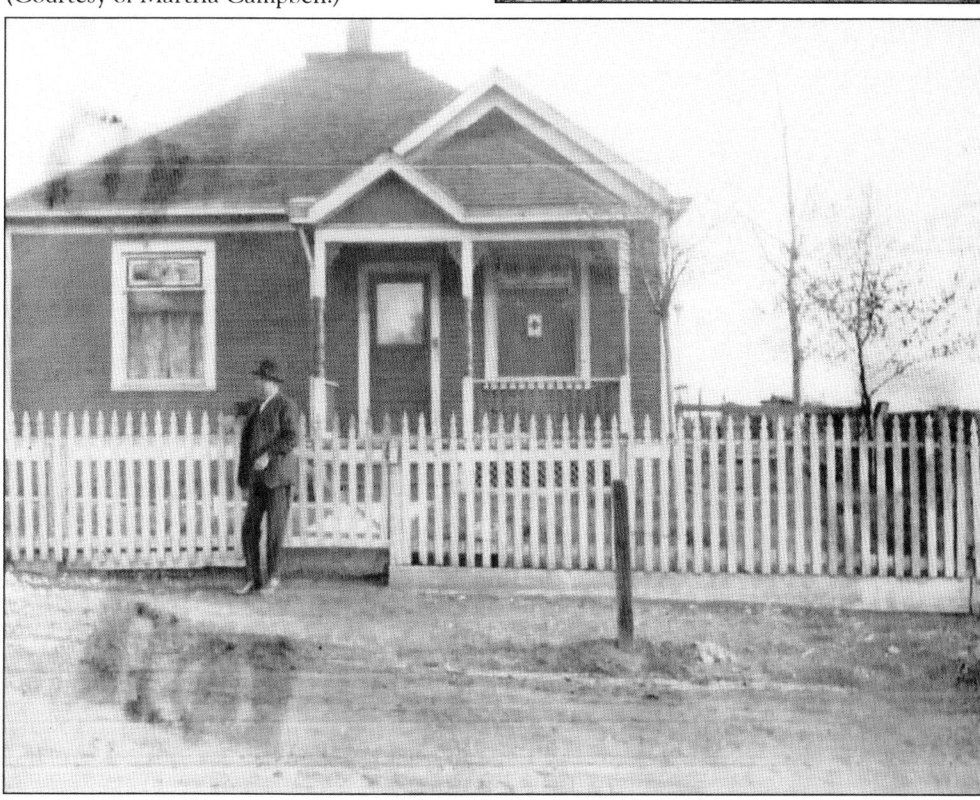

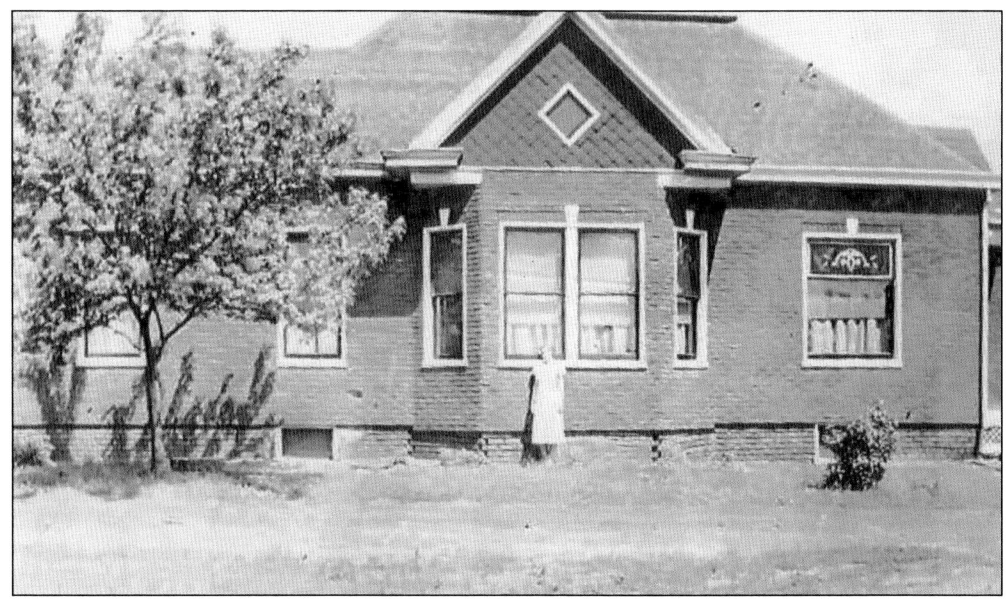

The house at 111 East Main Street belonged to Walter and Martha Meyer. There was a barn in the back of the lot next to the house where a few animals were kept. On certain nights, Walter held boxing matches in the barn. The person in the photograph is Martha Meyers. (Courtesy of Martha Meyer Campbell.)

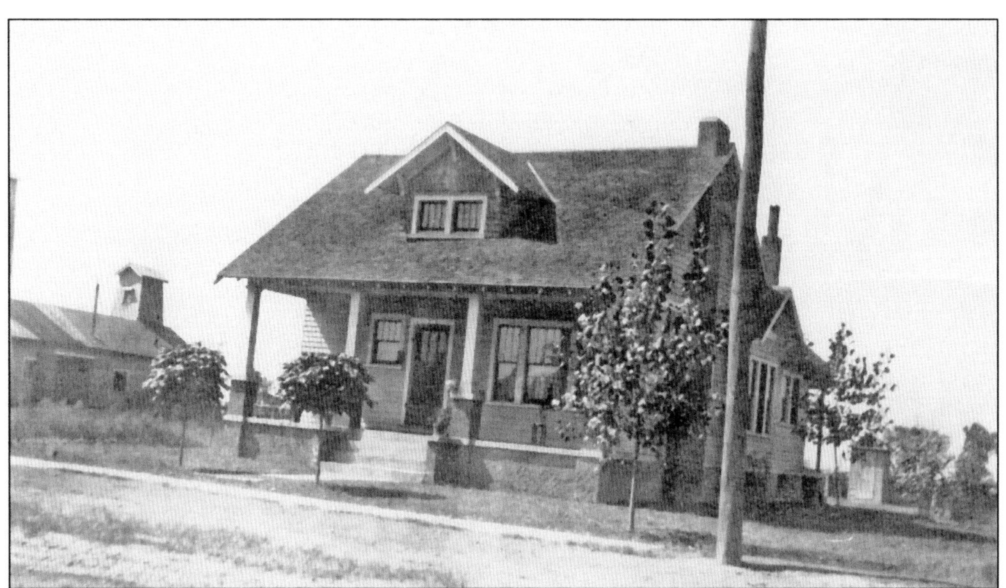

It is believed this house at 435 Broadway Avenue was the first in town with a poured foundation. The form marks are still visible in the basement. In the 1920s, the water wells belonged to the Western Cartridge Company, which shared the water with the residents of the village. The building on the left was erected over a water well for safety and to protect the equipment. (Courtesy of Dennis and Janet Newman.)

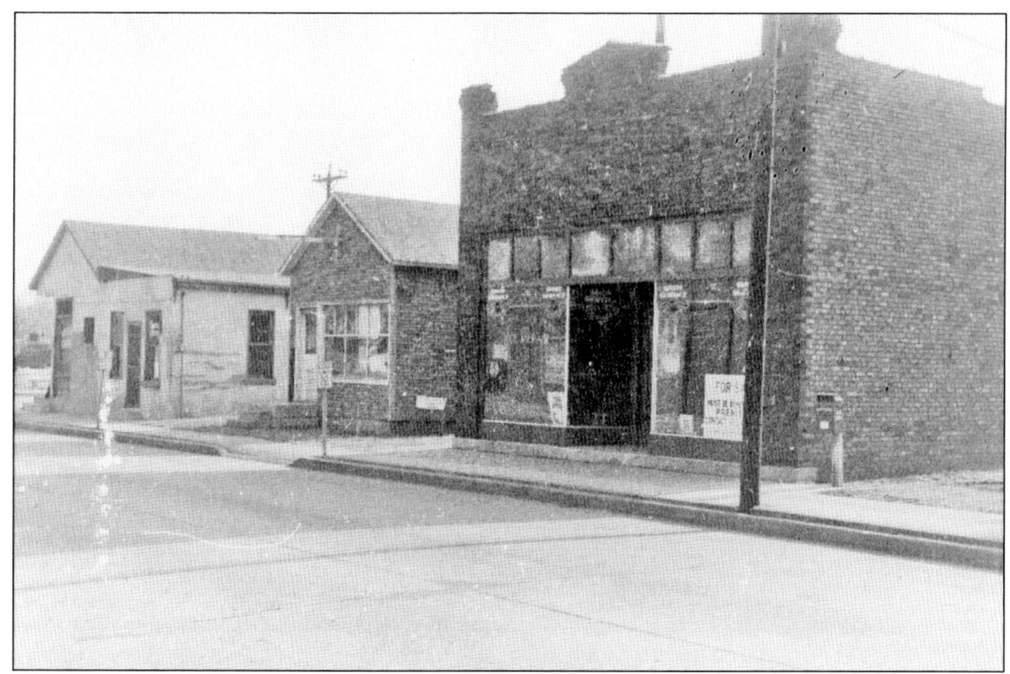

The brick building on the right was a post office in the 1900s. The building was on West Main Street at the site of the current municipal building. The small building in the center was Pedro Tchoukoleff's first shoe shop in 1928.

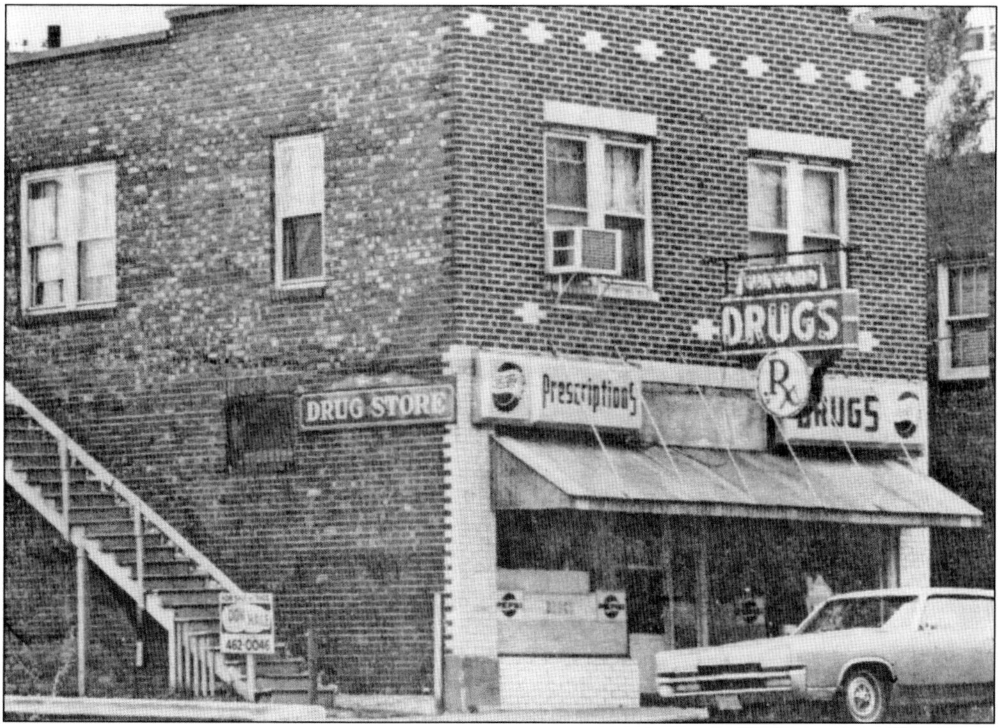

Vinyard's Drug Store was a landmark in the village beginning in 1924. Citizens could pick up drugs and necessities at the store. (Courtesy of Maurice Vinyard.)

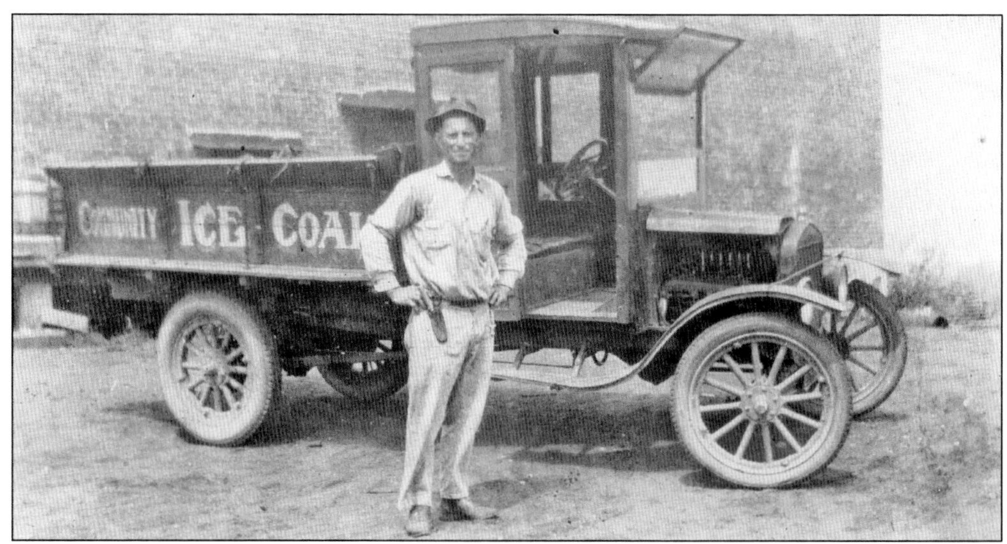

Community Coal and Ice was located on North Shamrock and Main Streets and was owned by Floyd Earl in the early 1920s. Around 1946, Herb Wilson purchased the business and ran it at that location until Glen Ralston purchased it in the 1960s. Ralston sold the business to his son Herb in 1992. The business has changed over the years from delivering coal and ice to the current seed, feed, and concrete ornamentals. The man in the picture is unidentified. (Courtesy of Herb Ralston.)

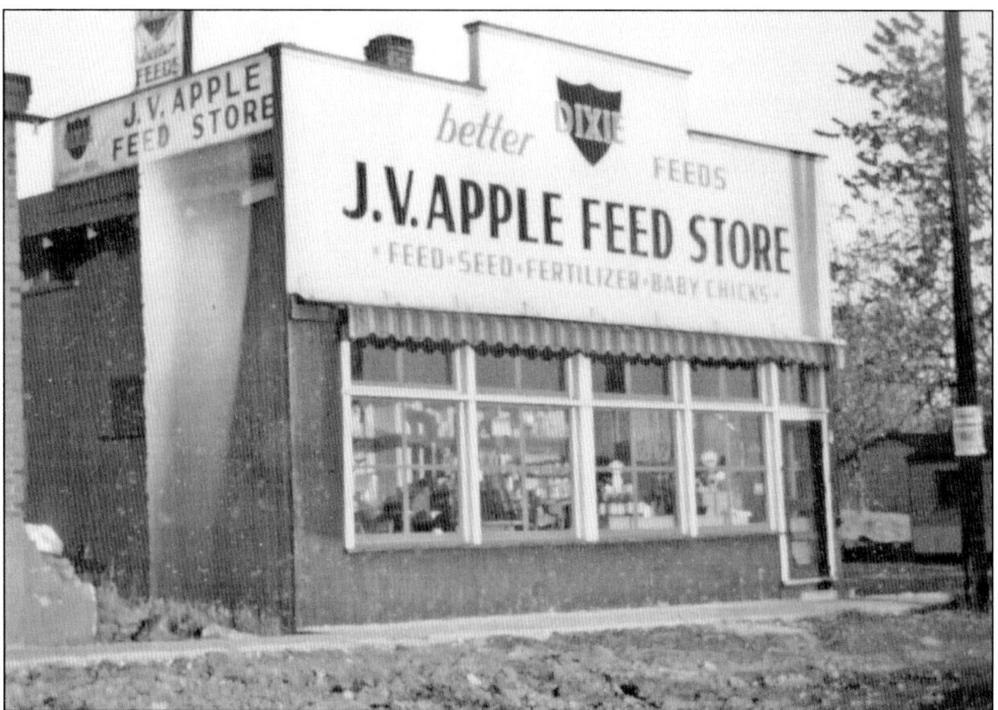

J.V. Apple Feed Store was in the 100 block of Old St. Louis Road (now East Alton Avenue). Jacob Apple ran the business from 1932 to 1939, selling feed, seed, baby chickens, and baby ducks. After his death, his son Joe ran the feed store until 1965 or 1966. He sold the store to an adjoining business, which tore it down to expand. (Courtesy of Carol A. Lawrence.)

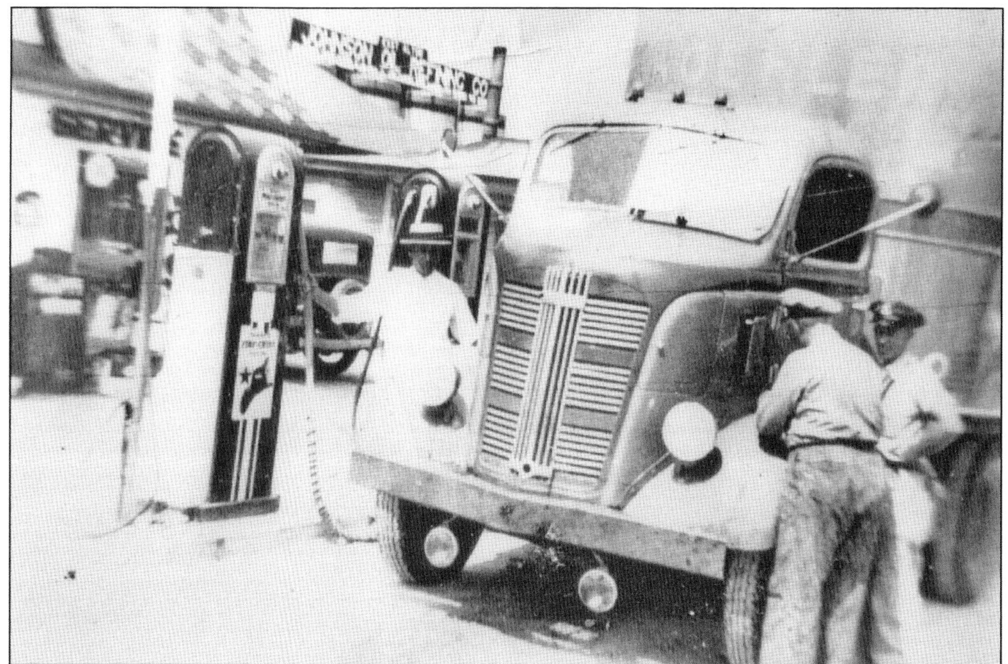

East Alton Johnson Oil Refining Company was at 559 St. Louis Avenue. The bulk plant was managed by O.H. Strode, and the service station was operated by Max Duvall. Both businesses were located at the same address during the 1930s. James Ringering is at the far right, with a Model A in the background. The other people in the photograph are unidentified. (Courtesy of the James Ringering estate.)

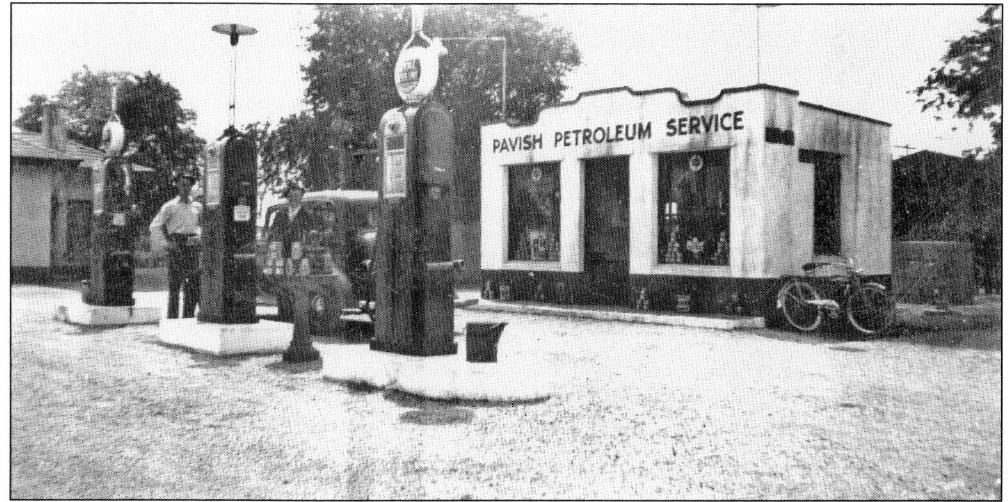

The White Rose Filling Station was on "Gasoline Alley" in the late 1920s. The section of Alton-Edwardsville Road along West St. Louis Avenue became known as Gasoline Alley due to the number of filling stations built there to serve the thousands of motorists who travel the roadway. The people in the photograph are unidentified. (Courtesy of Dolly Pavish Diaguid.)

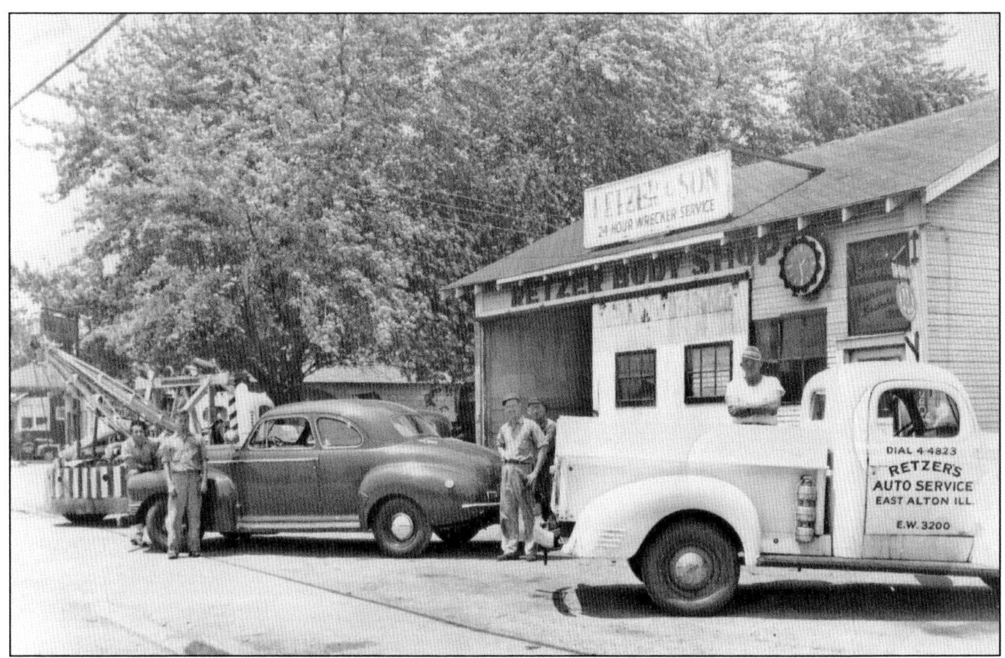

Retzer's Body Shop is pictured in the 1930s. The entrance to the shop was on West St. Louis Avenue between the Arlans Store and the East Alton Bowl Inn. From left to right are Norman Retzer, Marion Retzer, Marlin Retzer, unidentified, and Leo Retzer. (Courtesy of Tim and Chris Retzer.)

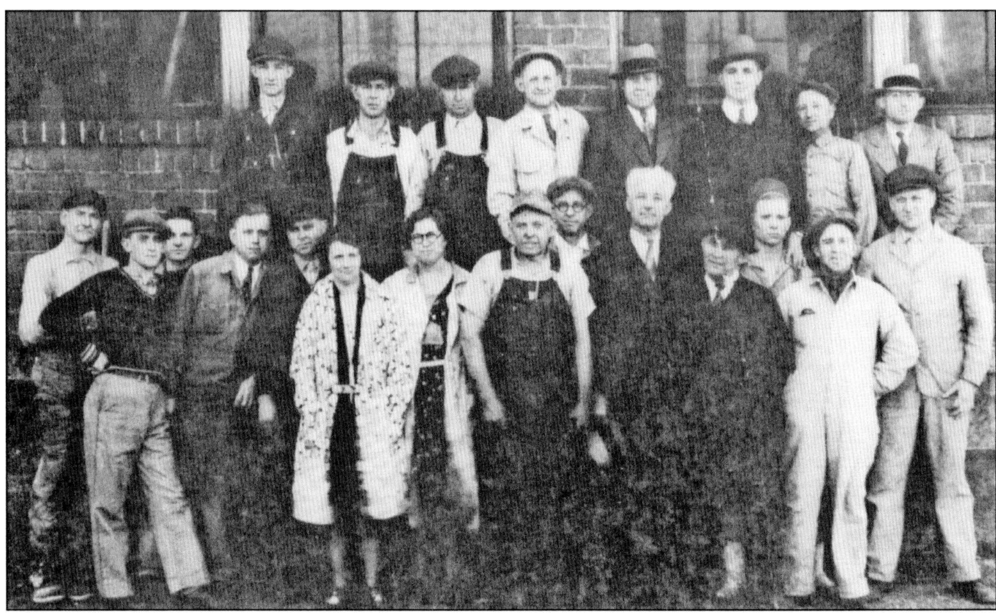

Employees of the Meadow Gold Dairy on East Alton Avenue are pictured in 1935. The American Legion Post 794 replaced the dairy at this location in 1967. From left to right are (first row) Dempsey Sawyer, Albert Junn, Ed Dorsey, Walter Eppmeyer, Russell Hale, Flora Riley, ? Smersley, Herman Adden, Jim Bell, Joe Triband, Charles Highfill, Vernon Elliott, unidentified, and Paul Johnson; (second row) Bing Ingold, John Eppmeyer, Gerhart Johnson, Lynn Kessinger, Lee Sawyer, Ray Highfill, George Elliott, and Gene Dorsey.

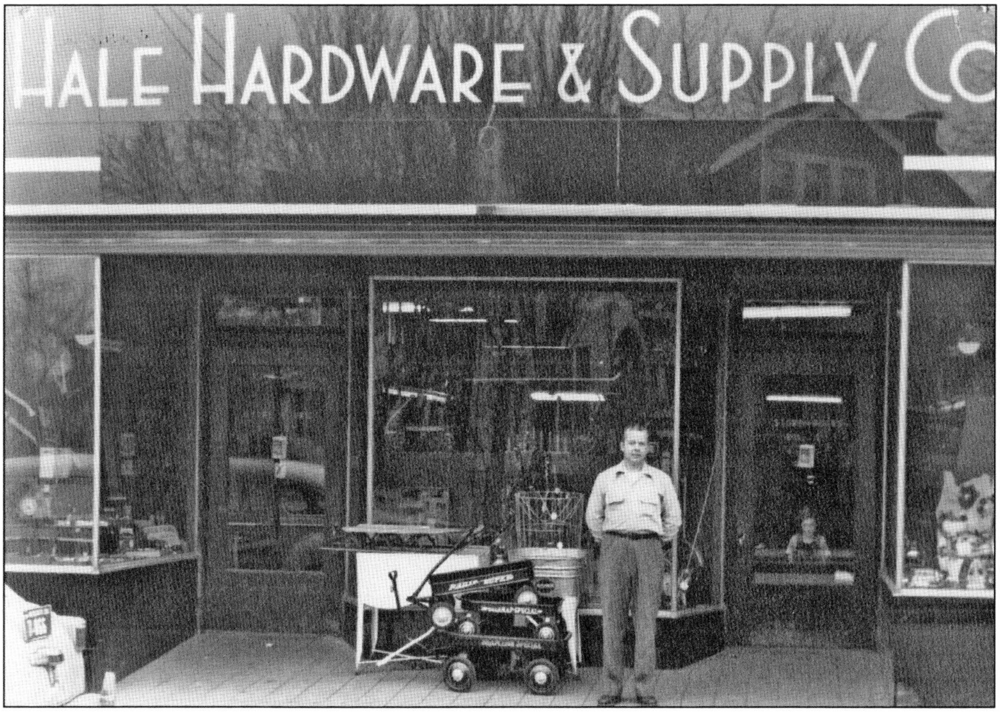

Lawrence "Lonnie" Darr is pictured standing in front of Hale Hardware and Supply Company in 1949. Hale Hardware, at 214 Smith Avenue, supplied citizens with household needs, tools, and toys for children.

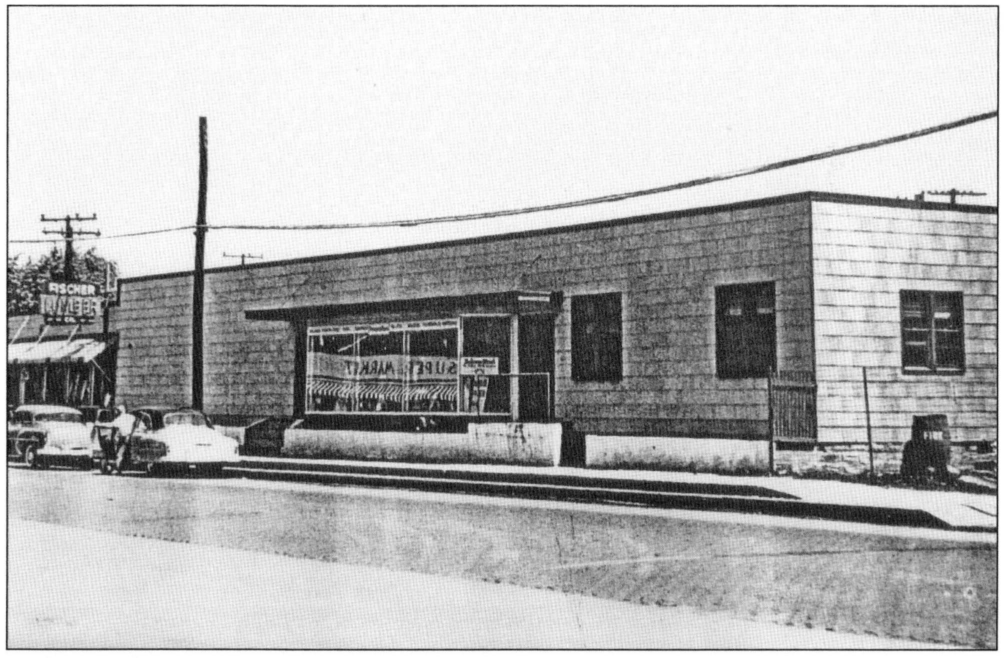

Fischer Lumber Company purchased Hale Lumber in 1941. Fischer is a four-generation family-owned business on Shamrock Street. It provides the community with various building supplies, items for remodeling homes, and help for customers with remodeling ideas.

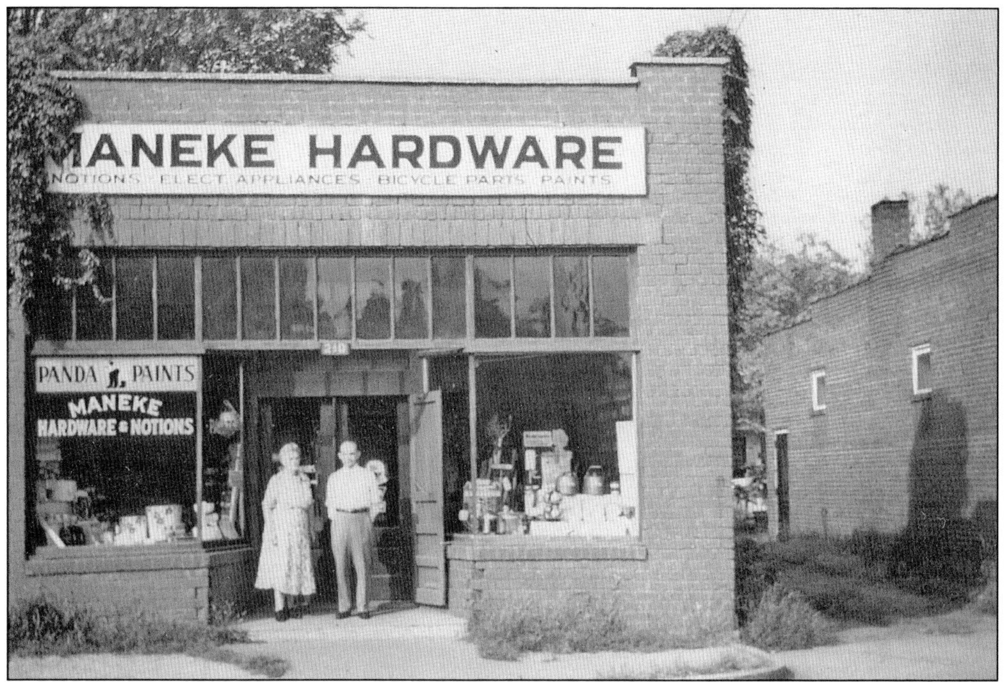

Fred W. and Mamie Maneke purchased the Mayfield Hardware Store on East St. Louis Avenue in January 1944 and renamed it Maneke Hardware. They lived in the back of the store for six years. The business closed around 1954. (Courtesy of David and Charlie Maneke.)

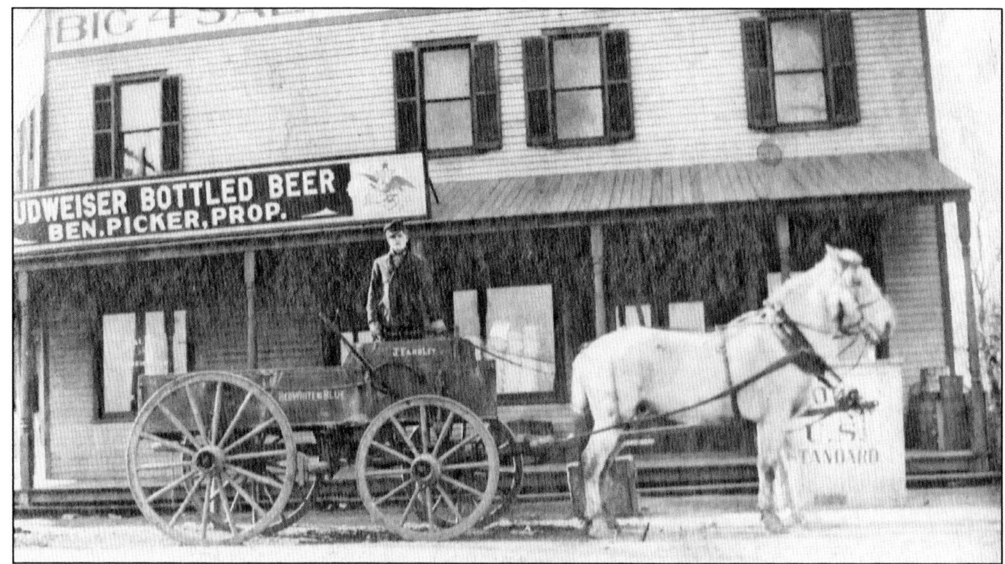

The original Big Four Saloon was located on Shamrock Street and burned down in the 1930s. Around 1947, Charles Dee Jones rebuilt the saloon, naming it the Big Four Tavern. Dee Jones and Mayor Charles VanPreter were good friends. Jones agreed to sell the Big Four Tavern property to VanPreter for the village hall. In 1966, Jones bought Ivan Enos Shoe Repair, on North Shamrock Street, to build the Little Four Tavern. John A. "Mick" Kleeman and Jess Tomerlin purchased the Little Four Tavern from Jones in January 1971. When Tomerlin decided to leave the business, Kleeman purchased his shares. (Courtesy of Roland Stulls.)

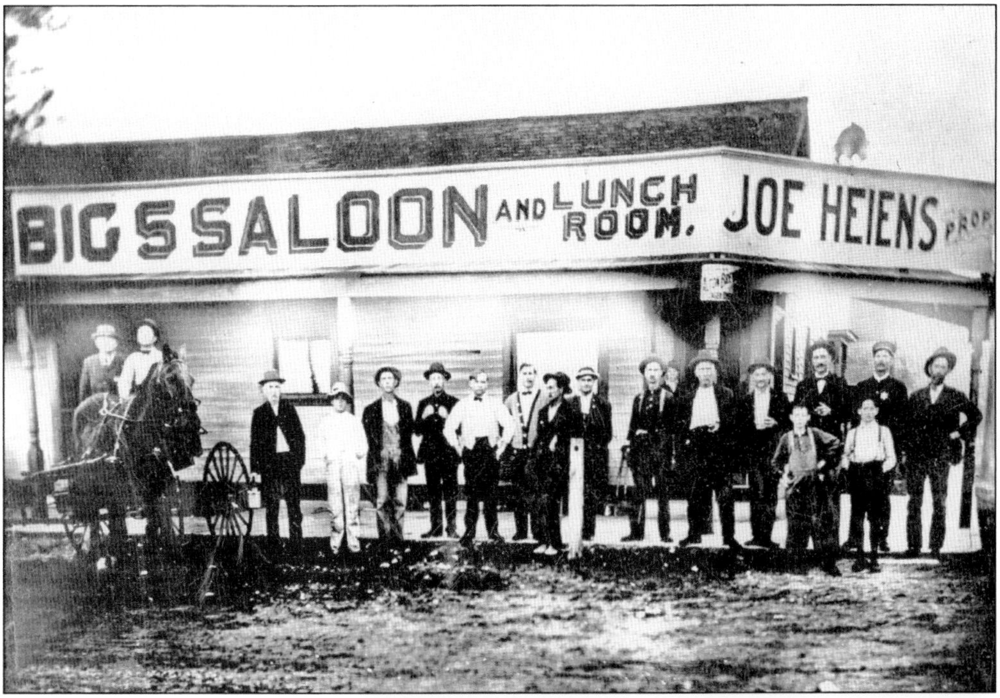

The Big Five Saloon was originally operated as a hotel and saloon by Joe Heiens at Shamrock and East Main Streets. The saloon business survived until Prohibition in the 1920s. In the photograph are, from left to right, Zephaniah "Boss" Silver, Ben G. Cooper, two unidentified, ? Crawford, two unidentified, Frank Titshnel, Harry Crawford, Dutch Rampenthal, unidentified, J.D. Nutt, Taylor Foster, two unidentified, Joe Heiens, town marshal "Chief" Franklin, and James Monahan.

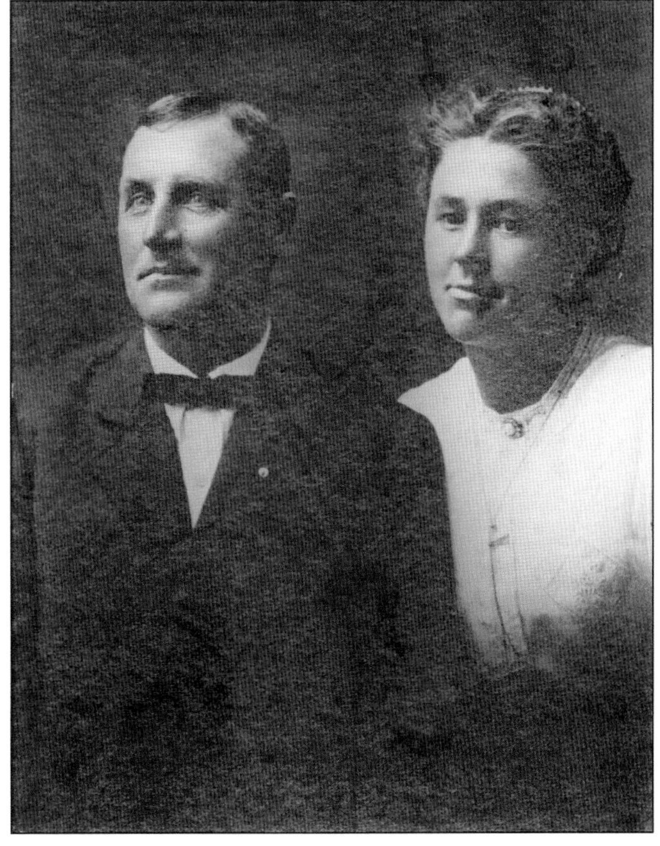

Edward J. Cooper was born in 1870 in Moro Township. After his marriage to Rosa, they moved to East Alton in 1915. Their home at 405 Broadway Avenue was one of the first houses constructed on the east side of the railroad tracks. (Courtesy of John Huff.)

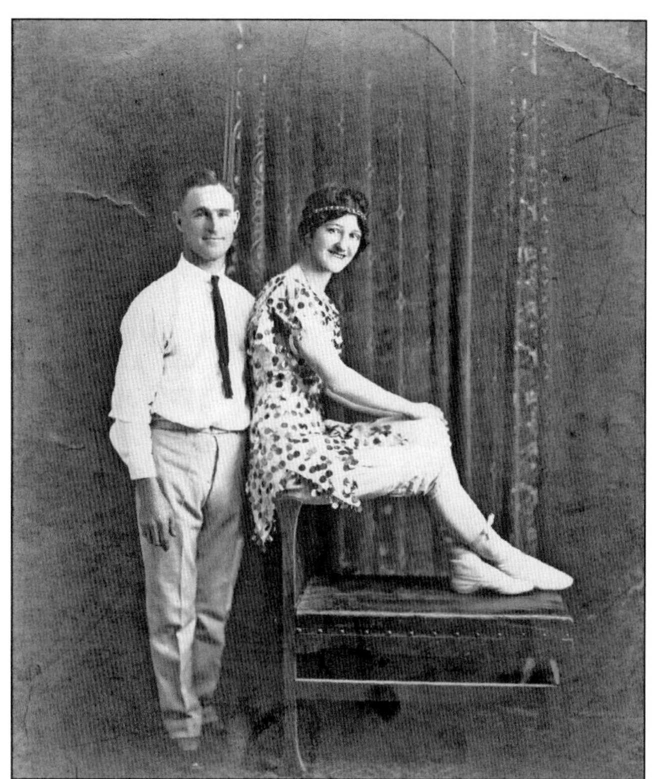

Edith Dyke was tutored by the grandparents of the renowned Harry James. In 1896, she married showman Ansel Smith. They started working on an aerial act that later toured internationally. Ringling Brothers, Hagenbeck and Wallace, and Norris Roe are three famous circuses and shows that presented their act. They toured the United States, including Hawaii, Canada, and several other. They also did three command performances for the King and Queen of England. After retiring, they lived on Bowman Avenue, and in the summers of the late 1930s early 1940s, their backyard was like a circus with all the neighborhood children being taught stunts by Ansel.

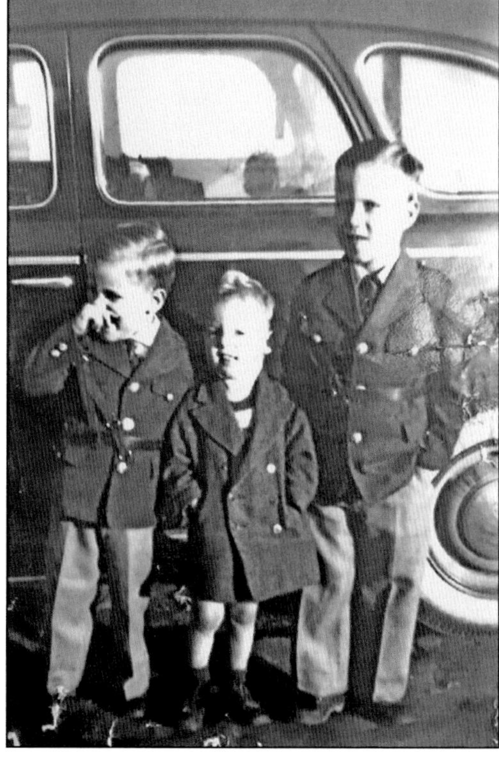

The three oldest Hinson boys are, from left to right, Charles, Howard, and Elgin "Sonny", standing in front of their family car. The photograph was taken in the early 1940s. Their parents were the late Naomi and Elgin Hinson Sr. They raised all six of their children at 422 Job Street. (Courtesy of Kelli Hinson Fletcher.)

Four

Growth and Change

World War II brought additional growth to the village. The Winchester Western Company (Olin) received contracts from the federal government, providing employment. The local federal headquarters were on Third Street, and housing was built near the headquarters for employees and their families working at the Winchester Western Company. The housing was to be temporary, but it was needed for service people returning after the war.

The war effort grew the population, and to accommodate the newcomers, enterprising citizens started new businesses throughout the area. With the increase in traffic, a number of gas stations and automobile businesses were started on West St. Louis Avenue. The locals called this area "Gasoline Ally" due to the number of gas stations along the road.

In 1935, a new post office was built, and the library was established. In 1956, a new fire station was built on Third Street to serve the east side of the village, and in 1951, the Citizens Building and Loan was built. Citizens served the community mostly through home and business loans. Wilshire Village, one of the earliest strip malls, was built in 1957. In the 1950s, two schools were built to address overcrowding.

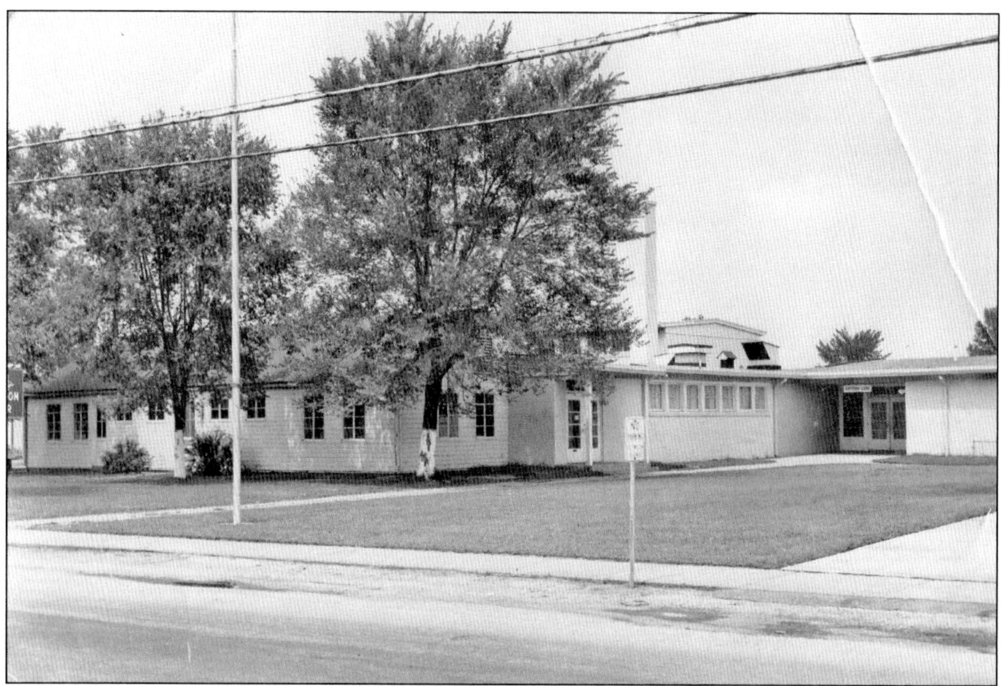

The above building was built in 1941 as a recreation center and headquarters for troops stationed in East Alton during World War II. The building was given to the village in 1954 and is maintained as a community and recreation center where various youth and adult activities are held. Realizing the need for addition room to serve the community, a gymnasium was added in 1979, and an auditorium was added in 1981. The center (pictured below) was renamed Keasler Recreational Center in 1978.

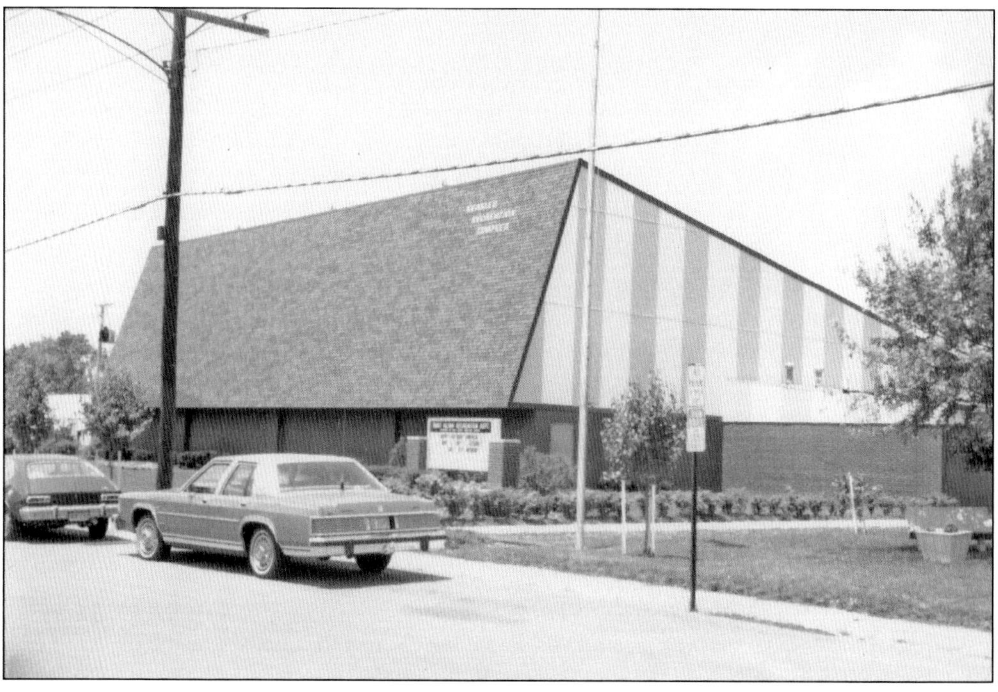

Dr. Everett R. Quinn took over the practice of Dr. C.A. Moore about 1930. Dr. Quinn was a longtime physician and East Alton medical officer. During World War II, he served in the Army Medical Corps. He returned to his East Alton practice after the war. He was assisted by his nurse, Nell McCrellis, for 45 years. This photograph was taken at Nell's retirement party in 1973. (Courtesy of Ted Lotz.)

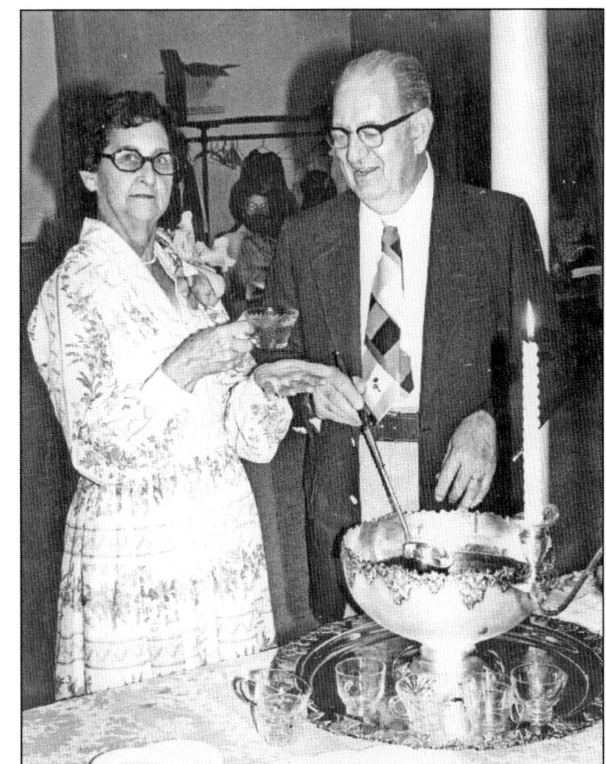

The new post office was built in 1935 on Smith Street. The old post office was on West Main Street where the current municipal building is located. (Courtesy of Maurice Vinyard.)

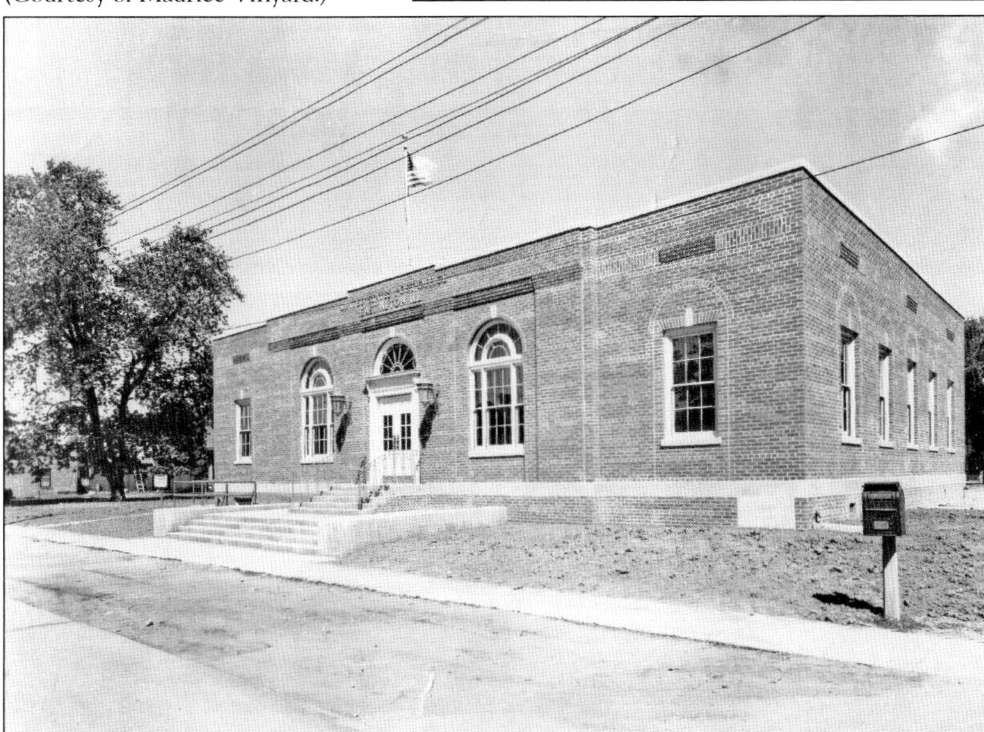

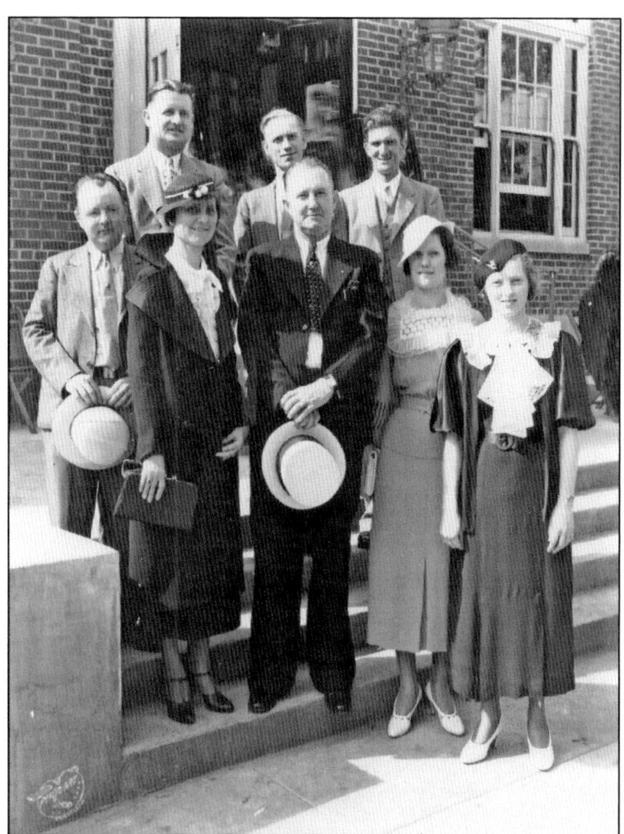

The new post office was dedicated on June 1, 1935. Staff members attending the dedication are, from left to right, (first row) William Bauer, Maude Quillen, Postmaster Lee Vinyard, Lena Robinson, and Lucille Reader; (second row) Clifford Cooper, Moren Joiner, and Lyman Crane. (Courtesy of Maurice Vinyard.)

The Ritz Theatre, on West St. Louis Avenue, was a popular gathering place from the 1930s to 1950s. In the 1930s, Thursday was children's night, with admission 10¢ and a bag of popcorn 5¢. The theater allowed organizations to use its facilities to hold benefits.

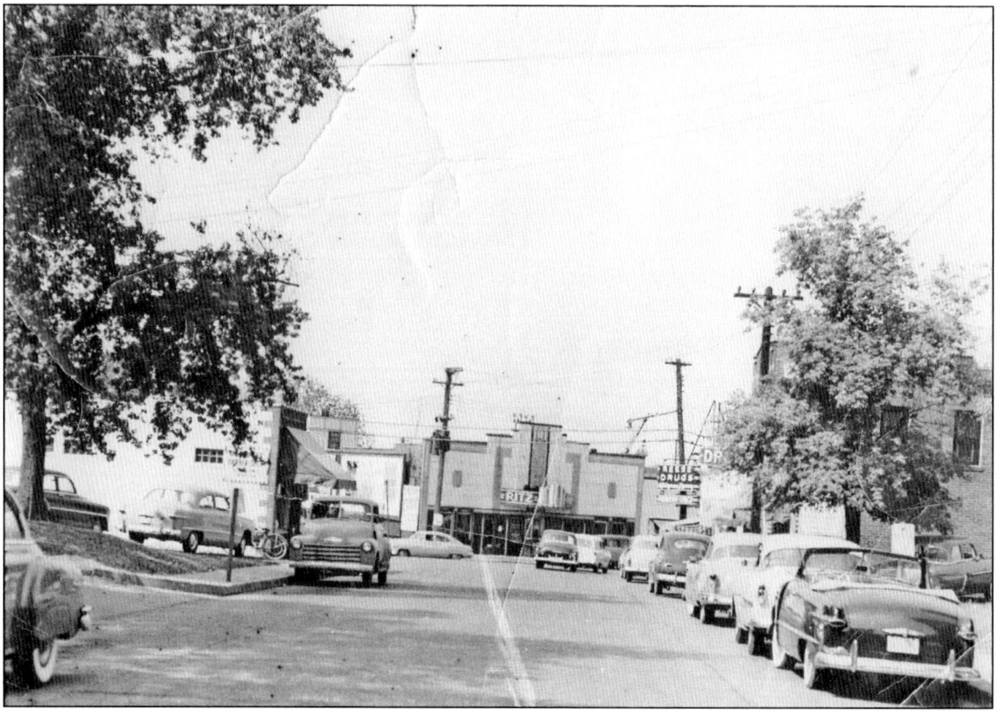

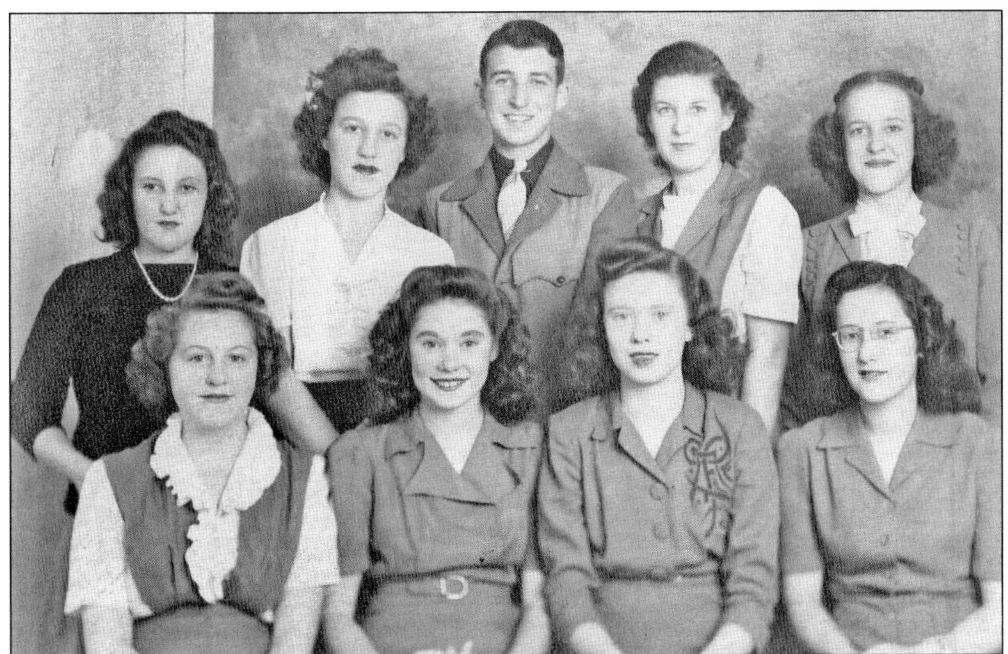

The Ritz Theatre was a popular gathering place in the early days. The employees who worked at the theater in 1944 and 1945 are, from left to right, (first row) Ramona Sawyer, Betty Withrow, Virginia Withrow, and Doris Townsend; (second row) Katherine Townsend, Bertha Lohse, Jack Grissom, Sally Moore, and Mildred Abner. (Courtesy of Bertha Lohse Baldridge.)

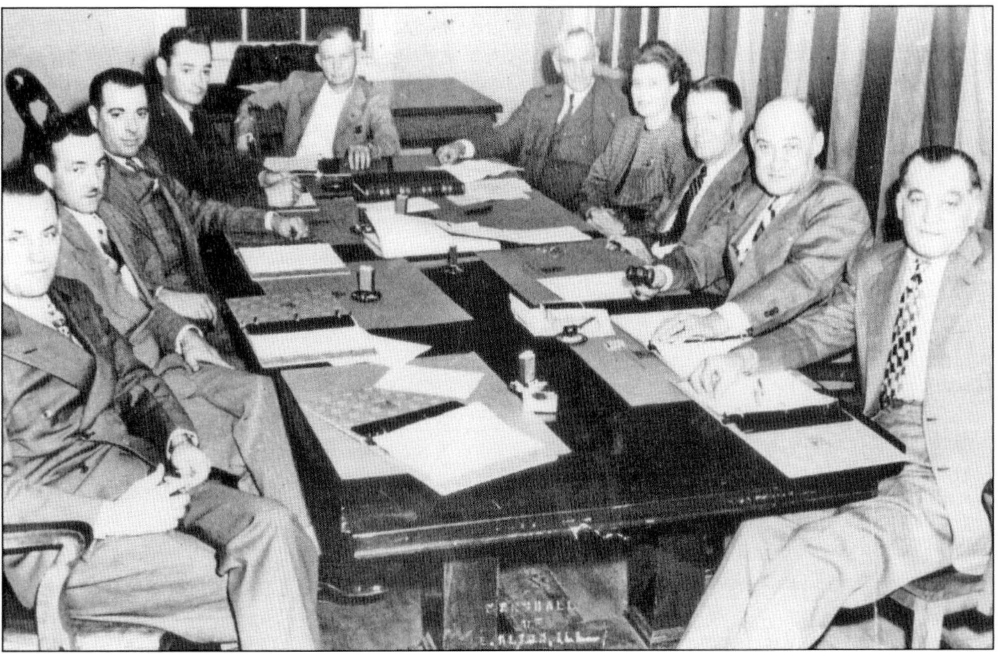

The city council meets twice a month to discuss village business. This meeting of the city council was held around 1945. Pictured from left to right are William Linkogle, Roschier Clinton, Albert Treece, Thad Fife, Thomas Redman, Judge William P. Boynton, Margaret Pruitt, Joe Nolan, Mayor Charles VanPreter, and William A. Keil.

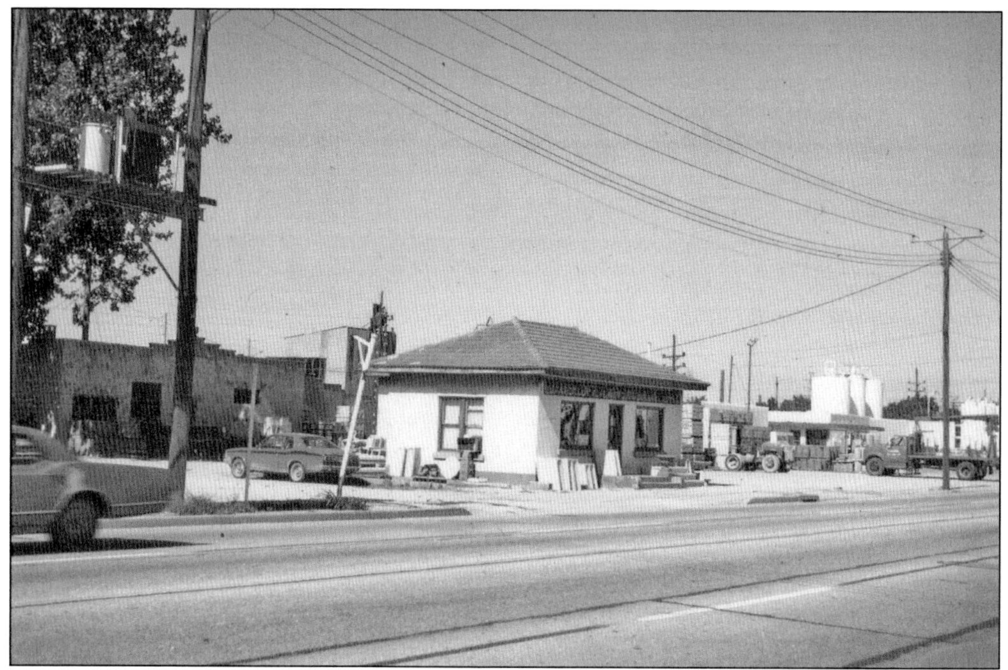

L.J. Pavish Concrete Works and Building Supplies was in business from 1929 to 1979. This company was located on West St. Louis Avenue between the Wood River and the viaduct. While Pavish was making concrete blocks for the foundation of his family home, people would stop to buy the blocks for their use. He recognized the need for building materials and started the concrete business. (Courtesy of Dolly Pavish Diaguid.)

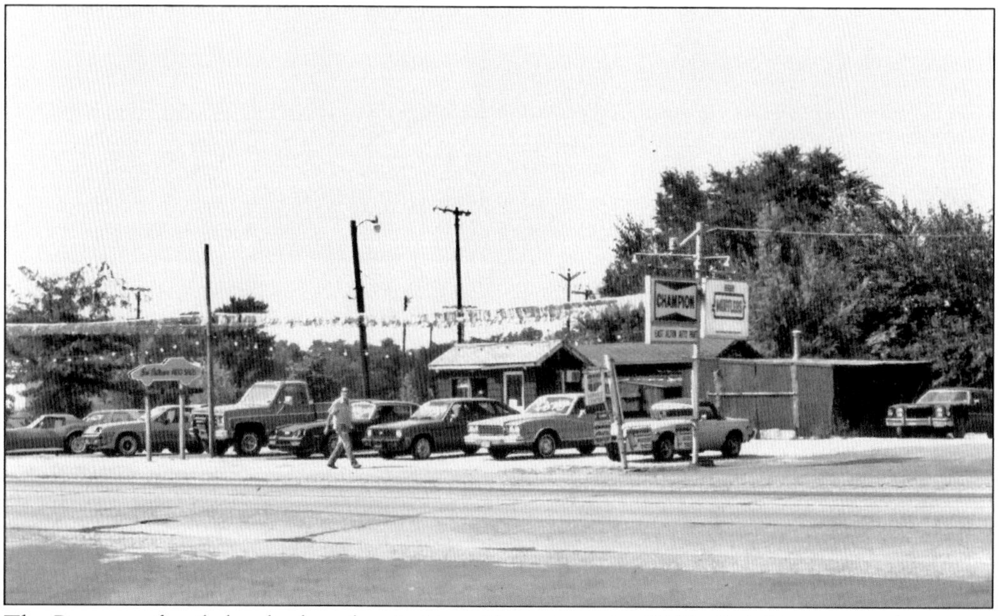

The Patterson family has had car lots in East Alton since the 1940s. Bob Patterson is known as the "Corvette Man" and has sold around 500 Corvettes over the years. He furnished the Corvette the Cardinals presented to Mark McGwire when he hit home run number 62 on September 8, 1998, breaking Roger Maris's long-standing record. Bob also deals in classic cars.

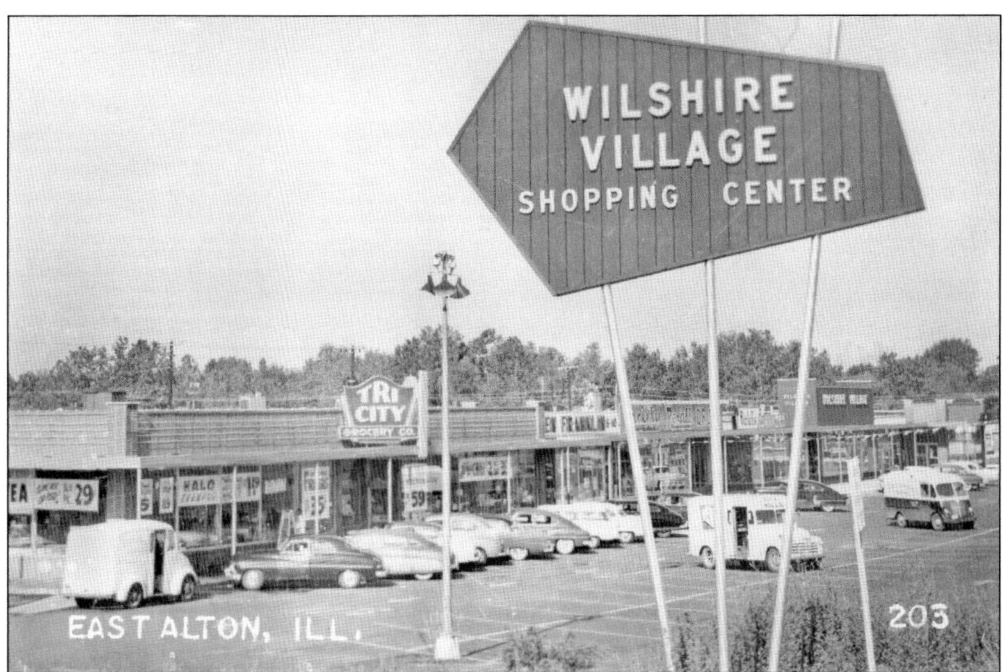

Wilshire Village Shopping Center was one of the first strip malls built in the area. A variety of stores at the shopping center provided residents of the village and surrounding cities with dry goods as well as necessary food items. The picture was taken in the late 1950s or early 1960s.

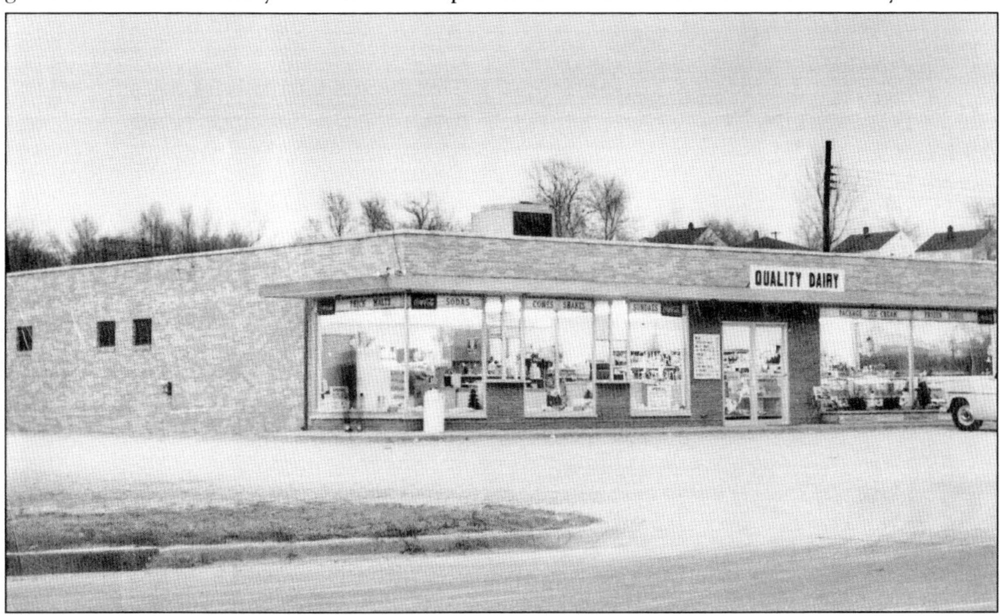

Henry Hahenkamp moved his dairy business from Moro, Illinois, to Berkshire Boulevard in the spring of 1955. Quality was the first building in the Wilshire Shopping Center. The dairy had seven daily routes delivering milk to homes, schools, and stores locally and in nearby towns. Quality quickly became one of the largest convenience stores in the area. Customers stood in line to buy ice cream cones, milkshakes, and sundaes. One summer, Henry's employees averaged 635 ice cream cones per day. He sold his business in 1978. (Courtesy of Jeanette M. Hahnenkamp Gentry.)

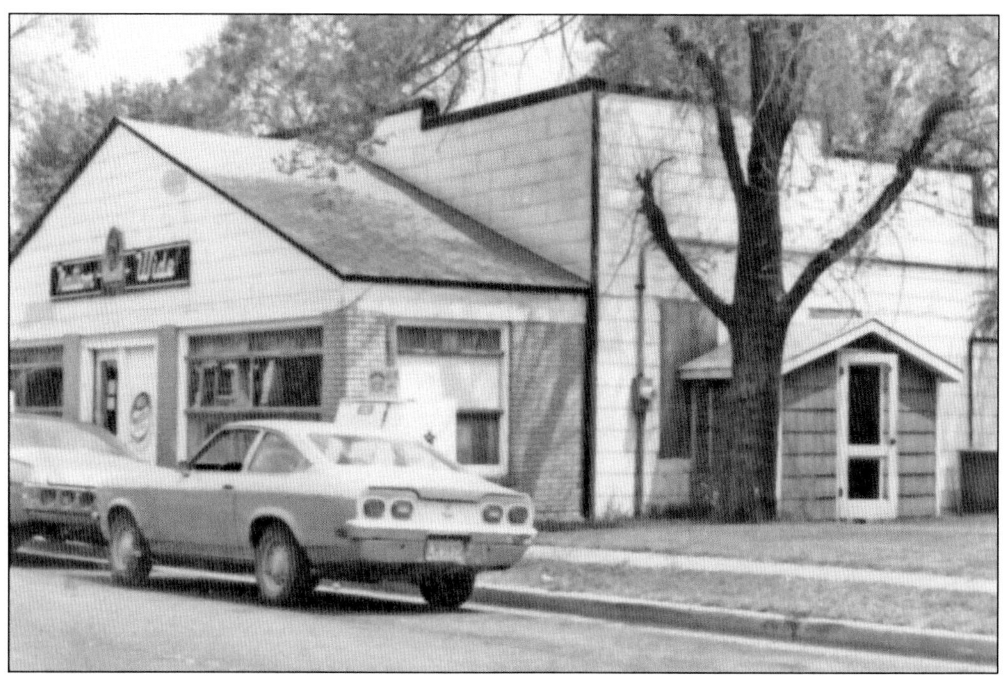

Holloway Market (above) was a member of Nation Wide, a consortium of independent grocery stores. Holloway's served the village until 1951. Sever's Market (below) is well known in the area. Marion "Bud" Sever purchased Holloway's Market in September 1951. Sever's is a small store that carries necessities and has a meat case full of quality hand-cut meats. Sever's is the last family-owned grocery store in the East Alton. "Bud" retired at the age of 80, and his sons David and Robert continue to run the store. (Both photographs courtesy of David and Robert Sever.)

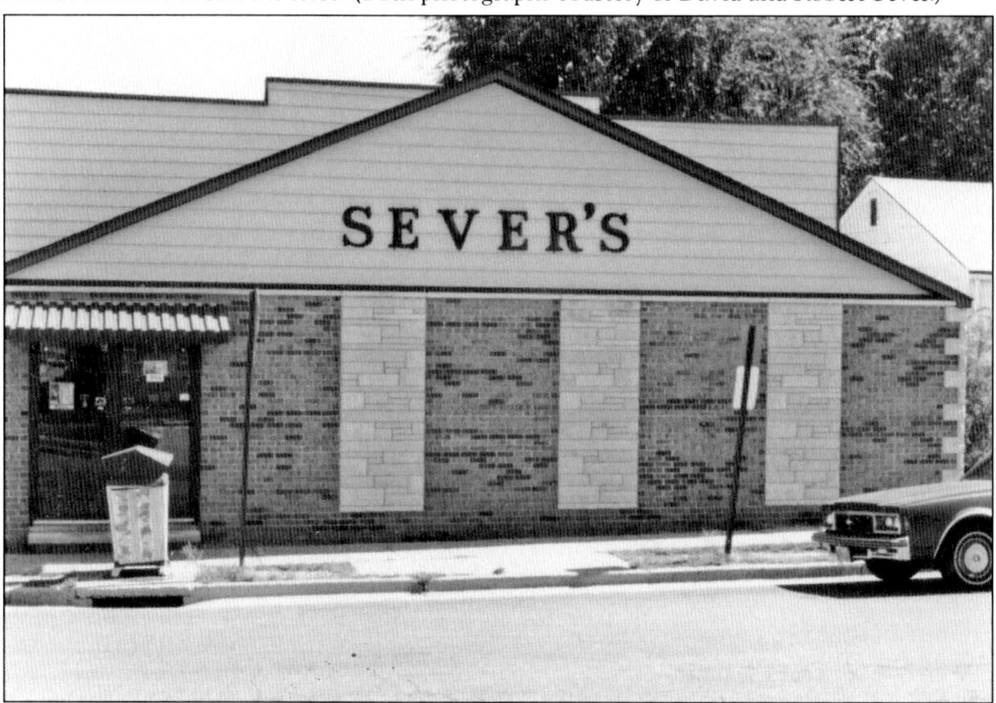

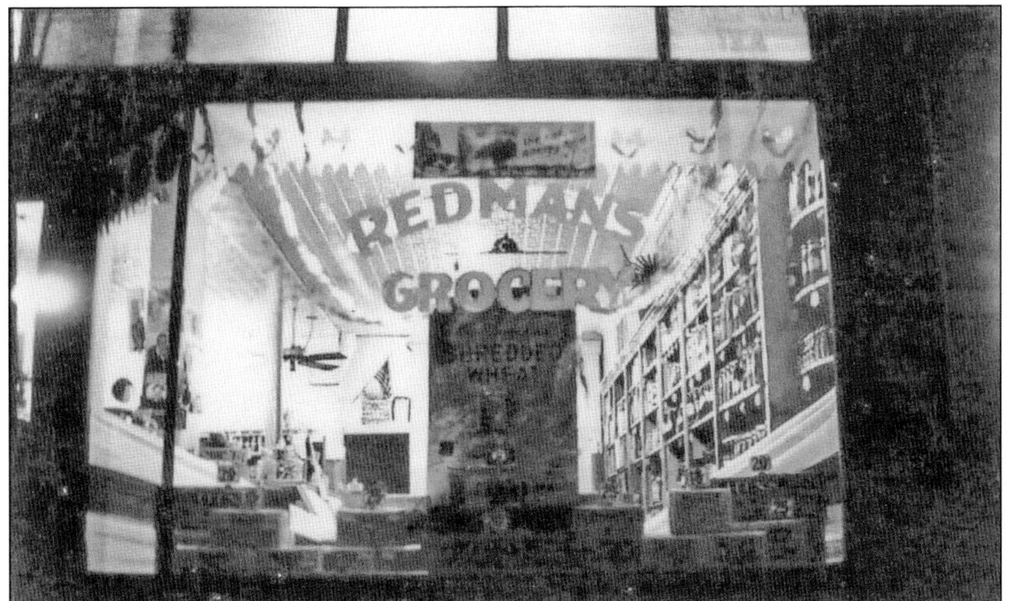

Redman's Grocery was built in 1917 at 335 Church Street. The store was run by Leslie and Eva Redman. Leslie passed away in 1952, and Eva continued to run the store until 1954. The building was converted into apartments around 1989. Redman was a village trustee in the late 1920s and early 1930s.

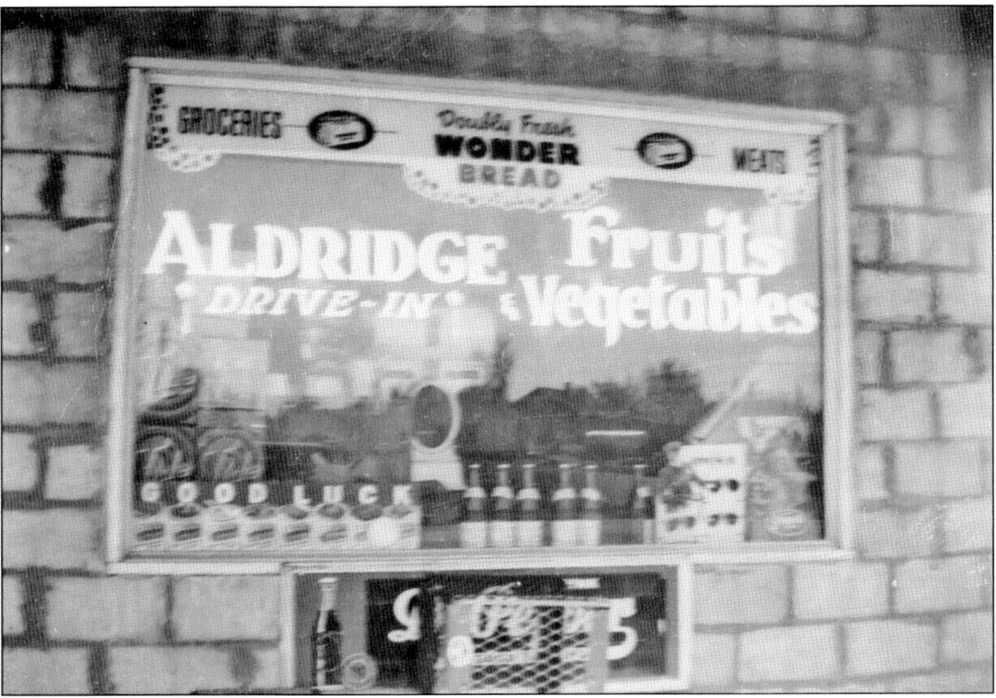

Aldridge Grocery, at 119 Fourth Street, opened in 1949. Robert Garrett and Lillian Manette Aldridge owned and operated the store. They lived in front of the store at 400 Washington Avenue. Their son Garrett Edward "Sonny" worked at the store until graduating high school. (Courtesy of Kim Aldridge, daughter of Garrett Edward Aldridge.)

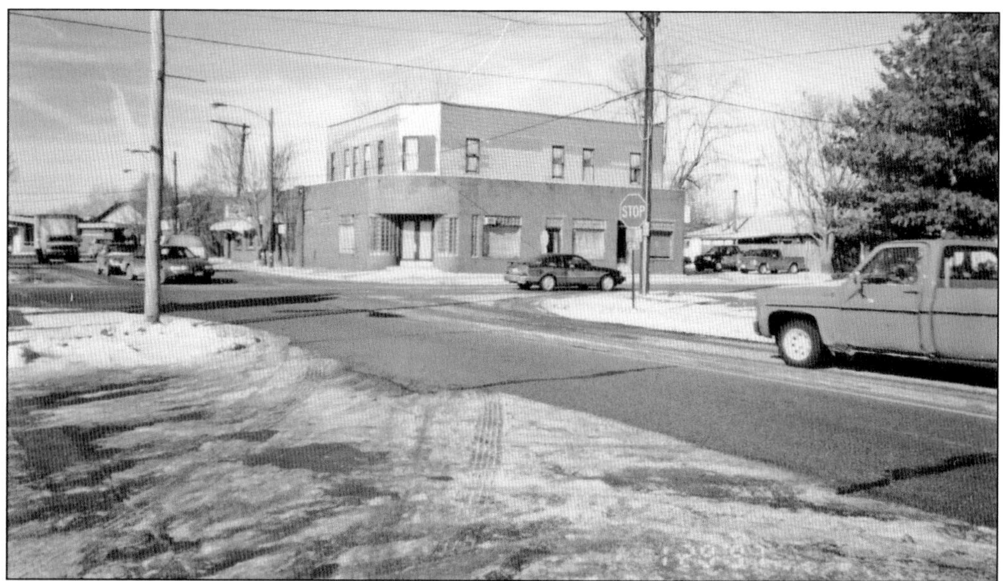

This building at Shamrock and West Main Streets has been the place of numerous businesses, including the Big Five Tavern, Shamrock Restaurant, and Park Hotel. The building was razed in the early 1990s, and the location is currently a small green space.

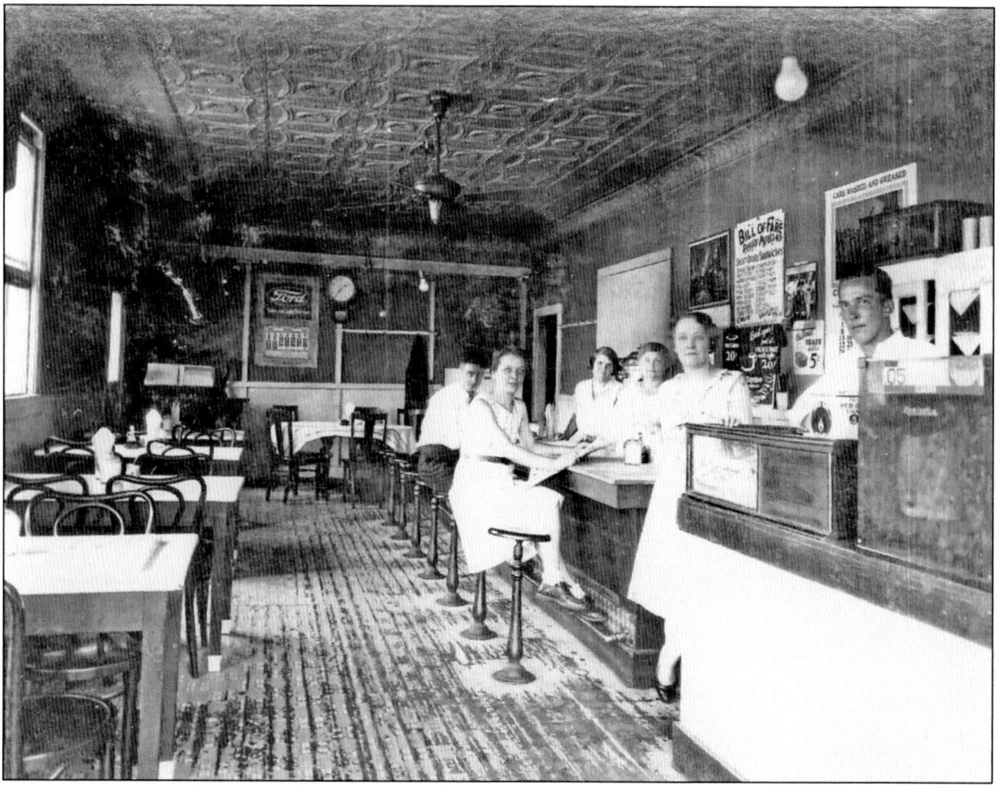

The inside of the Shamrock Restaurant is seen here. Martha Meyer was one of the cooks (second from the left behind the counter); others are unidentified. (Courtesy of Martha Meyer Campbell, granddaughter of Martha Meyer.)

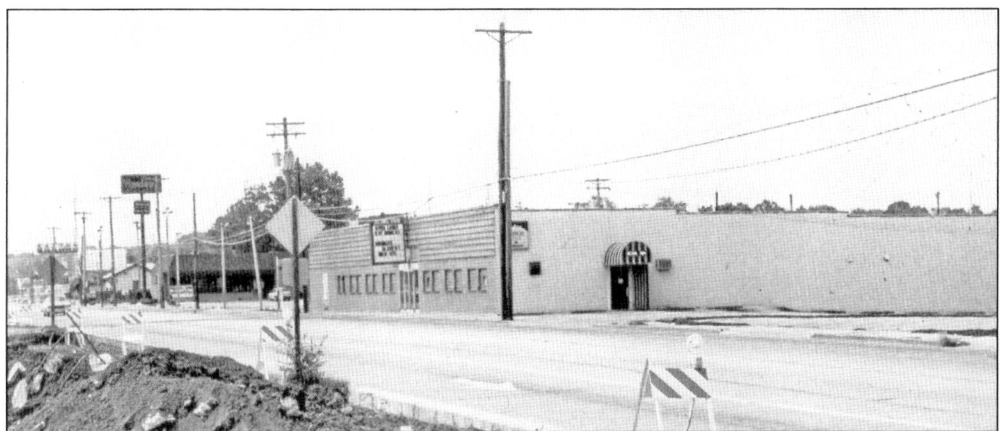

In 1948, Bowl Inn was opened by famed bowler Nelson Burton. Burton was inducted into the American Bowling Congress Hall of Fame in 1964. Bowl Inn was an ultra-modern 16-alley masterpiece of engineering. There have been various owners over the years. Owners Nancy and Denny Harrison closed the bowling alley between 2001 and 2002. Chris Staar opened Neon Works at that site in June 2005. Neon Works provides specialized lighting for cars, businesses, and homes.

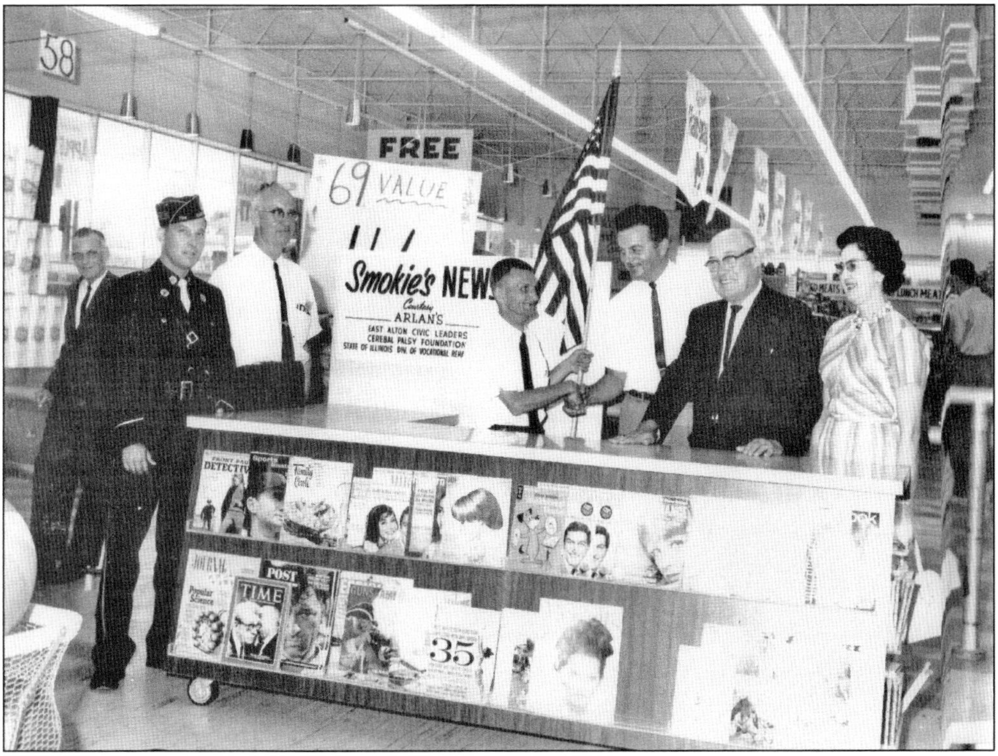

Martin "Smokie" Rhyne was well known in the village. Although handicapped, he worked at various newsstands, including at the Arlans store. He loved baseball and umpired Little League games at VanPreter Park. He was a frequent visitor at the Keasler Recreation Center. When the recreation center expanded, the old gymnasium was dedicated to Smokie. From left to right are Robert H. Brown from American Legion Post 794, Bill Linkogle, Martin "Smokie" Rhyne, James Johnson, Mayor Charles VanPreter, and unidentified. (Courtesy of Geno and Debbie Ballard.)

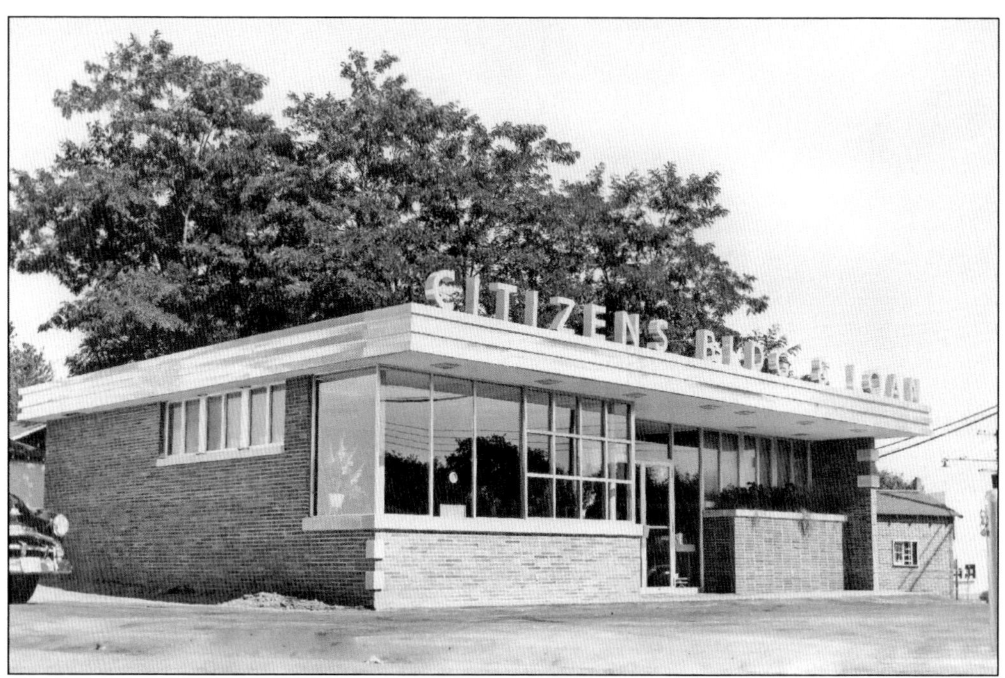

Citizens Building and Loan, on Smith Street, was dedicated on August 4, 1951. Citizens was owned by shareholders and gave back to the community, mostly through loans for property. A new building was constructed in 1964 near Wilshire Village Shopping Center. (Courtesy of Allen Hale.)

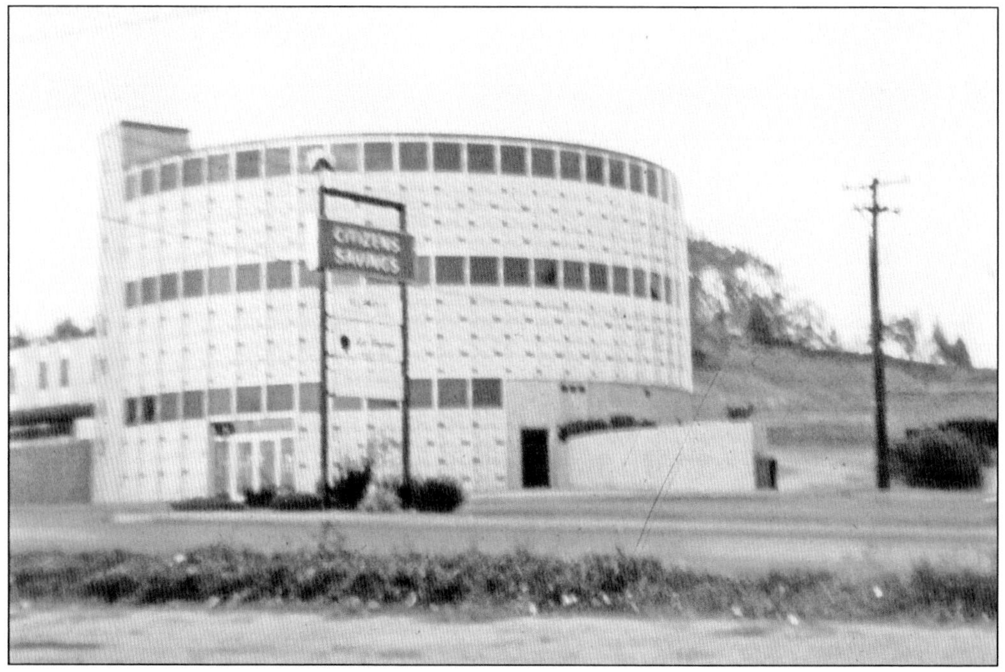

The new Citizens Building and Loan office was built in 1964. The building was unusual, with a round design and suspended bridge from the sidewalk to the entrance. Various businesses were located in this building. Citizens was closed in 1988 or 1989.

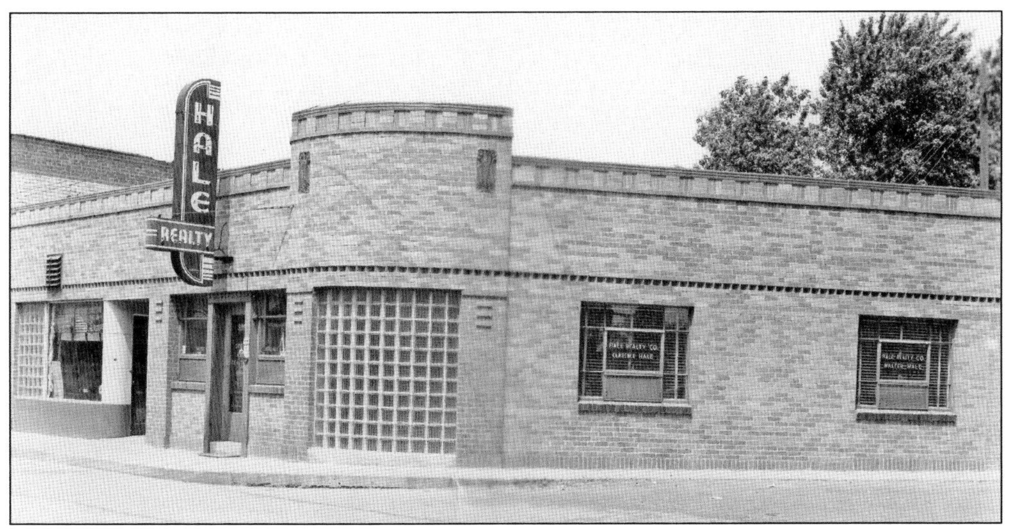

Bauer and Hale Real Estate and Insurance opened in 1918. Walter Hale Sr. left the partnership in the early 1920s and opened a real estate office in the Illinois State Bank. In the 1950s, Walter moved the Hale Real Estate offices from Illinois State Bank to the current location on Smith Street. Hale Realty is still in business. (Courtesy of Allen Hale.)

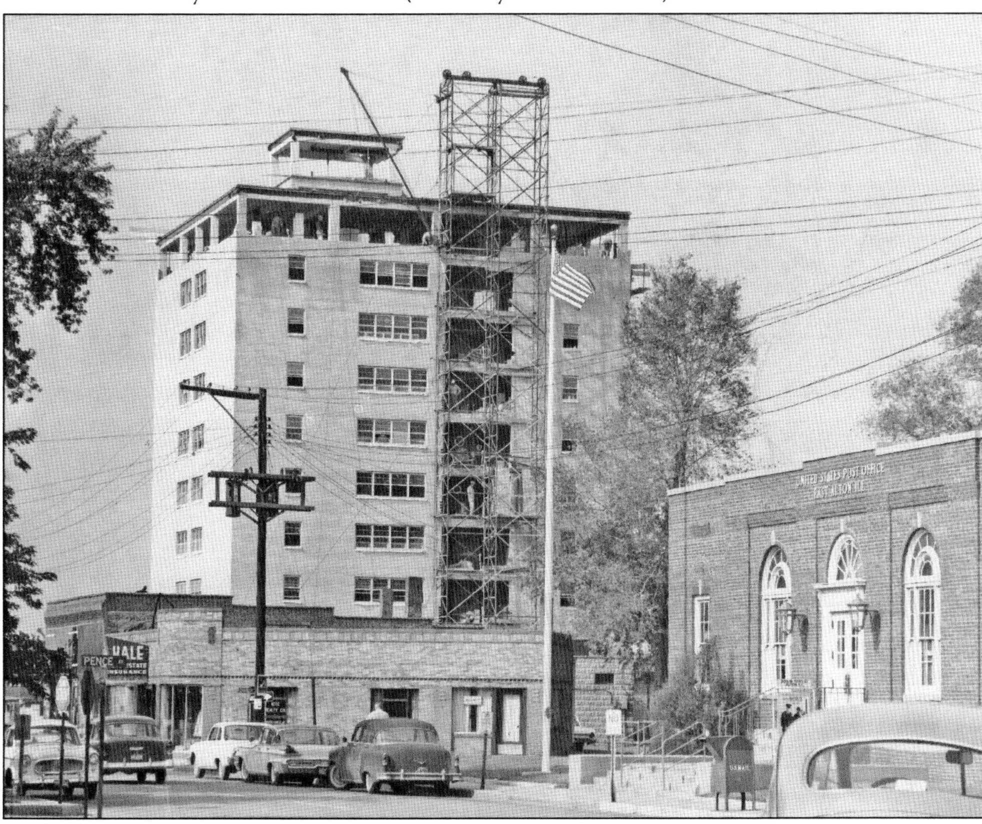

The Olin Home building was constructed in 1962 on Smith Street. The Olin Home is a federal housing unit that provides affordable housing for senior citizens. The East Alton Post Office and Hale Realty are also featured in this photograph. (Courtesy of Allen Hale.)

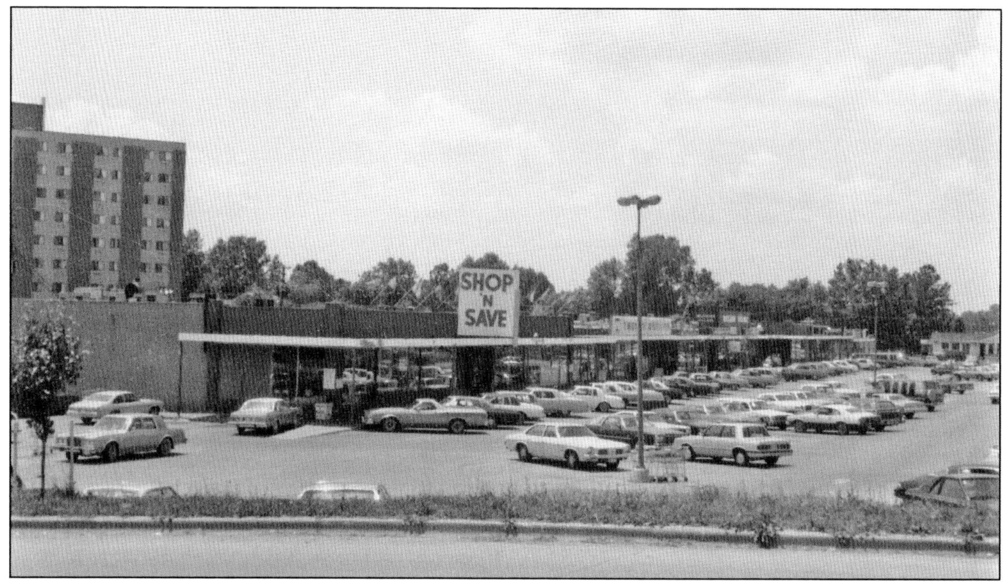

The high-rise on the left is the Township Village apartments on Valley Drive. These apartments allow senior and disabled citizens to live independently. The high-rise was built around 1980 near the Wilshire Village shopping center for the convenience of the residents.

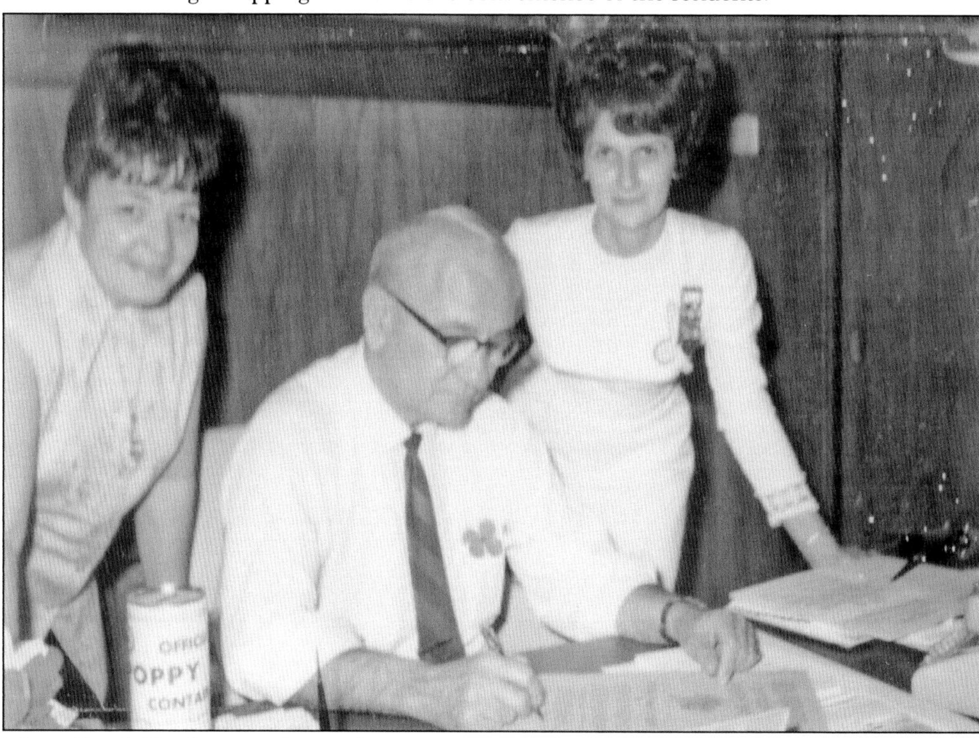

Mayor Frank Keasler signed a proclamation recognizing Poppy Days on Thursday and Friday of Memorial Day weekend in 1971. From left to right are poppy chairwoman Mavis Bracht, Mayor Frank Keasler, and Rosella Watts, president of the East Alton American Legion Auxiliary Unit 794. The poppies were sold at the bank, shopping centers, and industrial sites. (Courtesy of Rosella Watts.)

Five

FAITH AND VALUES

Church and religious groups flourished in Madison County. Prior to having a church building, most prayer and worship services were held in homes, the one-room school of Blackjack/Emerald, or the village hall. As the congregations grew, the need for a larger, more permanent location was addressed with the construction of a new building, with the members sometimes doing the work. In the late 1800s and early 1900s, it is reported that around nine churches were in the village.

The first to be organized was the First Baptist Church, first known as Wann Baptist, on July 2, 1891. The congregation started building its first church on Church Street in 1892 and required several years to complete. Henry Weigand, a deacon, lost his life trying to rescue others burned at the Wann Disaster. A memorial bell purchased out of dollar donations is in the First Baptist Church on Bowman Avenue. Engraved on the bell is "1893, Henry Wiegand, January 21, Memorial Explosion Dedication, 1894."

The First Methodist Church was organized 1899. The first structure built was a small white frame building on West Main Street. With continued growth, a brick building was constructed next to the first church on a lot purchased from Z.B. Job. The congregation now occupies its third building at Third and Kent Streets, where the first service was held in October 1961.

The First Assembly of God Church purchased the first building of the First Methodist Church on West Main Street around 1939. The church is still located at that site.

The First General Baptist Church, on Tomlinson Street and Berkshire Boulevard, was established in the summer of 1931, during the Depression. The present building was completed in 1956, with church members doing much of the work. The 7-by-12-foot lighted cross in the steeple and the Sunday morning chimes have become landmarks in the community.

Over the years, the churches have provided services for the community by adding vacation Bible school, lunch in the summer, quilting clubs, as well as organizations and help for the needy.

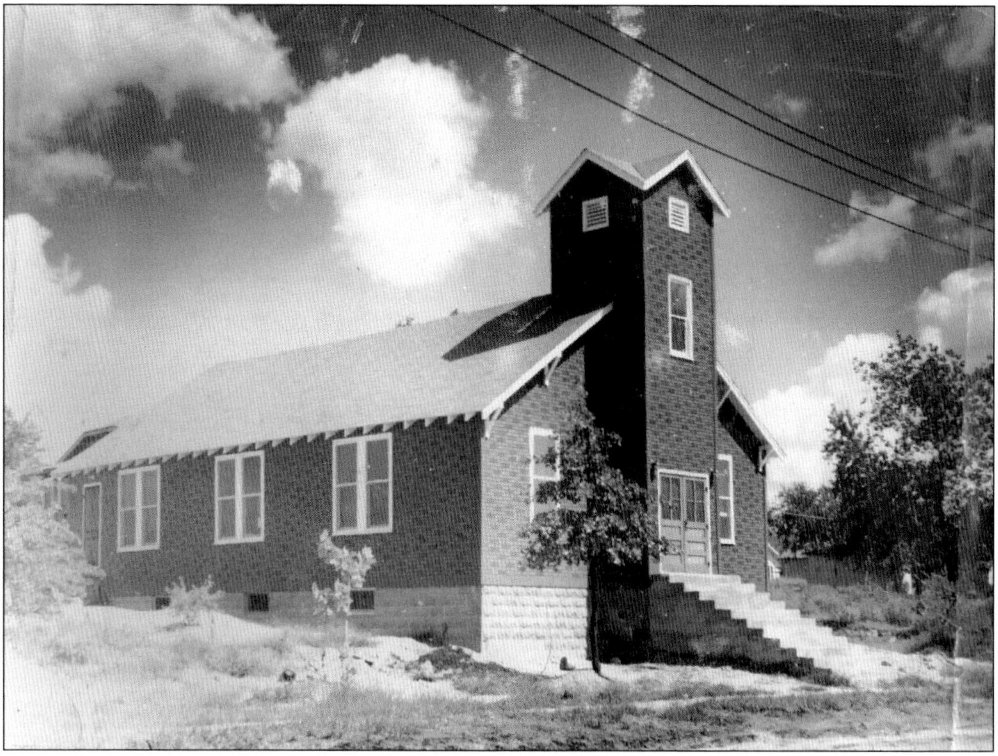

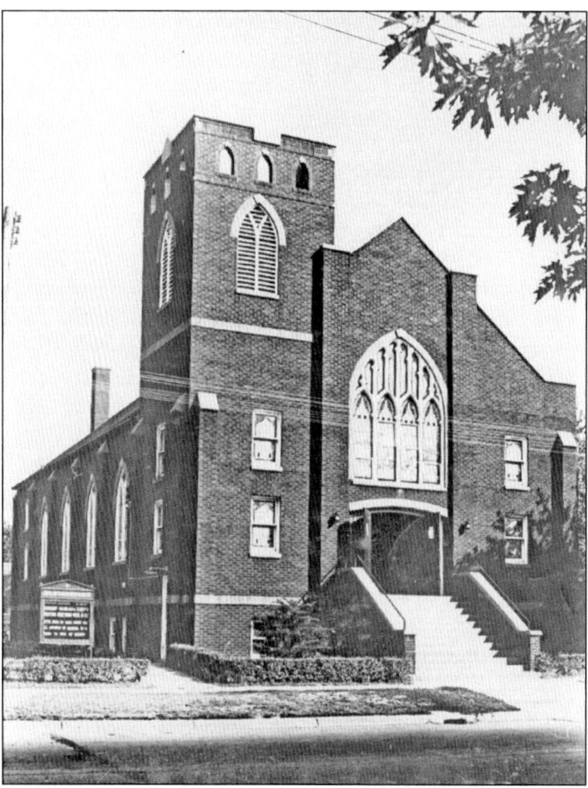

The First Baptist Church (above) was the first official church of East Alton, organized on July 2, 1891, with 21 members. The church was known as Wann Baptist because of its proximity to the Wann side track near the Alton Junction. In 1893, the first church building was erected on Church Street on land donated by Z.B. Job. Pictured at left, the building on Bowman Avenue is the second church building.

The beginning of the First United Methodist Church goes back to July 1899. The first services were held at the old village hall. The church was organized with 18 charter members. They purchased a lot at 325 West Main Street, and on November 30, 1902, the cornerstone was laid.

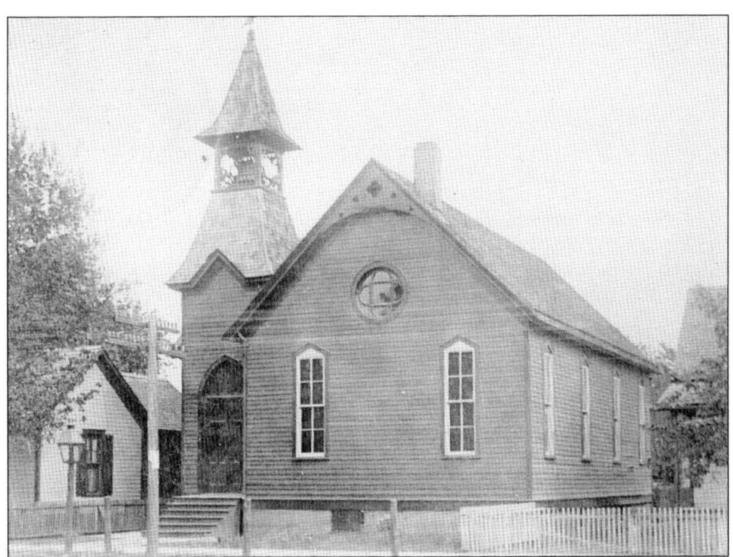

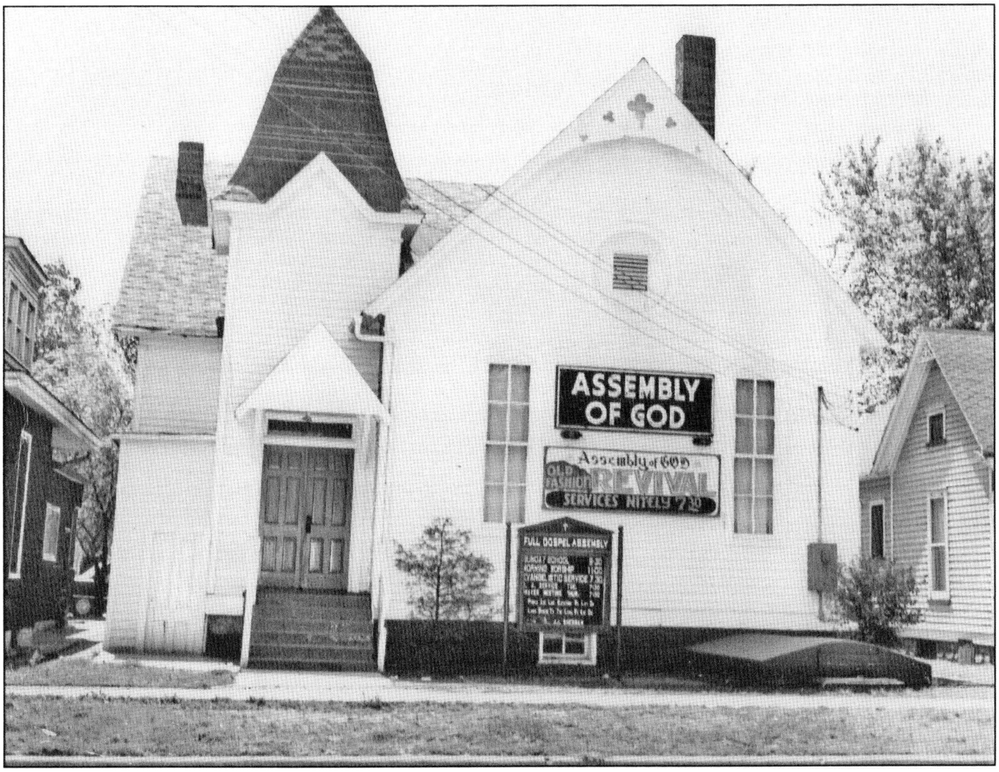

The First Assembly of God Church on West Main Street was organized around 1939. This building was the first location of the First Methodist Church in the early 1900s. The First Methodist Church constructed a new building next door to this one. The First Assembly of God Church bought this building and is still located here. Betty Pittman was the first person baptized in the church.

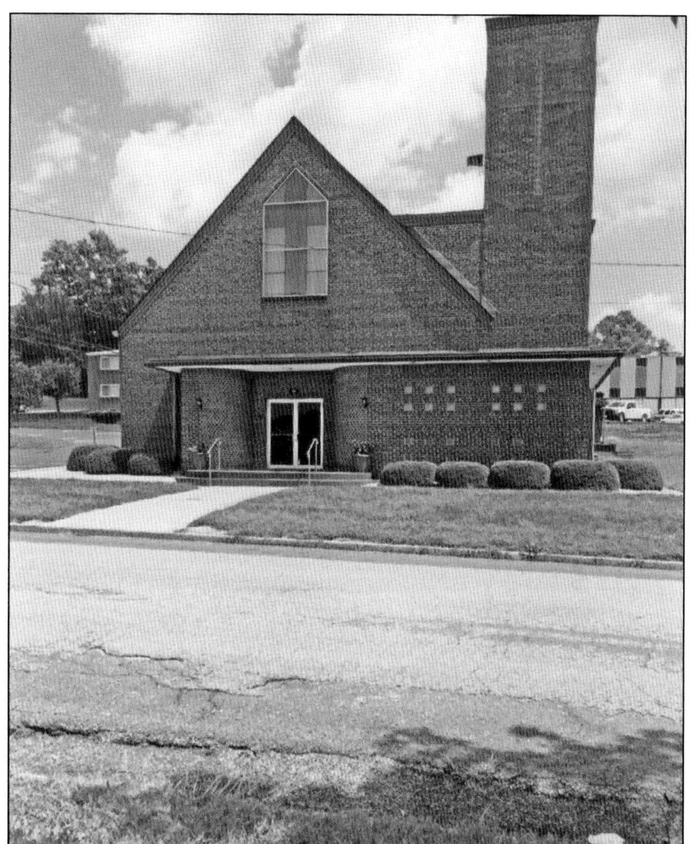

The First General Baptist Church, on Tomlinson Street and Berkshire Boulevard, was established in the summer of 1931. Church members constructed the present building in 1956. The steeple's lighted cross and the Sunday morning chimes are community landmarks.

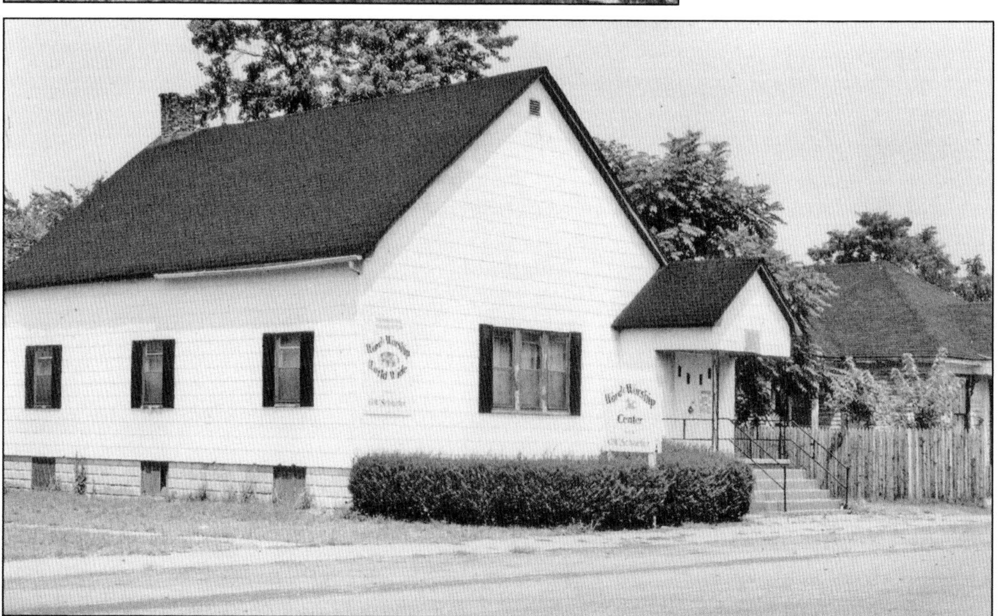

The World Worship World Wide Church rented this building on Church Street from the Junior Order of United American Mechanics Drill Team of East Alton. Over the years, the club rented the building to organizations and churches. The club provided books for area schools in 1945.

Six

To Preserve and Protect

The East Alton Police Department was no different in structure than any other early American law enforcement organization.

After incorporation in 1893, one of the first things the board did was form the Police Committee to address law and order. The position of constable of police was appointed by the Police Committee, which was in turn appointed by the village mayor.

In 1898, James Weiss, serving as village marshal, was employed by the village and the Big Four jointly. Weiss was the first East Alton officer to lose his life in the line of duty.

A significant change came in the 1930s, when the force was increased from one man to three.

The East Alton Fire Department was organized on May 28, 1921, with organizing instructions being given by Simon Kellerman Jr. of Edwardsville. The firefighters were all volunteer.

After completing a two-mile road paving project, the citizens held a party to celebrate. The funds raised at the celebration went toward a 1921 hose reel cart. The hose reel cart was the first piece of firefighting equipment acquired. A Reo truck was purchased in 1926, and as needs continued, a 1947 White truck was purchased. The first firehouse was built in 1927 in the back of the village hall, and a second firehouse was built in 1956 on Third Street.

The ladies' auxiliary was organized November 22, 1926, to support the firefighters. Enthusiasm lagged, necessitating reorganization in October 1949. Membership in 1950 was 11.

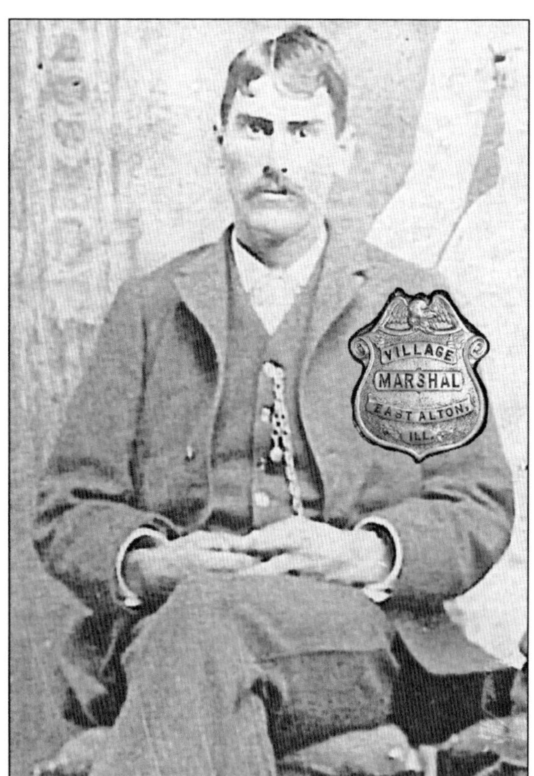

On July 6, 1898, James Weiss, serving as village marshal, was shot and instantly killed by one of four men whom he was ordering from the Big Four Railroad property. He was employed by the village and the Big Four jointly to patrol the railroad station to stop the almost nightly robberies. He was the first East Alton officer to lose his life in the line of duty. (Courtesy of Darren Carlton.)

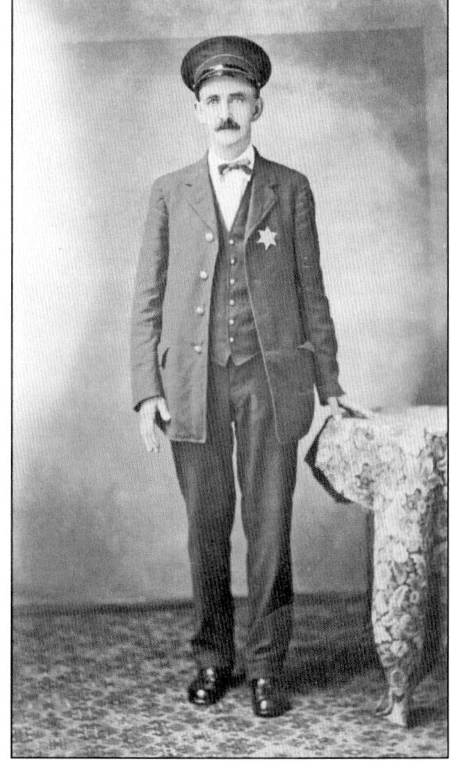

Henry (Hank) Feldwisch was an appointed town marshal (constable) from the 1900s to 1920s. He was responsible for lighting the oil lamps throughout the village and cranking a siren by hand to announce curfew.

John Orval Cannedy was employed by the Village of East Alton as a special police officer. He worked as a pipefitter for the Western Cartridge Company and was granted a leave of absence from 1925 until 1927 to serve as the East Alton chief of police. He was the first police officer to patrol the village on a horse. (Courtesy of Eva Faye Cannedy Zeisset.)

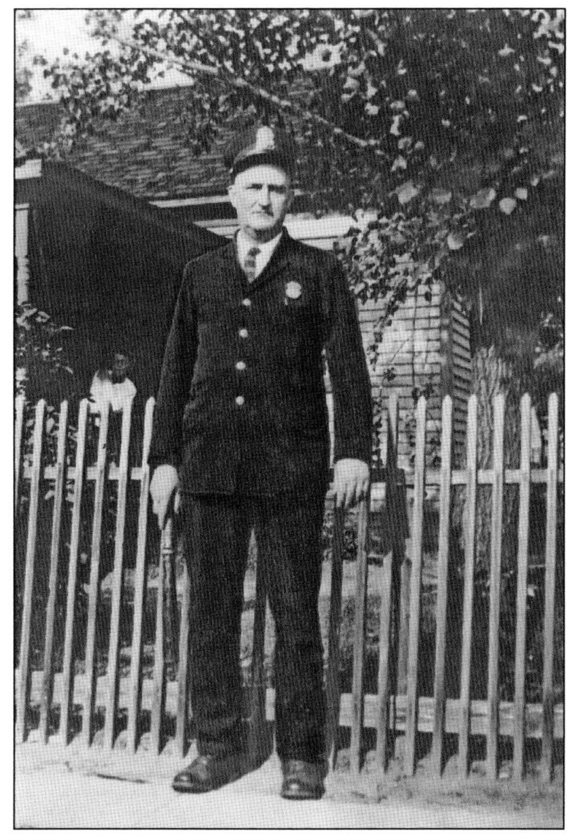

Robert (Bob) Green Sr. was the first motorcycle policeman in East Alton. Green is in front of the old village hall on a Harley-Davidson. He served as a motorcycle policeman in 1938 and 1939. After leaving the police department, he worked as a security guard at Olin Corporation and later at Illinois State Bank. On August 6, 1973, he captured a robber at Illinois State Bank and received a nonfatal wound during the confrontation. (Courtesy of Robert Green.)

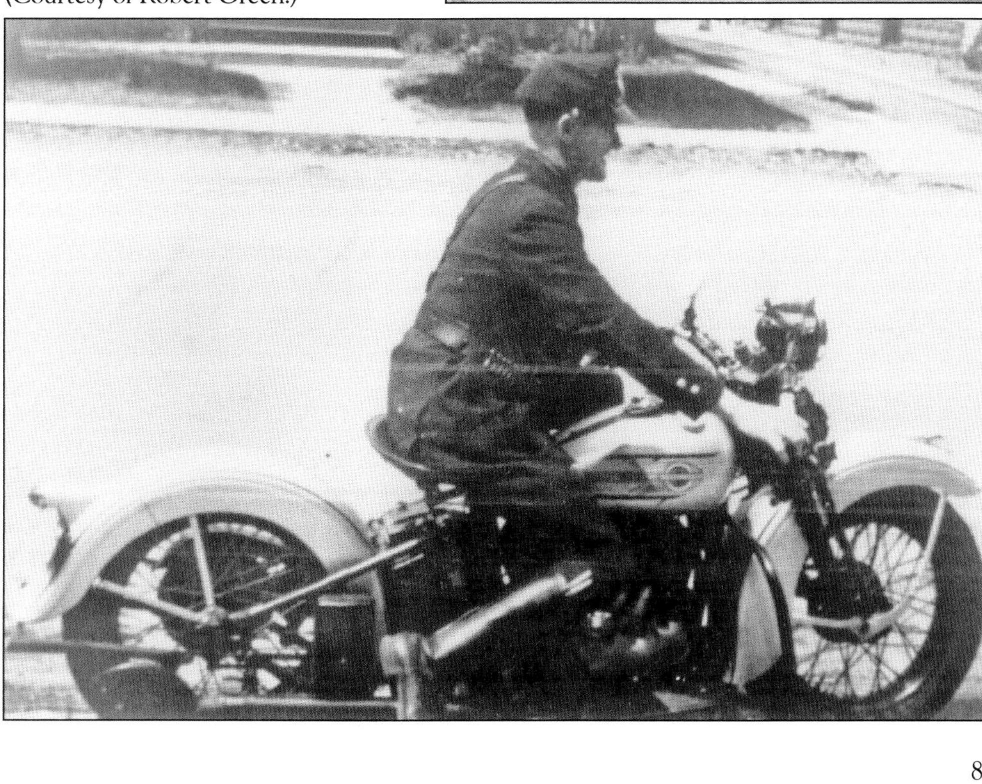

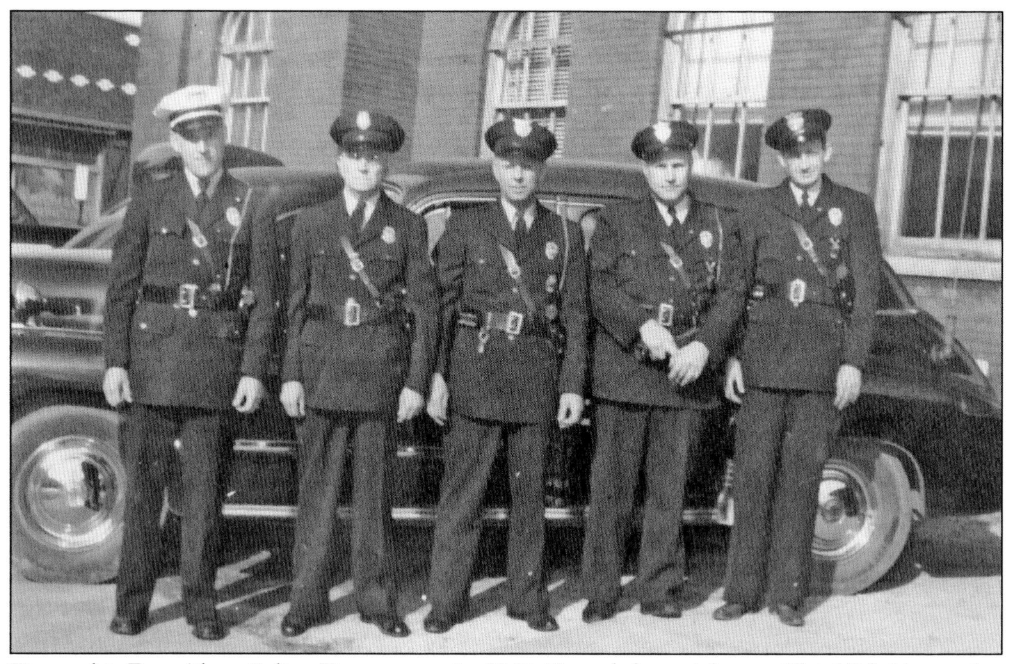

Pictured is East Alton Police Department in 1949. From left to right are Chief Ed Abernathy, Fred McCauley, Homer McPeak, Harold Riggins, and Herbert "Slim" Scoggins.

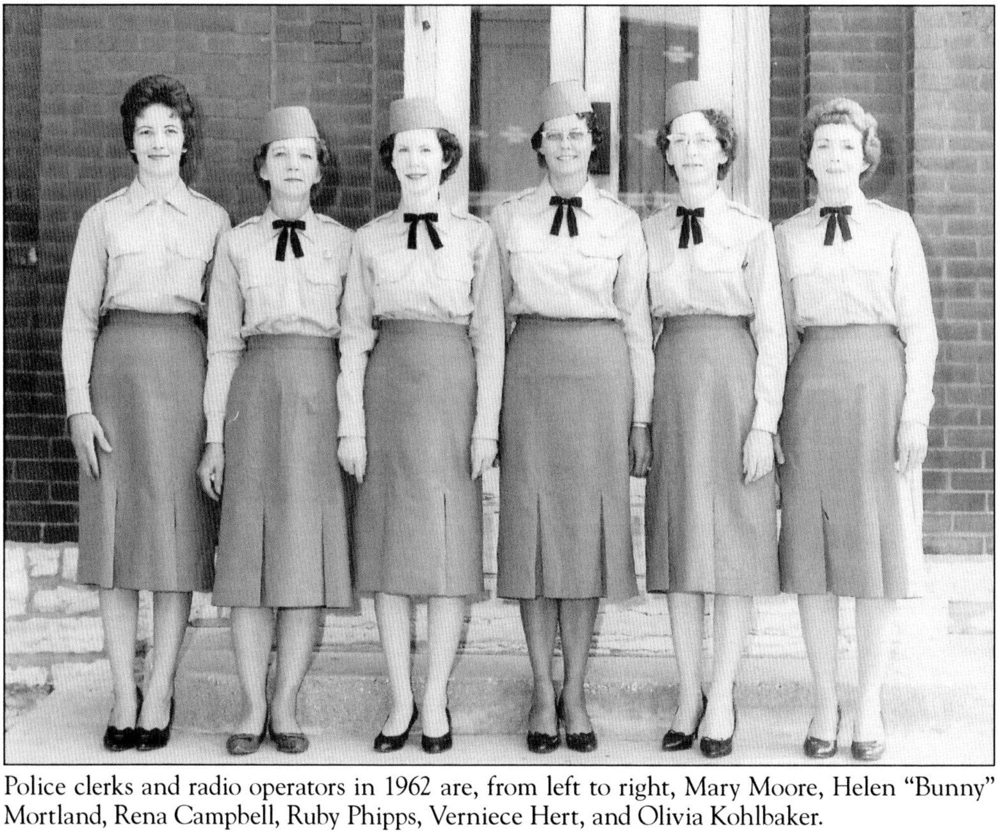

Police clerks and radio operators in 1962 are, from left to right, Mary Moore, Helen "Bunny" Mortland, Rena Campbell, Ruby Phipps, Verniece Hert, and Olivia Kohlbaker.

Charles (Chuck) Cope was a member of the police department and volunteered for the fire department, serving the village for over 60 years. James Earl Ray, who murdered Martin Luther King Jr., was arrested by Charles Cope and Chaten Gleenwood (not shown) when Ray attempted to rob National Cleaners. Ray was held in the East Alton jail. (Courtesy of Charles Cope.)

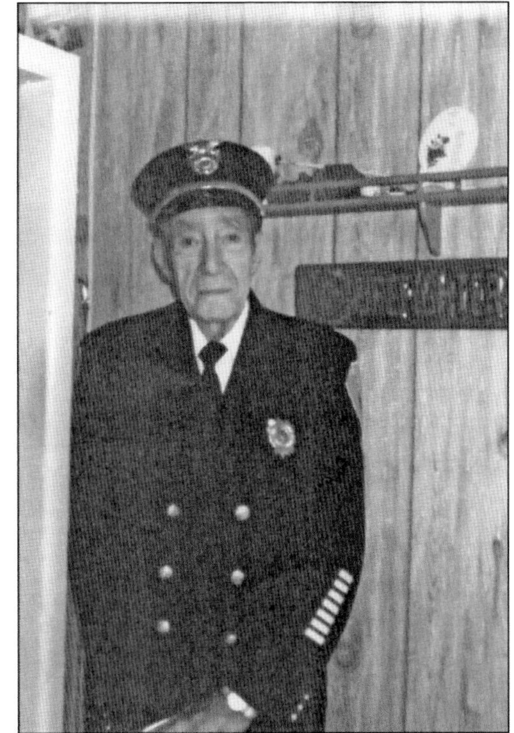

The police department is pictured in 1962. From left to right are (first row) Olivia Kohlbaker, Helen "Bunny" Mortland, Chief Harold Riggins, Verniece Hert, and Evelyn Mahanay; (second row) Ross Riley, Don Hubach, Ebert Grimes, Ron Berry, and Don McPherson.

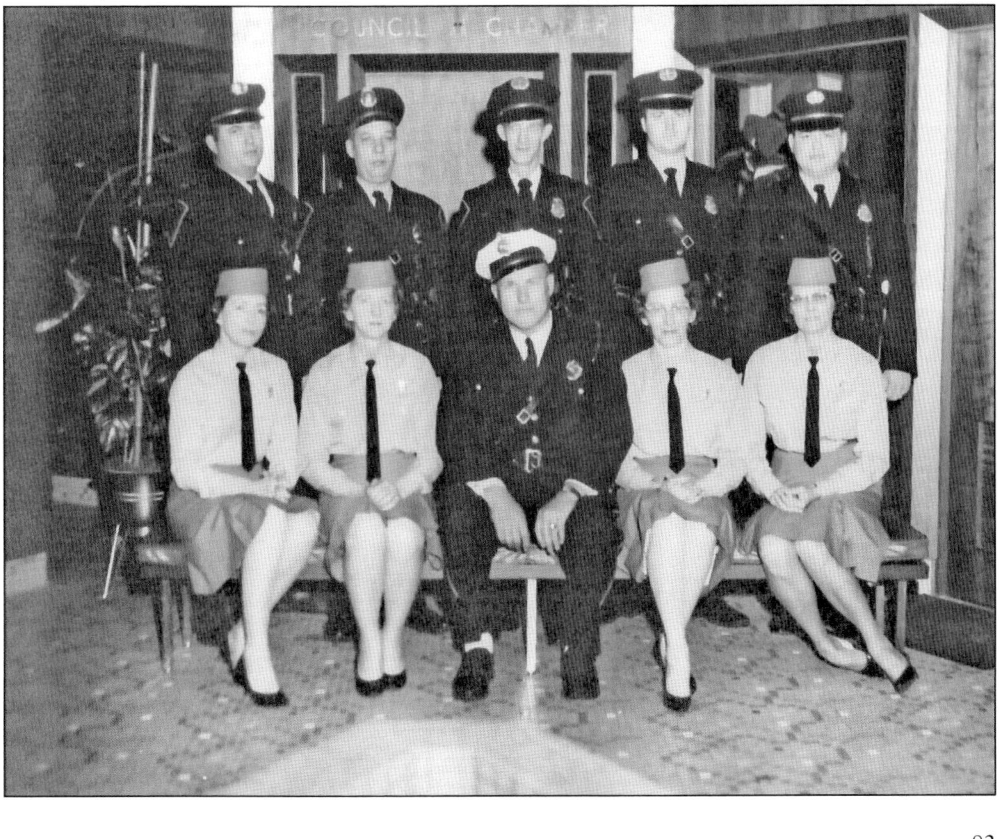

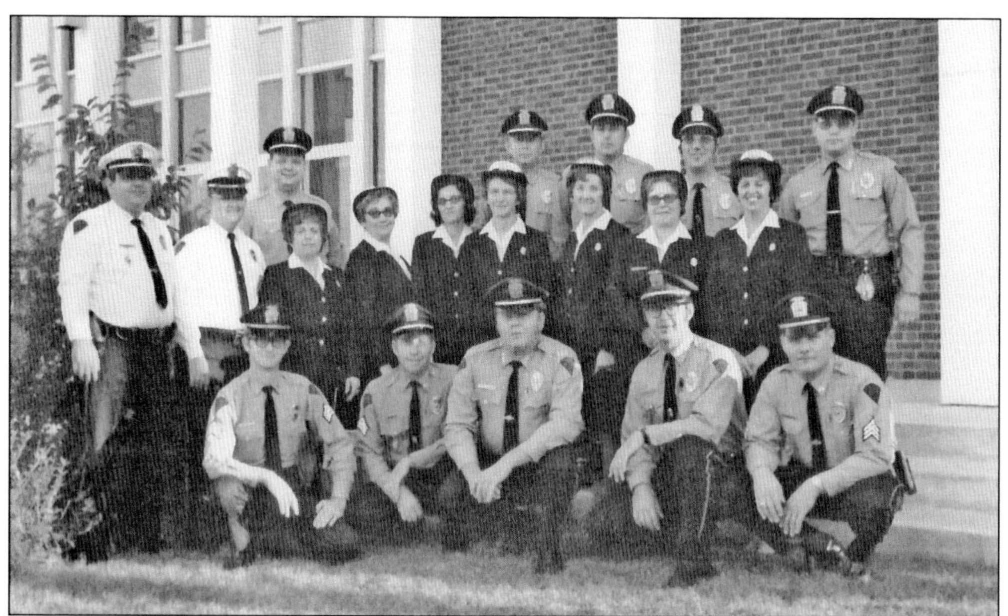

Police department staff in 1974 are, from left to right, (first row) Michael Urban, John Crotty, Mike Bristow, Pat Taylor, and Dennis Childs; (second row) clerks and radio operators Marilou Vandiver, Irene Harpole, Evelyn Mahanay, Verniece Hert, Ruby Orr, Betty Kinder, and Celina "Tiny" Snider; (third row) Capt. John Browning, Chief Fred Bright, Carlos "Doby" Gillis, John Wheeler, Ron Berry, Tom Hettick, and Shannon Hobbs.

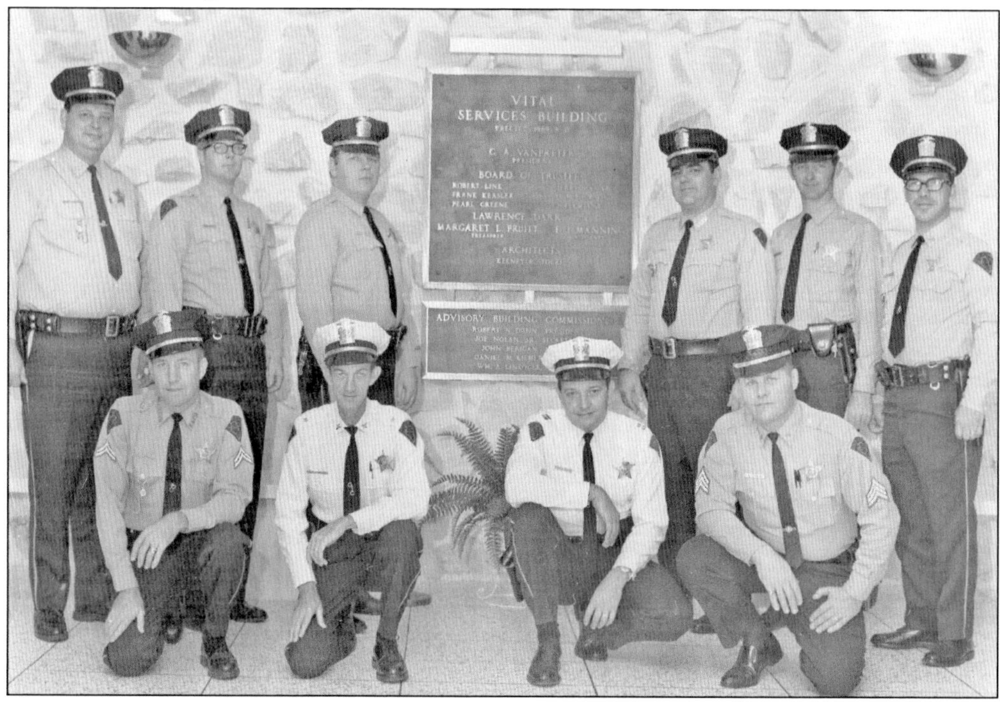

Pictured from left to right, the police department in 1979 included (first row) John Crotty, Ebert Grimes, James Billingsly, and Dennis Childs; (second row) Carlos "Doby" Gillis, Doug ?, Mike Bristow, John Browning, Mike Urban, and Tom Hettick.

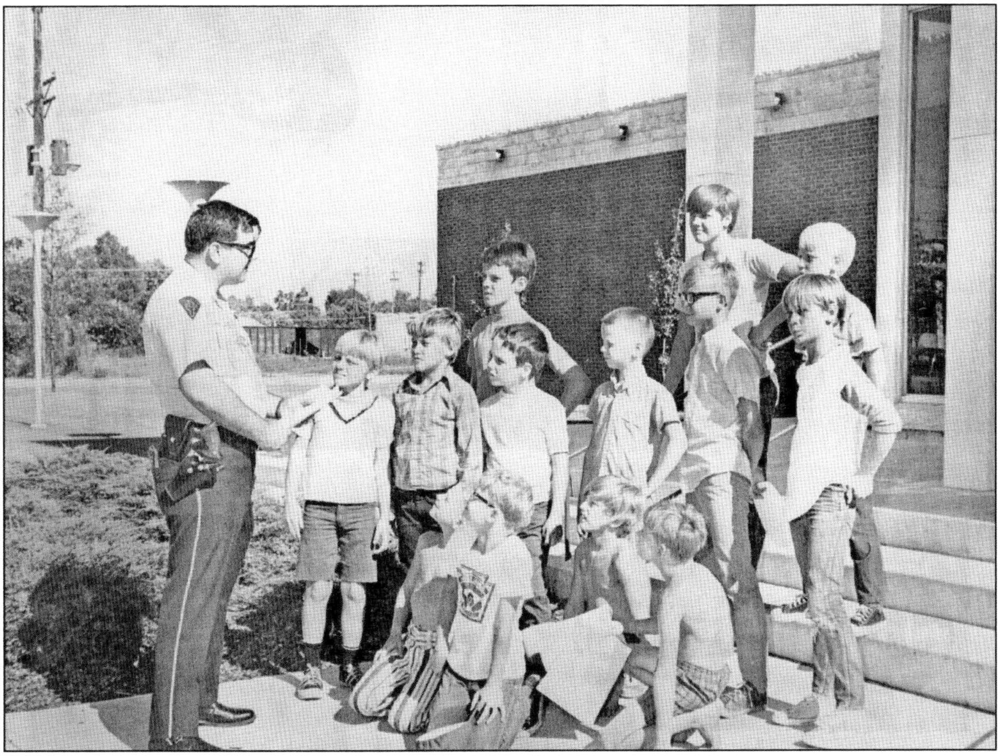

John Browning is pictured in 1974 speaking with children to promote the Alton Youth Camp. Police officers promoted the camp as a positive activity for children. (Courtesy of Darren Carlton.)

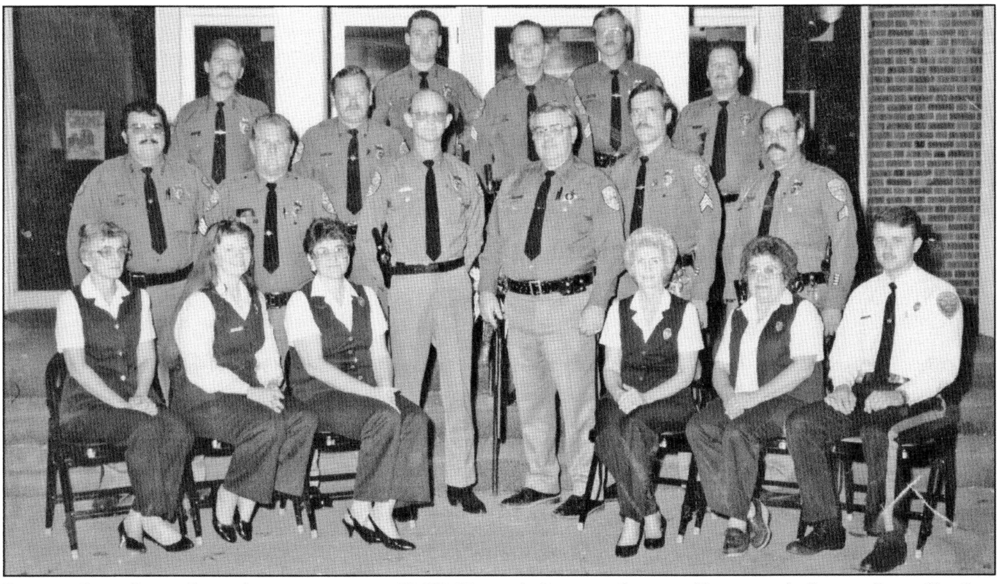

Pictured is the police department in 1987. From left to right are (first row) dispatchers Evelyn Mahanay, Vickie Greene, Janet Behr, Donna Austin, Marilou Johnson, and Dwynn Isinghausen; (second row) Mike Rexford, Sgt. Dennis Childs, Chief Michael Urban, Capt. John Browning, Sgt. Robert Greene, and Sgt. Shannon Hobbs; (third row) Mike Joiner, Jack Moore, Scott Middleton, Sgt. Carlos "Dobie" Gillis, John Hohnsbehn, and Richard Brown. (Courtesy of Darren Carlton.)

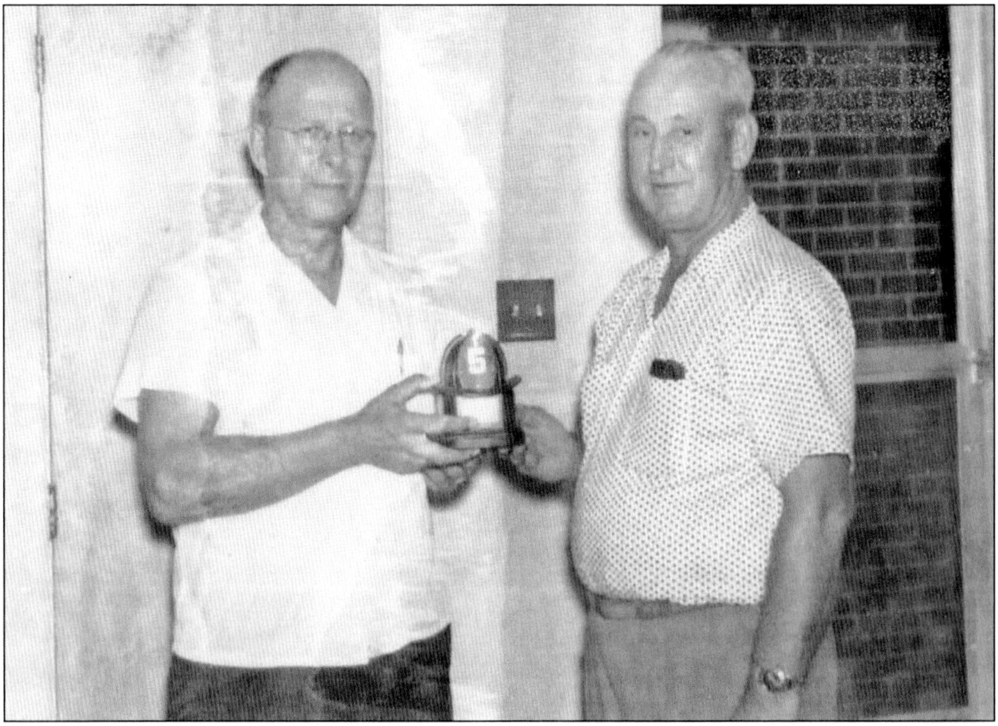

Around 1945, Mayor Charles VanPreter hired the first two full-time firefighters. Homer McPeak (left) was the first paid fireman, and Cecil McCown (right) was the second. Prior to McPeak and McCown, the department consisted of all volunteers. (Courtesy of Annabell McPeak Gibson.)

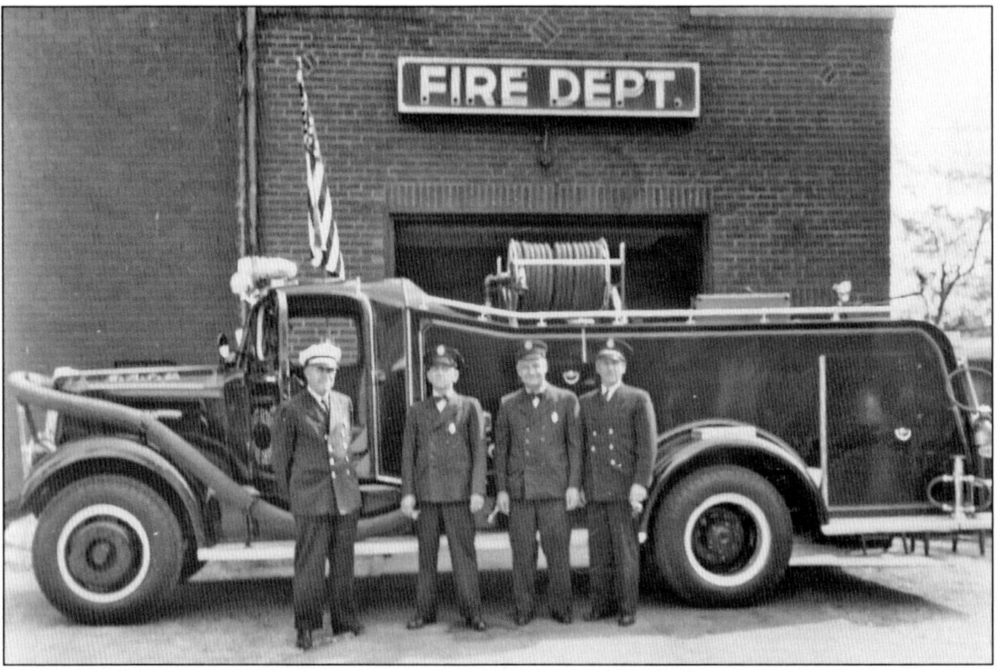

The original firehouse was built in 1927 in the back of the village hall. Standing in front of the new 1946 White pumper are, from left to right, Otto Vroman, Ed Bauer, A.E. Jones, and G.B. Robinson.

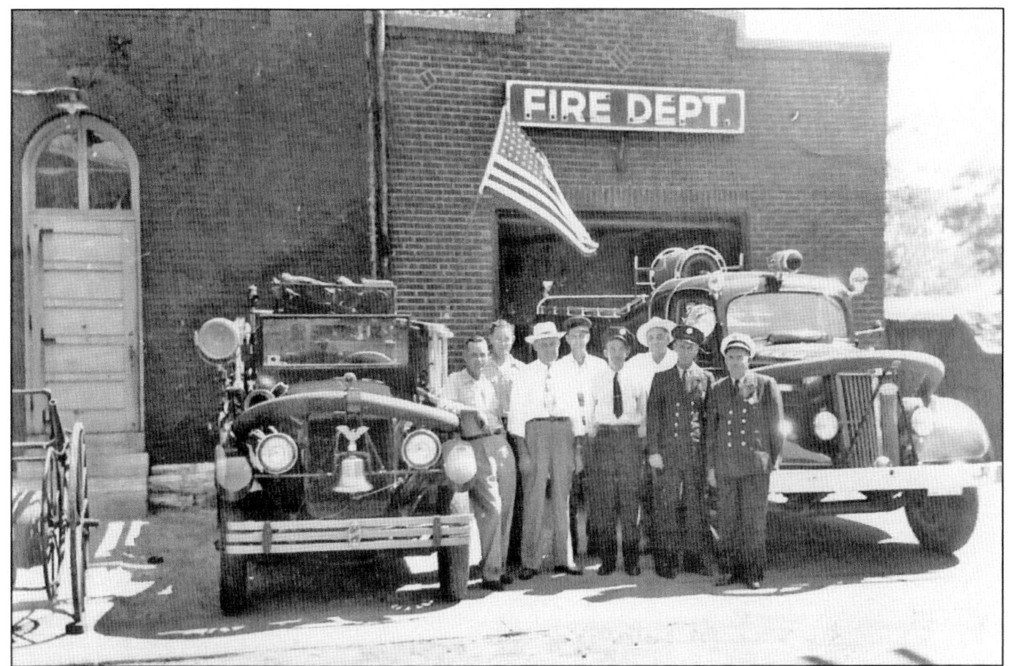

This lineup of firefighting equipment represents a half-century of progress in the village's fire protection. On the left is one of the first hose reel carts from 1921. Next to the reel cart is the 1926 Reo pumper, and to the right of the Reo is a 1947 pumper that replaced the 1926 engine. Featured in the photograph from left to right are Bill Linkogle, Thad Fife, Charles VanPreter, unidentified, Simeon Harp, unidentified, Cecil McCown, and Leonard McPeak.

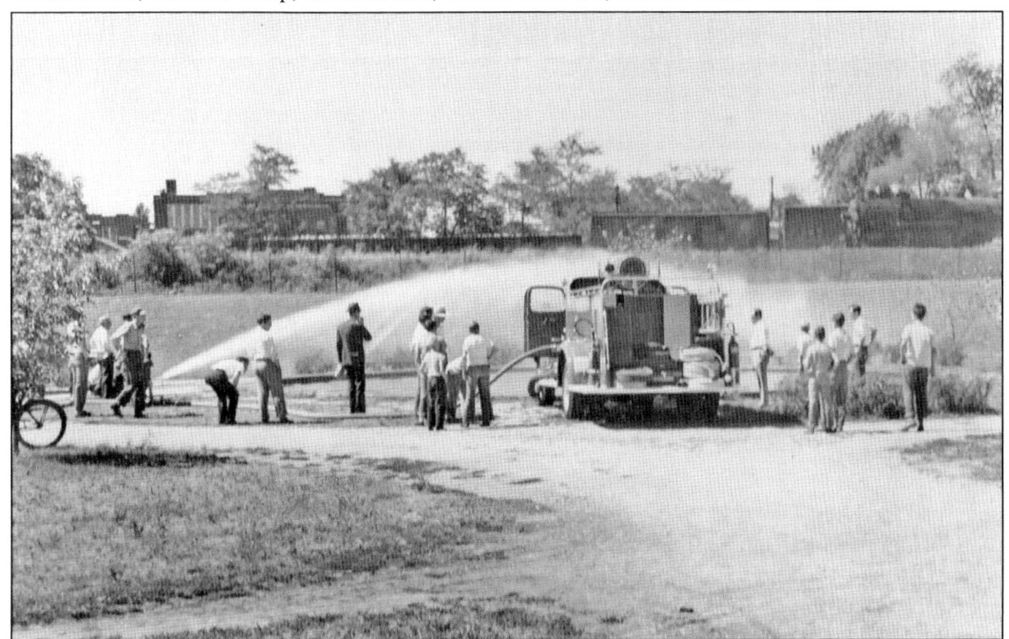

The new 1946 White pumper fire truck is being demonstrated at VanPreter Park in 1947. In the background, a train is on the railroad track beside Shamrock Street. (Courtesy of East Alton Fire Department.)

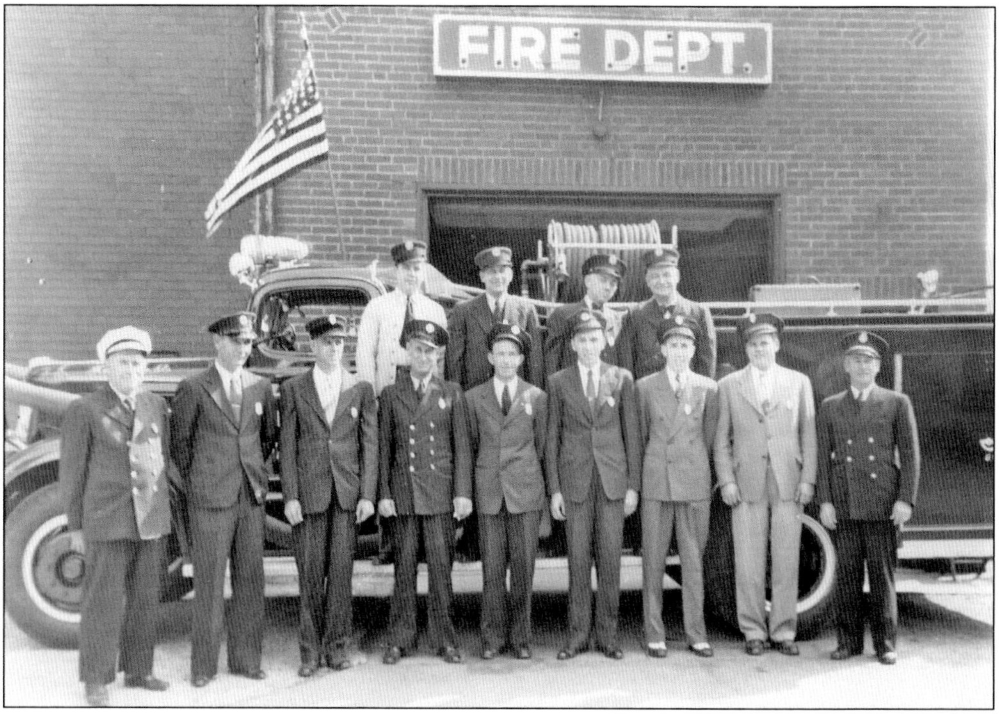

Firefighters pictured in November 1947 are, from left to right, (first row) Otto Vroman, Frank Keasler, Edward Johnson, Cecil McCown, Simeon Harp, William Whiteside, Vernon Vroman, Vergil Gentry, and G.B. Robinson; (second row) Lawrence "Lonnie" Darr, Ross Trowbridge, Edward Bauer, and A.E. Jones.

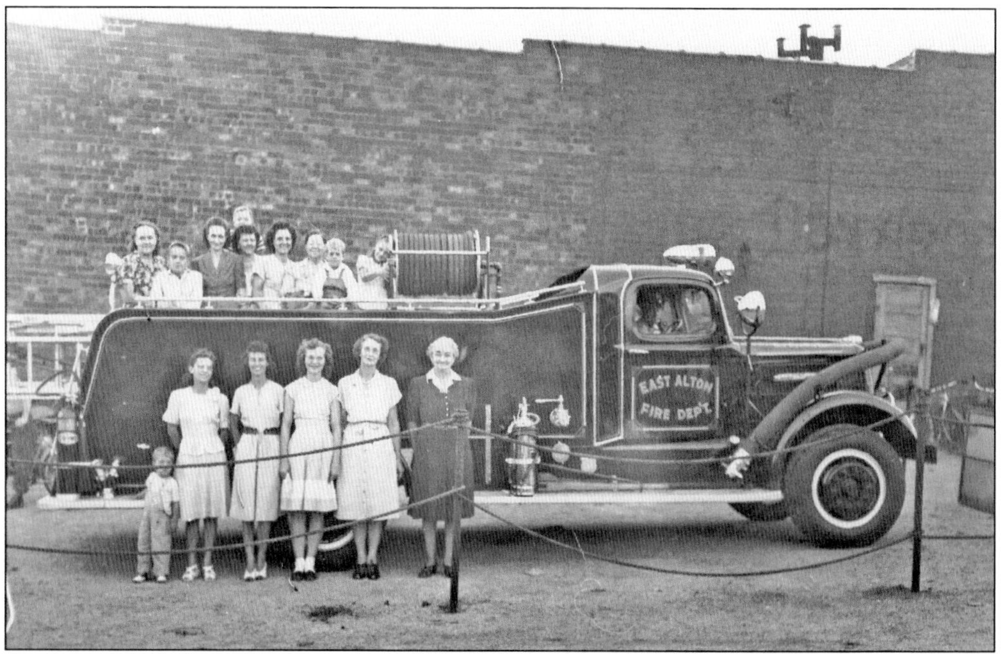

It is believed this is the women's auxiliary in front of the first firehouse. The auxiliary supported the firefighters in community activities. This photograph was taken around 1947.

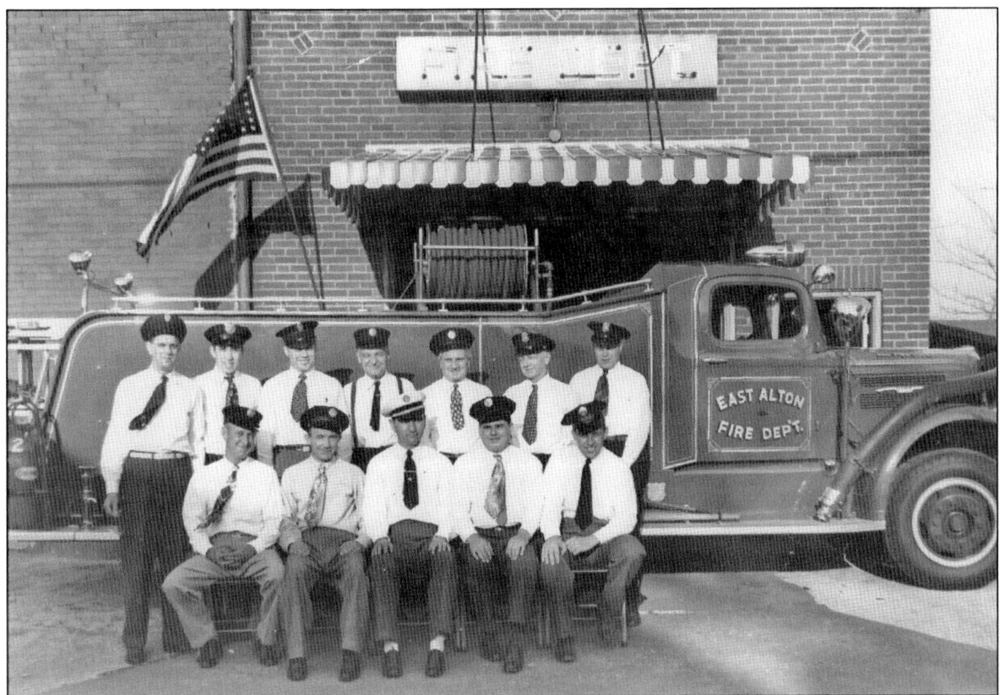

Fire department staff are pictured in 1949. From left to right are (first row) Cecil McCown, Simeon Harp, Chief Frank Keasler, Virgil Gentry, and Dick Sneed; (second row) Edward Johnson, Vernon Vroman, Charles Thomas, Earl Jones, Harold Blackburn, Edward Bauer, and Edward Bickmore.

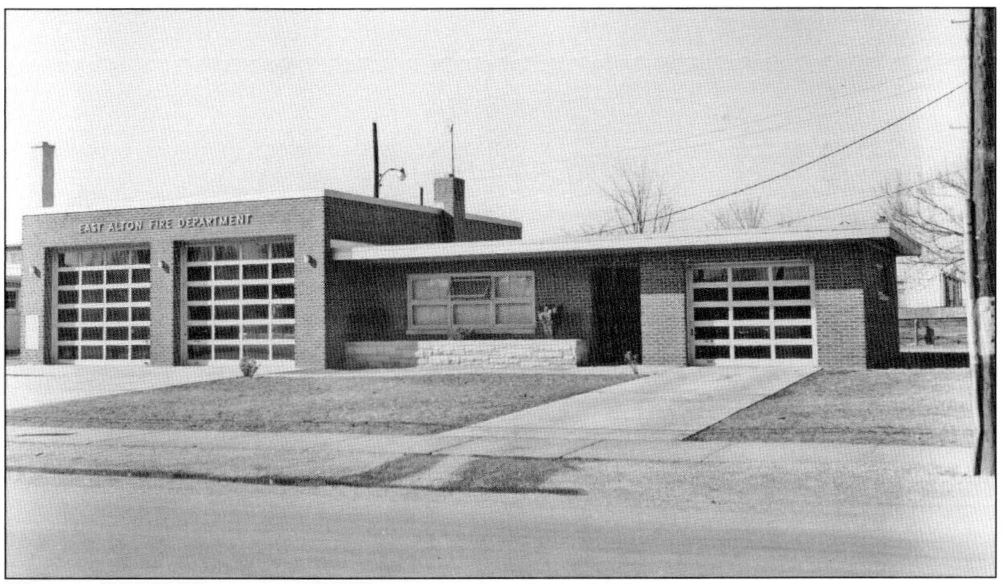

Train tracks ran through the center of East Alton, splitting the village in half. With a train on the tracks, fire trucks were unable to get to a fire on the east side of the village. In 1956, Station Two was built on Third Street, providing coverage throughout the village. Since the use of the railroad switch was greatly diminished, Station Two on Third Street was closed in 1998. The building was razed in January 2014. (Courtesy of the East Alton Fire Department.)

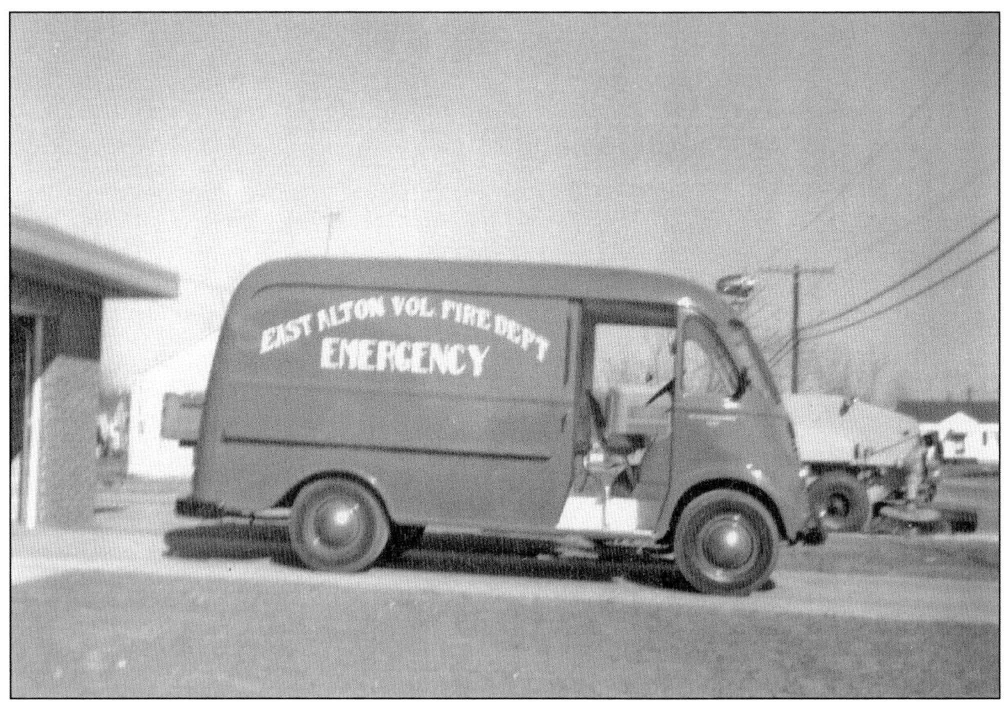

Pictured is the emergency vehicle housed at the 1956 Station Two location. This vehicle was used much as today's smaller fire trucks, carrying emergency medical supplies.

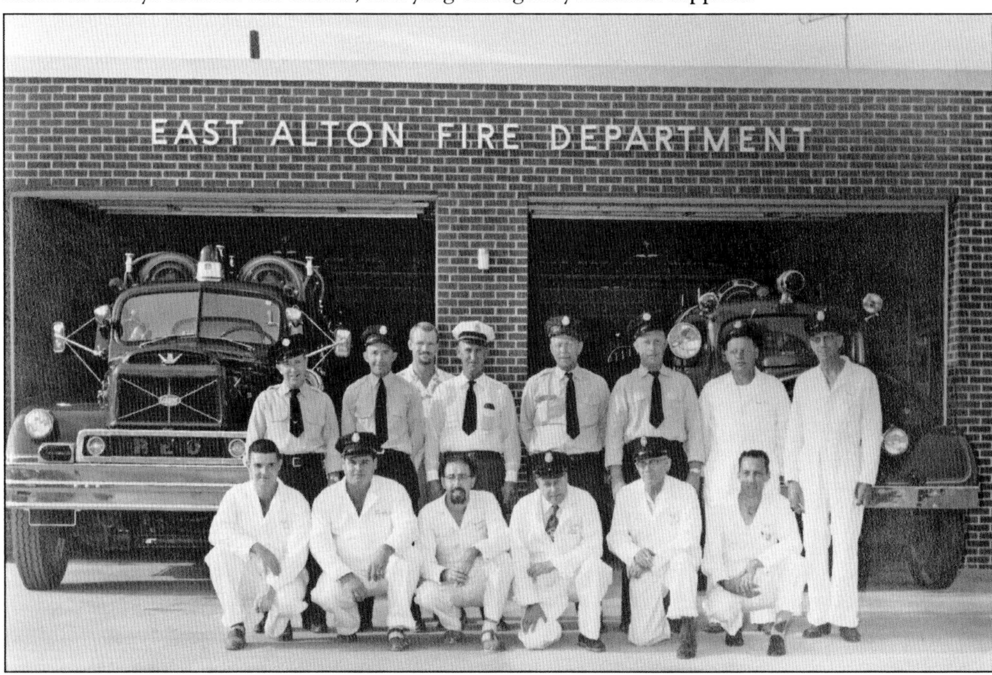

These firefighters at Station No. Two on Third Street in the 1960s are, from left to right, (first row) Marcell "Chuck" Zeisset, Norb Federle, Vernon Vroman, Ed Bickmore, unidentified, and Ralph Bartlett; (second row) Lee Satterfield, Simeon Harp, Mel Brock, Cecil McCown, Homer McPeak, Fred Johnson, Melvin "Bud" Vandalia, and Bill Whiteside.

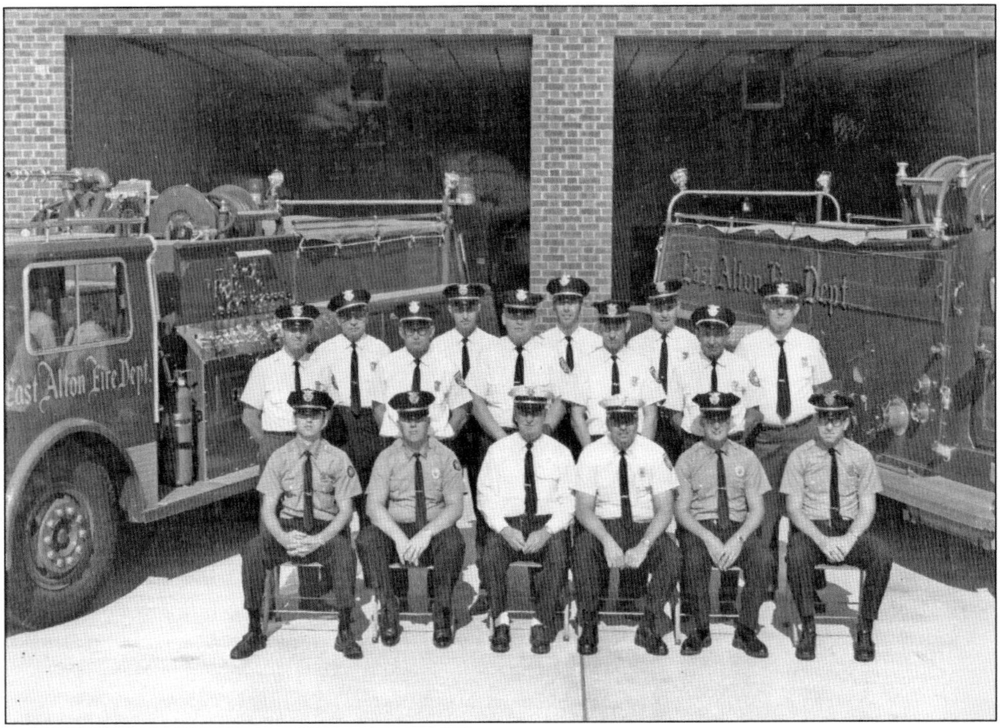

Firefighters at the firehouse on Shamrock Street in 1971, from left to right, include (front row) William Shewmaker, John Streeper, Chief Cecil McCown, Assistant Chief James Johnson, Dale Shirley, and Ed Ballard; (back row) Ron Pendt, Melvin "Bud" Vandalia, Larry Harp, Marvin Jones, Larry Wiegand, Bill Hert, Bob Killebrew, Norb Federle, Simeon Harp, and Marcell Zeisset.

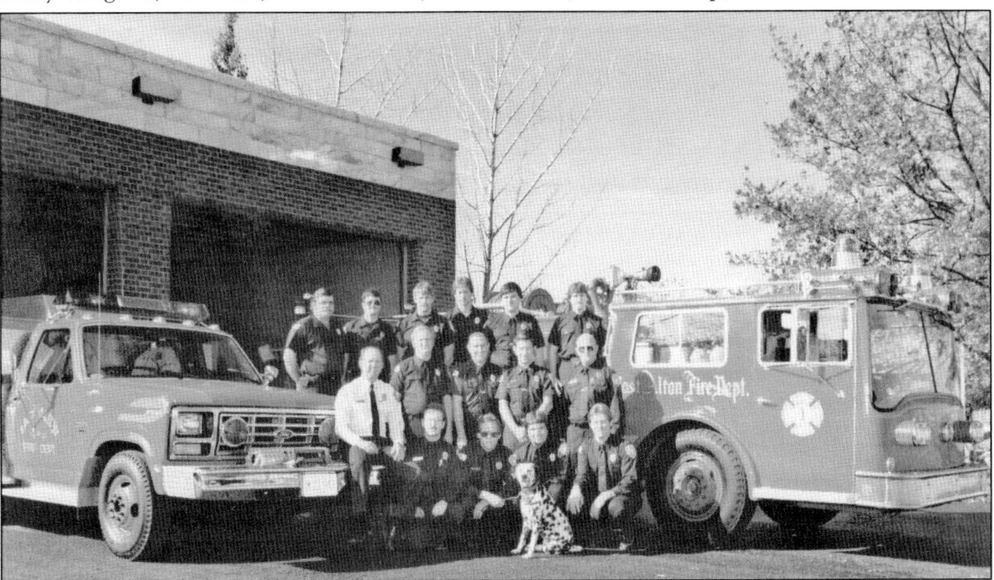

The fire department in 1985 is, from left to right, (first row) Roger Werts, Randy Mortland, Joe Stratton, and Duane Rose; (second row) Bill Shewmaker, Bill Roe, Marvin Jones, Bob Killebrew, and Dale Shirley; (third row) Earl Ziegler, Rick Wilkinson, Steve Foiles, Kevin Cartee, Mike Rhodes, and Rodney Palmer. In front is Cinders, the firehouse mascot.

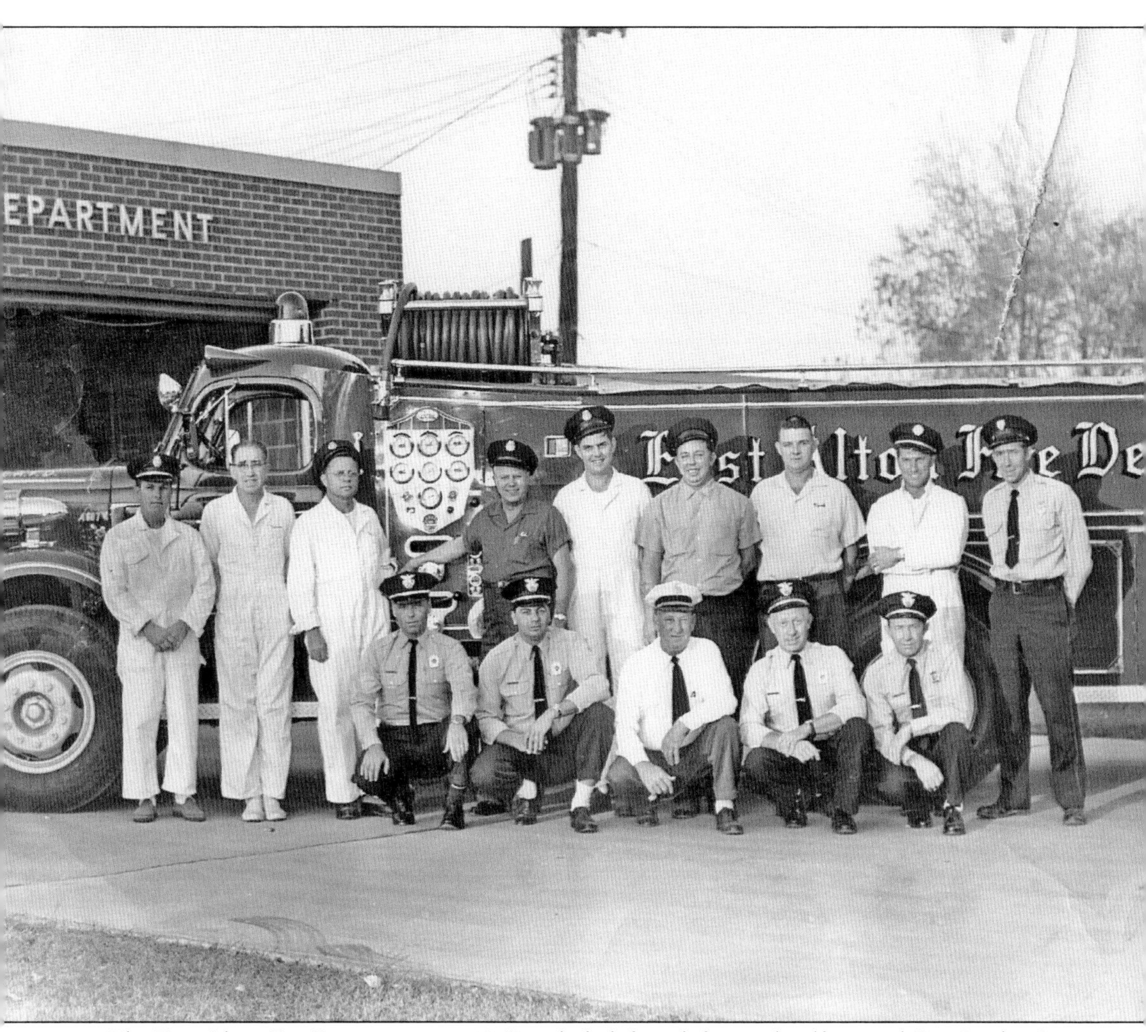

The East Alton Fire Department in 1967 included, from left to right, (first row) Ray Boyles, James Johnson, Cecil McCown, Fred Johnson, and Simeon Harp; (second row) Bill Mathis, Vernon Vroman, Melvin "Bud" Vandalia, Ed Bickmore, Norb Federle, Russell Ferguson, Marcell Zeisset, Dick Dawson, and Charles (Chuck) Cope. (Courtesy of Jimmy Johnson.)

Seven

AN EDUCATED CITIZENRY

The first school in Emerald was a crude one-room log cabin at Main and Shamrock Streets, commonly known as a "blab" school because the students studied aloud. The floor, benches, and furniture were made of split logs. In 1864, there were eight to ten pupils enrolled. This school was abandoned during the early 1880s. Emerald or Blackjack School was built on land donated by Zephaniah Silver where the current Washington School is located. Lincoln School was built in 1919. In 1926, the upper floor was divided to provide space for junior high students, and a gymnasium was added. In 1929, the board of education let a contract to build the first four rooms of the Francis G. Blair School. In February 1936, seven rooms were added to the original structure. The final eight rooms were added in 1942.

With overcrowded conditions at the elementary schools, it became necessary to build additional schools. The East Alton Junior High was built in 1952 to accommodate seventh- and eighth-grade students. Eastwood and Niagara Elementary Schools were constructed in 1958.

The PTA was organized in 1917 with John Jones as the first president. Although its operations may not have been too extensive, it paved the way for the present organizations.

The Mothers' Club was organized in 1935 by mothers who wanted to help families struggling during the Depression. The club provided food for needy families; helped the schools by providing supplies for the classes; sewed band uniforms; planted trees at schools; and carried out many other projects to enhance student education.

The East Alton Public Library was established in 1935, which allowed the citizens to acquire knowledge and experience life through its books.

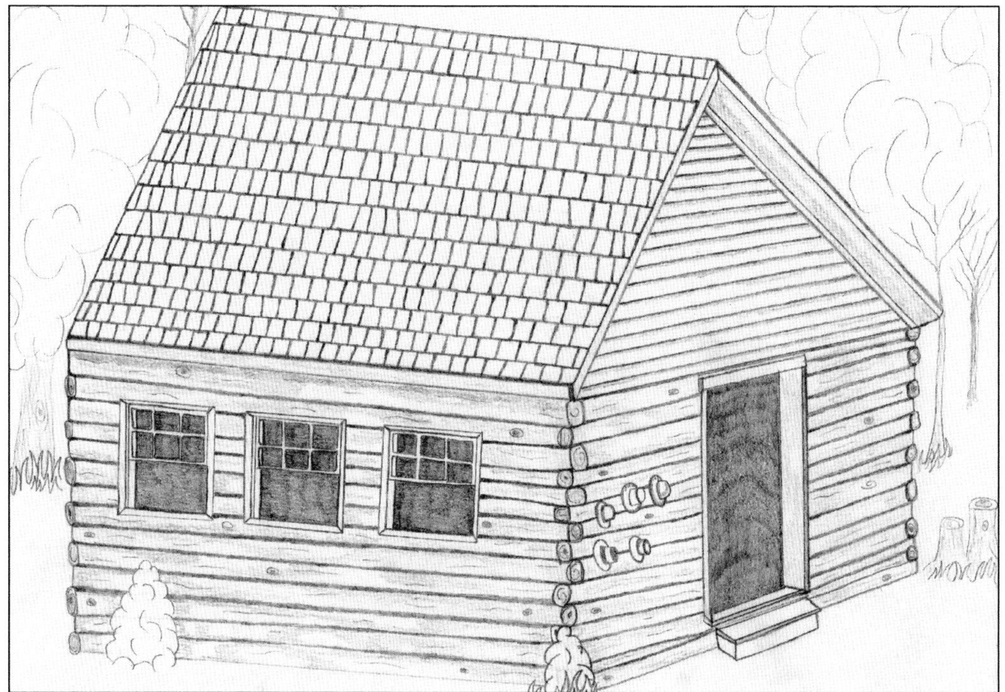

The first known school in the settlement of Emerald was a crude, one-room cabin on the corner of Main and Shamrock Streets. The floor, benches, and furniture were split logs, and an open fire place heated the room. Because the students recited their lessons aloud, the school was known as a "blab school." The school began in 1864 with one teacher and 8 to 10 students. This school was abandoned in 1870 when it was replaced by the Blackjack School, also known as the Emerald School, built on the site of the present Washington School. The land the Blackjack or Emerald School was built on was donated by Zephaniah Silver. This sketch by Tim Ross depicts the log-cabin school.

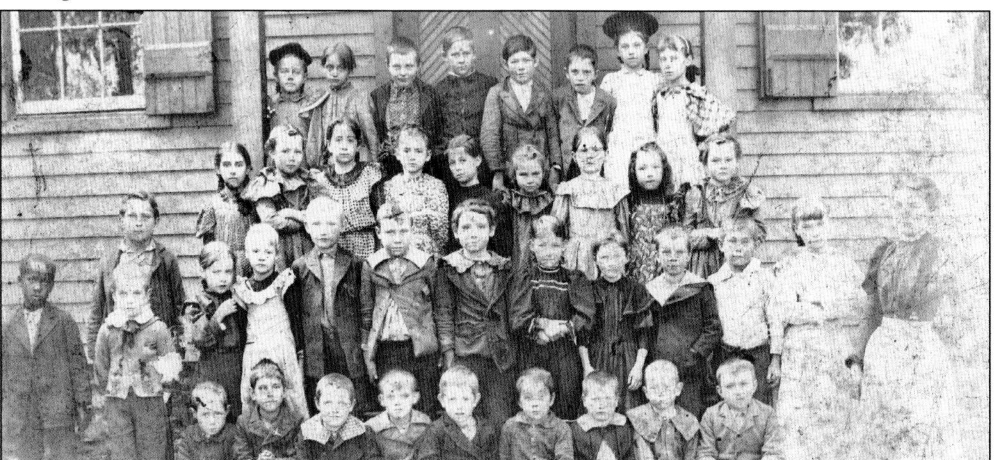

After the one-room school was abandoned, the Emerald School was built on the site of the present Washington School. Emerald School was also call Blackjack School, because it was set in a grove of blackjack (scrub oak) trees. It is believed this picture is of the Emerald/Blackjack School in 1897. This school is where the election was held to incorporate the village of East Alton. (Courtesy of Ronald Stull.)

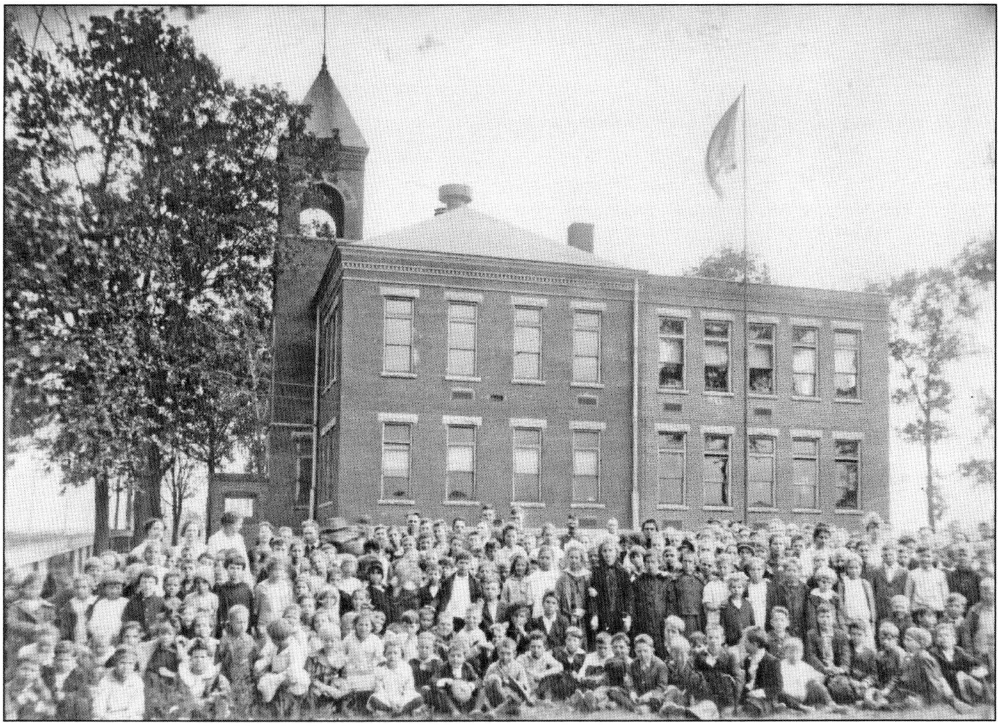

Schoolkids are pictured at Washington School. The four-room Washington School was built in 1903 to replace the Emerald/Blackjack School. An additional four rooms were built in 1912. Additional rooms were built as the population grew. The building was razed in 1964.

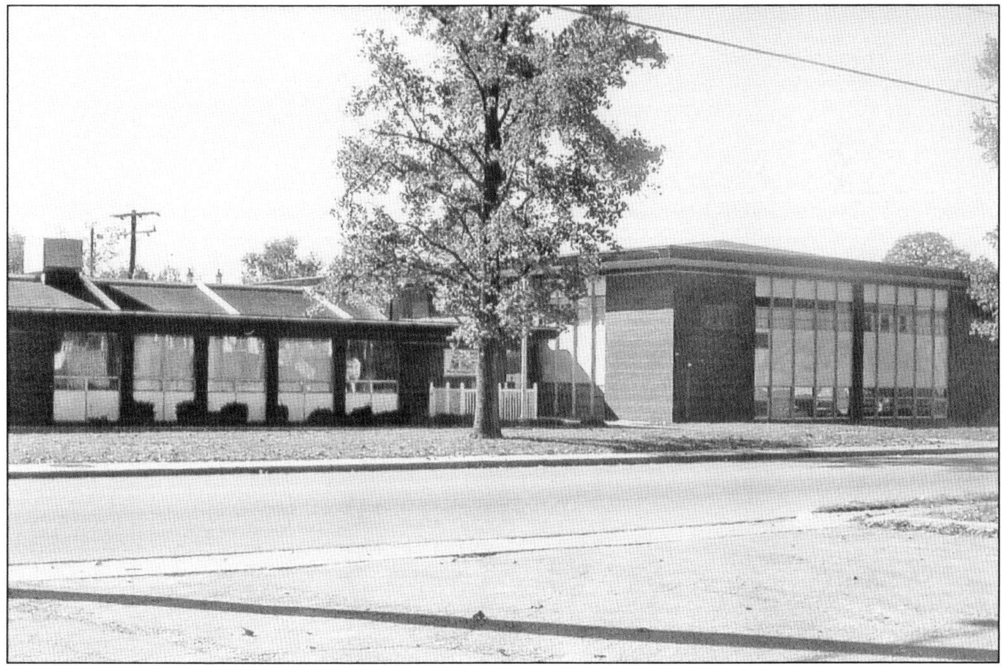

The new Washington School was built while classes were held in the adjacent old school. The new Washington School was built and opened in 1964.

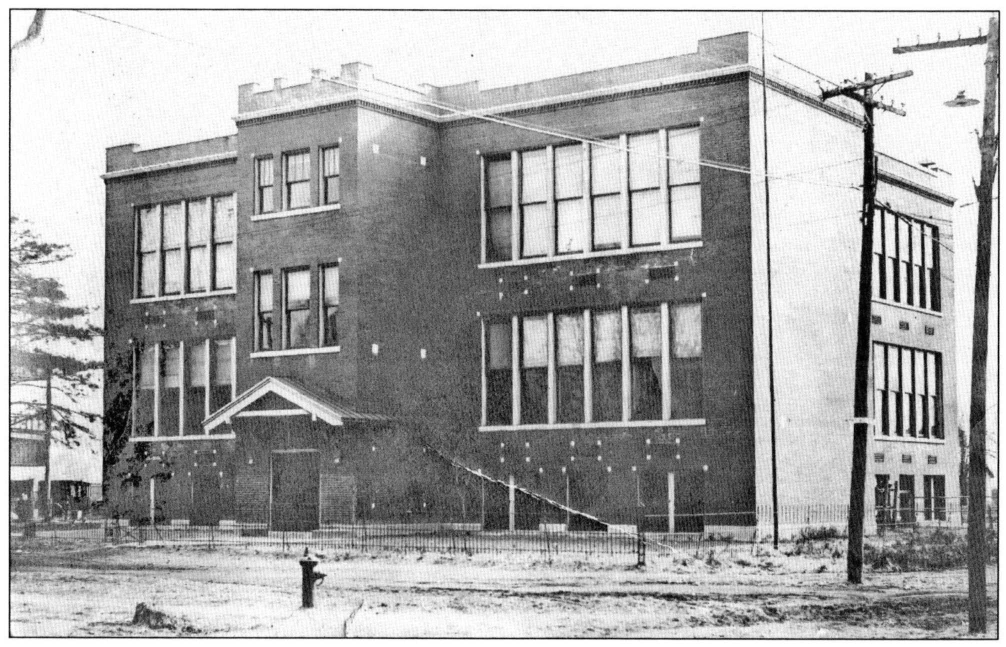

The Lincoln School (above) was built in 1919. Seven years later, a gym was added, and the upper floor was divided to provide space for junior high students. A new school (below) was built while classes were held in the old building. The old building was razed in 1970. After World War II, the population declined and it became necessary to consolidated schools. In 1989, the new school (below) was closed.

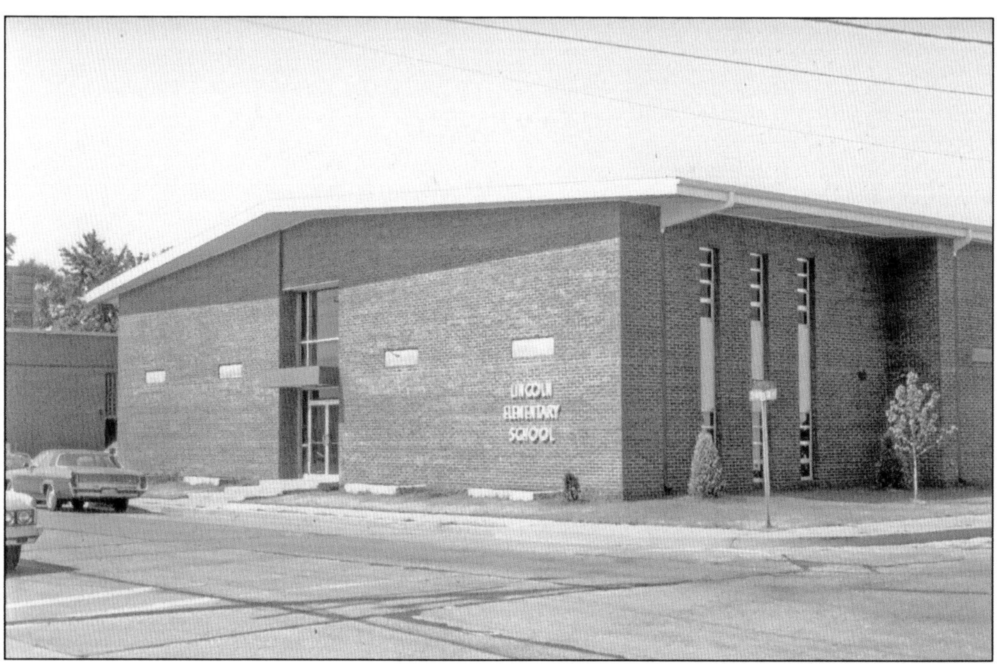

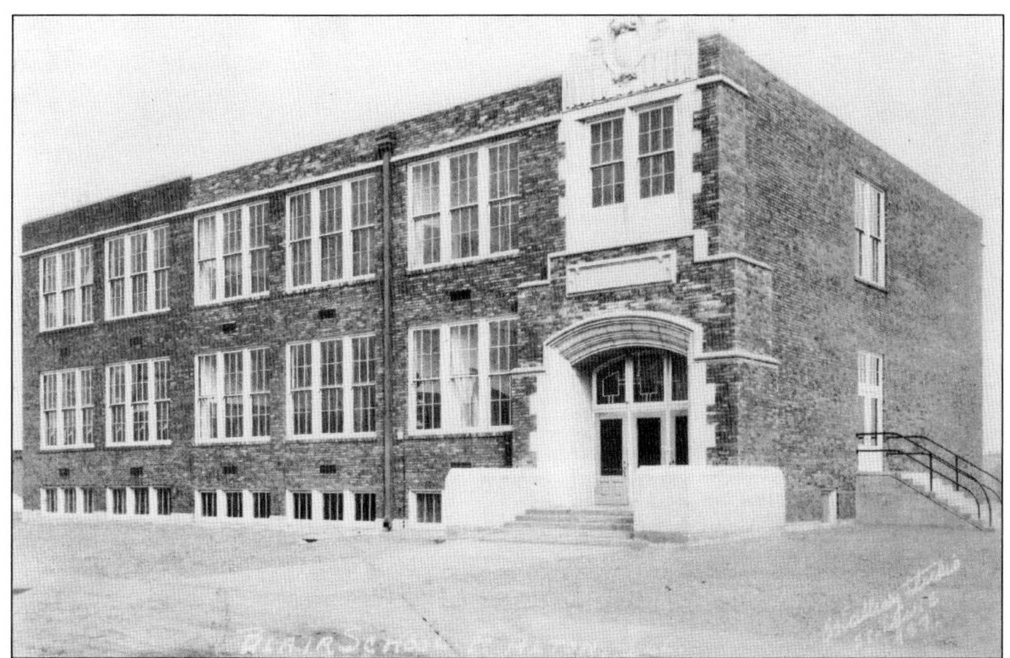

On July 2, 1929, the board of education let a contract to build the first four rooms of the Francis G. Blair School, better known as Blair School (above). In February 1936, seven rooms were added. The population continued to grow with the war effort, and in 1942, the final eight rooms were added to Blair (below). Blair still accommodated kindergarten through the sixth grade and the special education students of the district. Blair School was also where the band program of the district began. This building was razed in 2001.

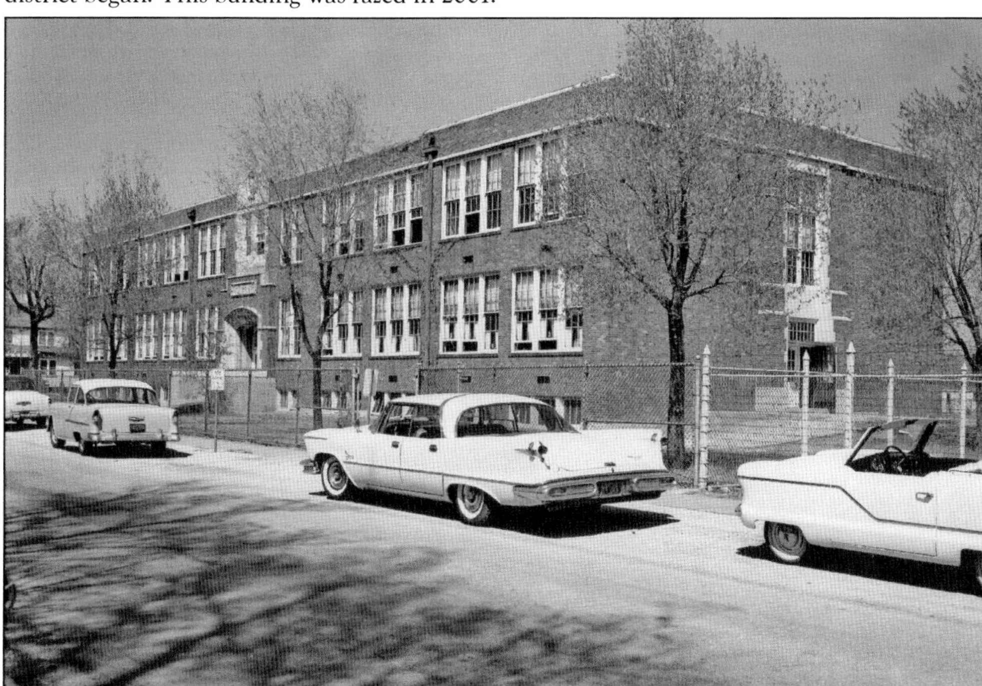

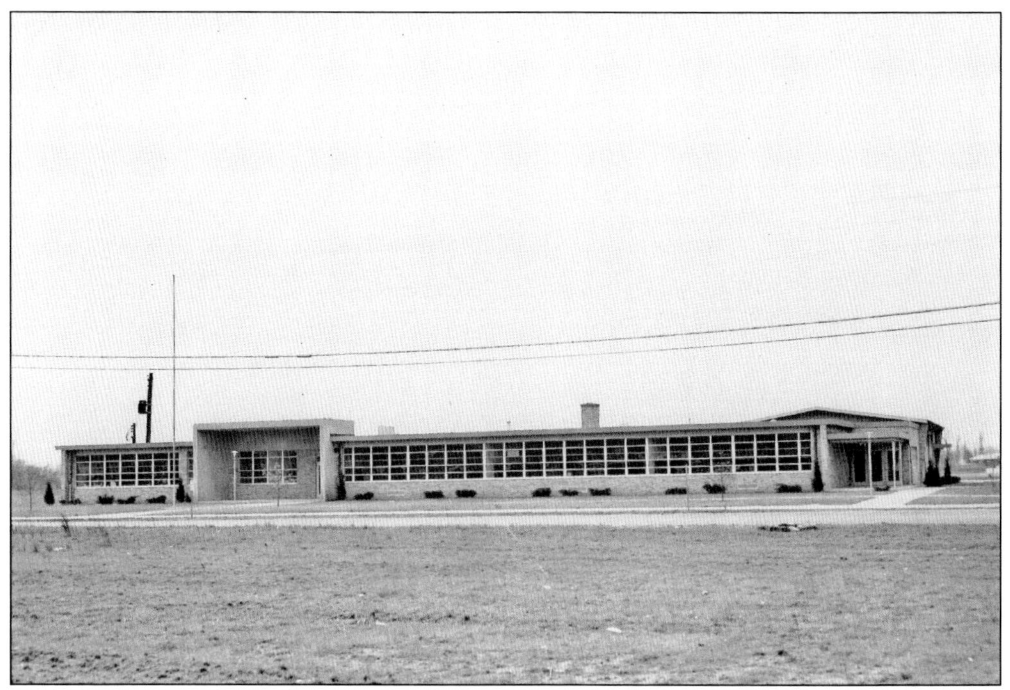

With the continued growth of the village, it became necessary to build additional schools to provide the children with a good education. Eastwood Elementary (above) and Niagara Elementary (below) were constructed in 1958. With declining population, it became necessary to consolidate schools. Niagara was closed in 1975.

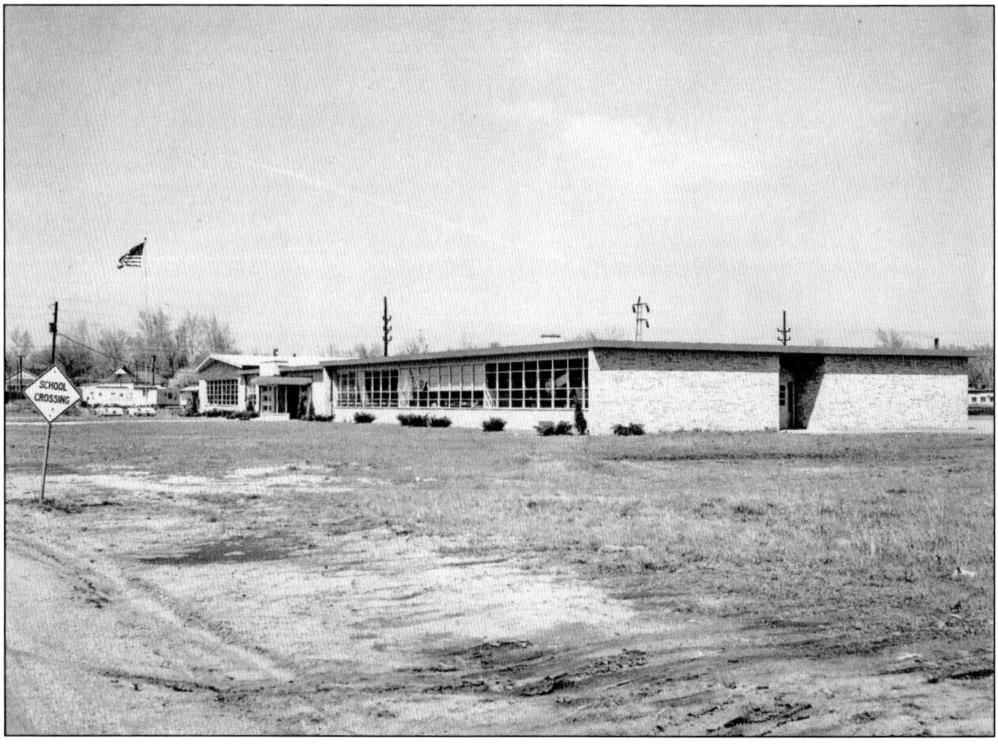

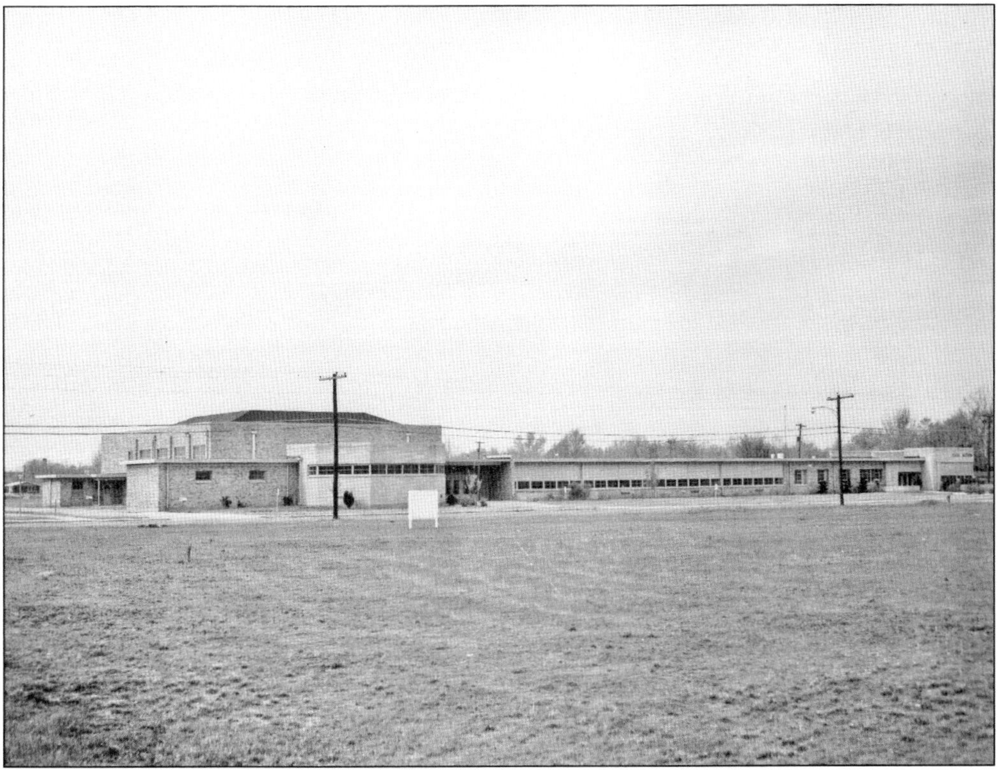

With the overcrowded conditions at the elementary schools, it became necessary to construct another building. The East Alton Junior High was built in 1952 to accommodate the seventh and eighth grades.

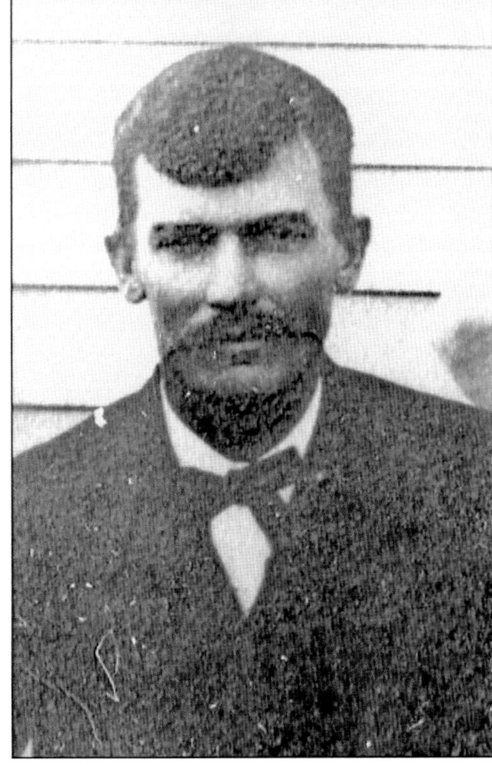

George F. Smith served as school board president from December 1905 to April 1909. While he was serving, the only school in East Alton was Washington School. (Courtesy of Sheryl Smith Ferry).

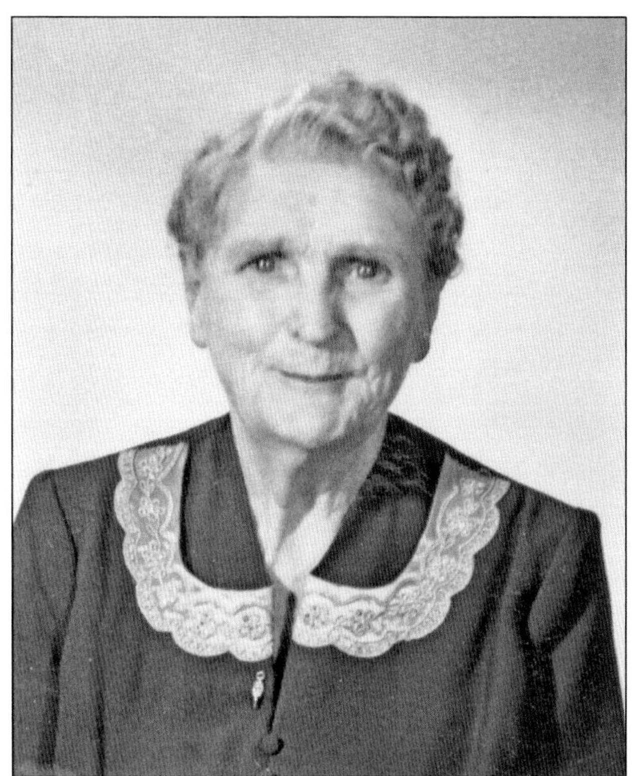

Florence Day was born in 1881. She became a bride, a mother, and a widow in one year. She came to East Alton to teach in a one-room school building. Later she become a school principal, a position she held until her retirement in 1948. She was influential in organizing the Parent-Teacher Association, the Mothers' Club and the East Alton Woman's Club, serving as the first president of the latter two. She established the hot lunch program in the schools.

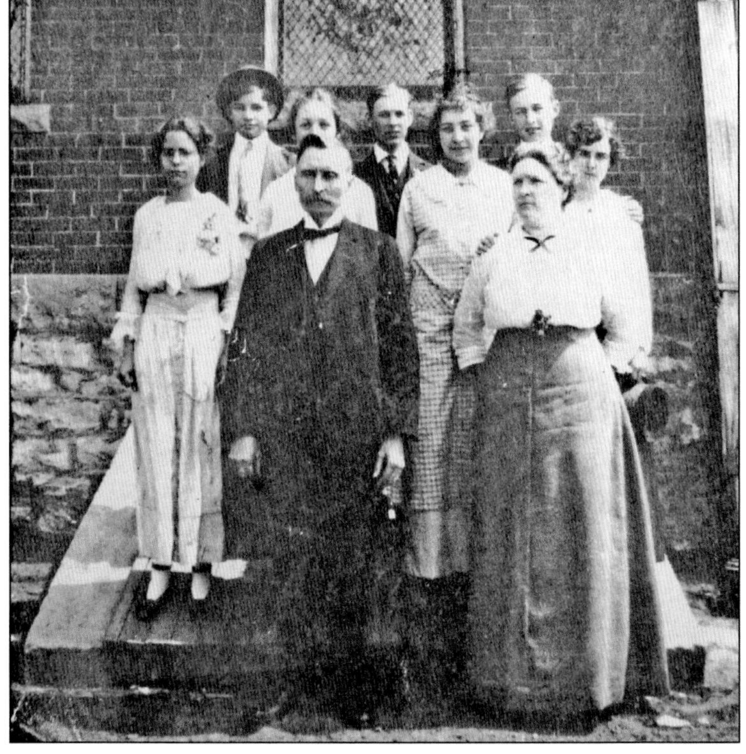

This group of students represented the eighth-grade class of Washington School in 1915. From left to right are (first row) Michael Mallory (principal) and Florence Day (teacher); (second row) Lillian Leitner, Bessie Bragg, Clara Futhey, and Marie Grider; (third row) Charles Ingold, Aaron Robinson, and Charles VanPreter.

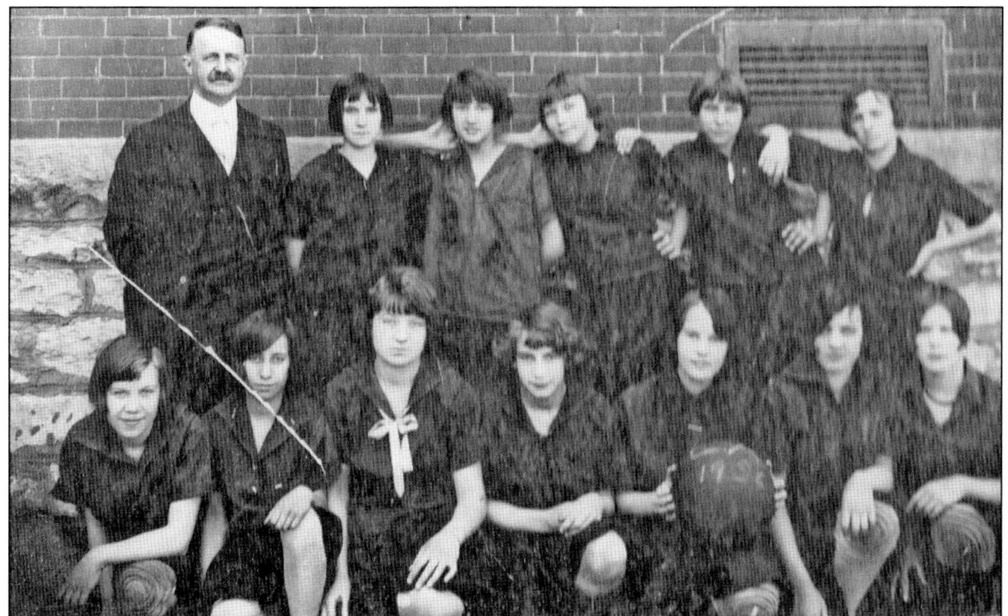

The 1926 girls' basketball team is, from left to right, (first row) Verna Bright, Dorothy Treece, Viola Kruse, Myrtle Reimer, Virginia Duvall, Maude Blake, and Sybil Miller; (second row) W.I. Wilson (coach and superintendent of schools), Dolly Witt, Grace White, Florence Wonnacott, May Deitzel, and Esther Thorp.

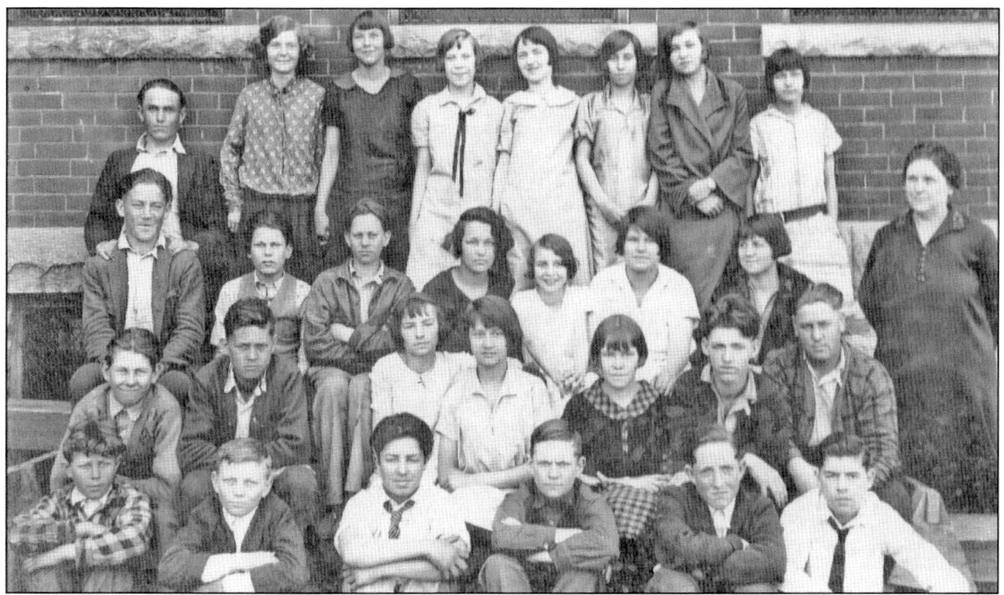

Students at Washington School in 1927 are, from left to right, (first row) Edward Pickard, George Adams, Robert Slayton, Harold Hord, Earl Lawrence, and Martin Vroman; (second row) Clayton Glass, Earl Fairbanks, Charles Wilson, Ruby Holland, Ethel Rowson, Flossie Fry, Irene Morgan, and Florence Day (teacher); (third row) Robert Ghent, Fred Drysdale, Esther Thorp, Grace White, Marguerte Stuchersch, Leonard Parsons, and Walter Sons; (fourth row) Carrol Blange, M. Dempsey, Florence Wonnacott, Verna Bright, Dorothy Cantrell, Dorothy Treece, Lucy Harolston, and Dorothy Bauer.

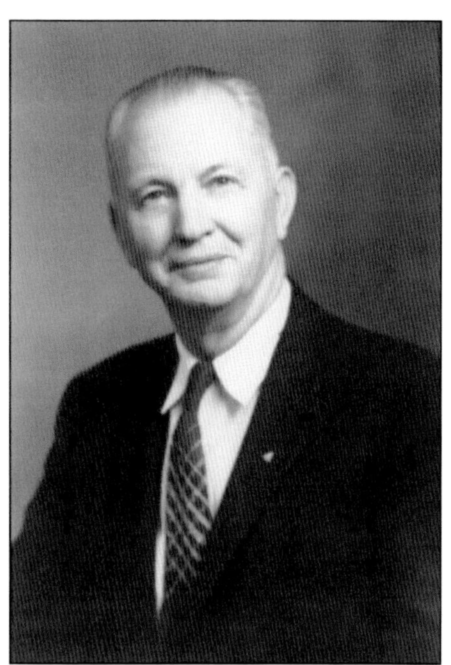

Prof. Charles T. Gabbert accepted the position as superintendent of the elementary schools in 1936. He had a hand in just about every project concerning the youth. He was active in many civic organizations, such as American Legion, Boy Scouts, and fraternal organizations. He was on the board of the recreation center and was an assistant for the civil defense housing division during World War II. He received many awards for his work improving education, such as a lifetime membership in the Illinois Congress of Parents and Teachers. He retired in 1962 after 26 years as superintendent.

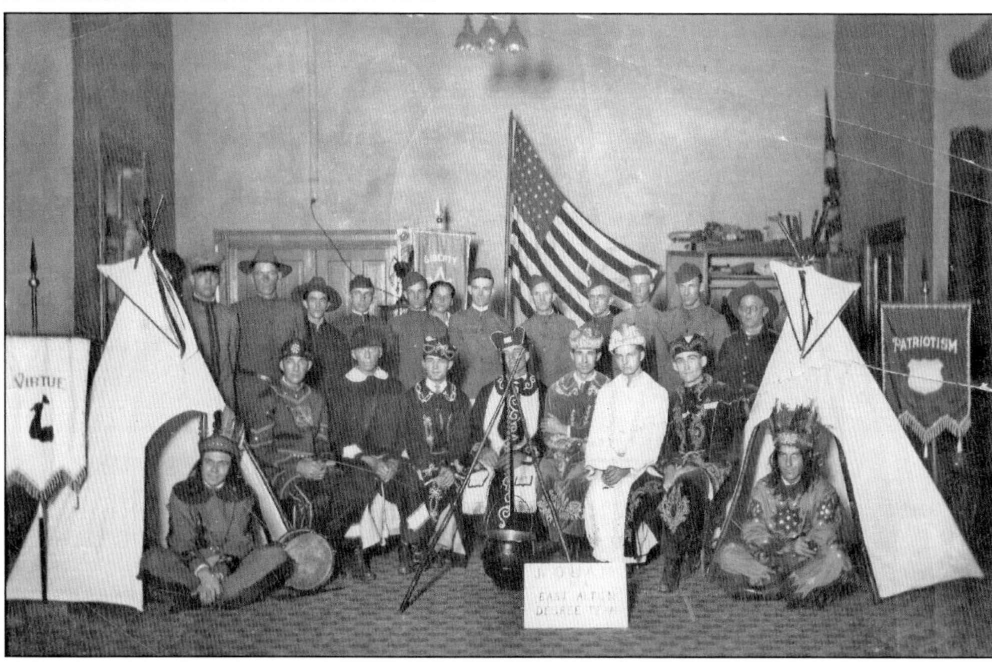

The Junior Order of United American Mechanics (OUAM) Drill Team of East Alton performed throughout the area in the early 1920s. The OUAM carried army-surplus rifles. Their goal was to protect schools, the Bible, and the United States. They would go to schools to perform and hired Chief White Eagle and his tribe members to perform with them. The organization was dissolved after World War II. Some of the people in the photograph were identified as John Unterbrink, Ray Haven, Alvin Cannedy, Leo Johnson, Bill Ringering, Albert Unterbrink, Everett Miller, Perry Johnson, Elmer Schoniswise (back row, second from left), and J.B. Harrison. The exact placement of the other people is not known. (Courtesy of the Ringering family.)

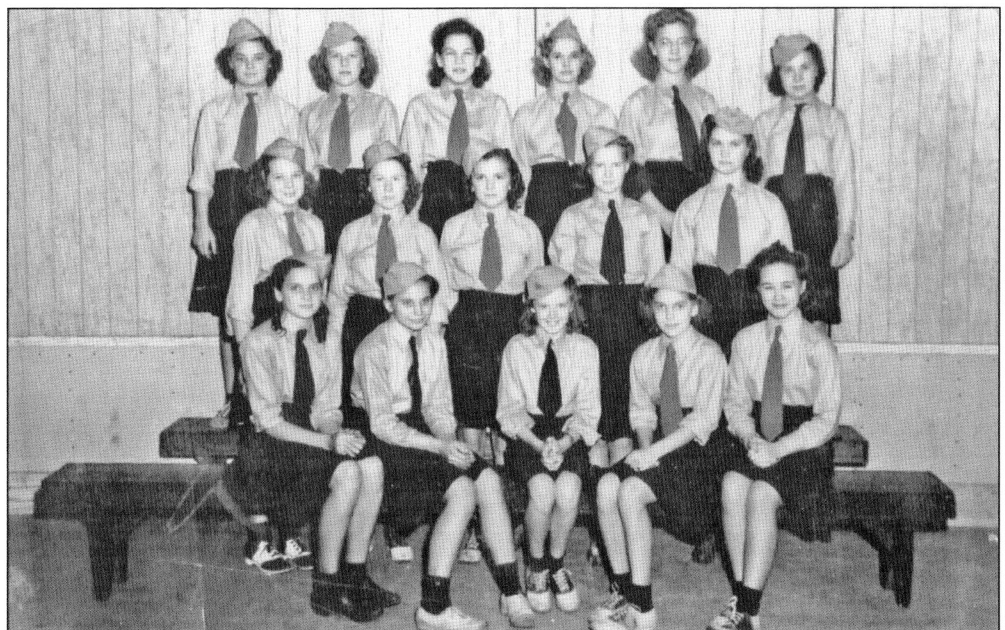

The East Alton Club sold World War II bonds and stamps. This photograph was taken at the Ritz Theatre on West St. Louis Avenue. From left to right are (first row) unidentified, Joan Jackson, Dolores Tweedy Kessler, Colleen Dorsey, and unidentified; (second row) Arianne Ringering Lynch, two unidentified, Meva Johnson Hartsock, and ? Alvarez; (third row) four unidentified, Betty Damsey Feers, and unidentified. (Courtesy of Dolores Kessler.)

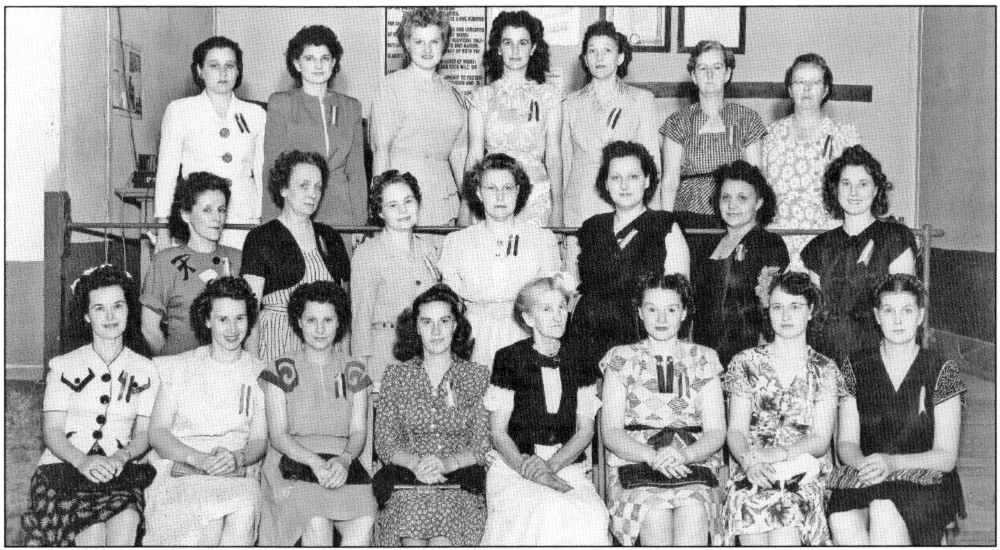

Pictured are the Daughters of America, May Flower Council Number 5, Edith Smith Class of June 1946. Daughters of America was organized in 1912 by women in the village. It was a national organization of members having an ancestor who helped to secure the independence of the United States. Some of the members recognized in the photograph include, from left to right, (first row) Iva Wildt, Billie Wildt, Gwen Parker, unidentified, Edith Smith, and three unidentified; (second row) six unidentified and Marguerite "Sis" Keasler; (third row) all unidentified. Also pictured, though placement is unknown, are Eurea Lawrence, Ada Jones, and Bonita Walmsley.

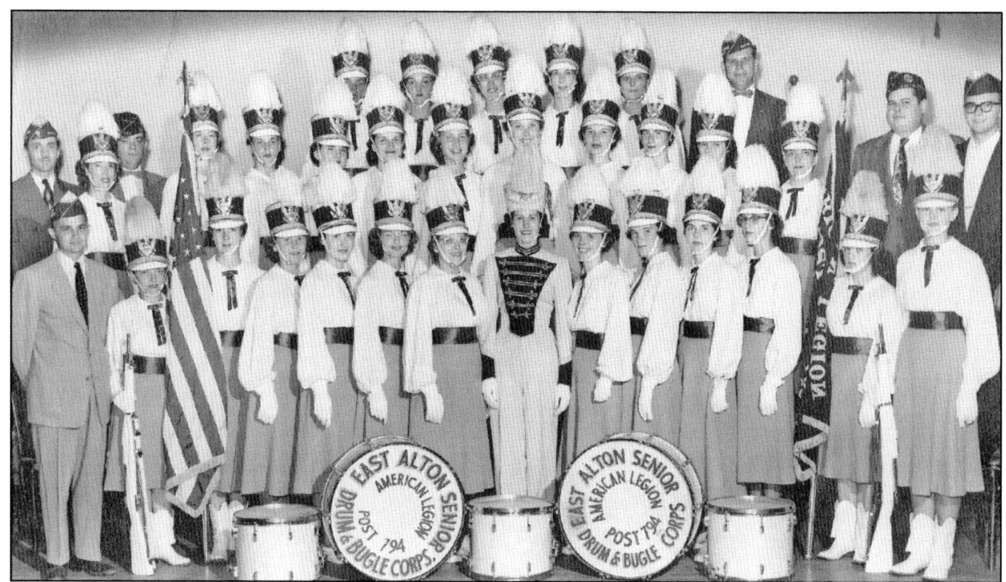

The Drum and Bugle Corps was organized in 1950 by girls over 21. The girls performed at various functions and in competitions, doing intricate marching patterns while playing an instrument. The people in the picture are unidentified.

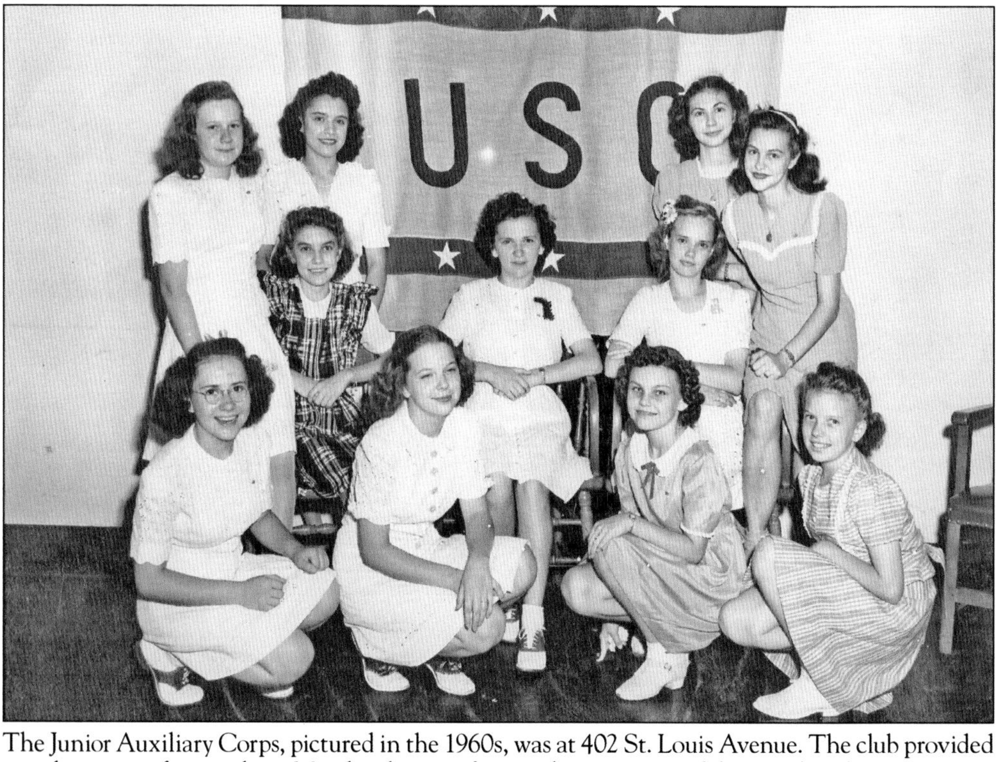

The Junior Auxiliary Corps, pictured in the 1960s, was at 402 St. Louis Avenue. The club provided social activities for members. Membership was free, with 80 percent of the members being Western workers. From left to right are (first row) Mary Ellen Means, Aria Ann Ringering, Lois Dorsey, and Latherina Darr; (second row) Colene Dorsey, Erma Parker, and Lucille Talkington; (third row) Virginia Hanks, Alice Fears, and two unidentified. (Courtesy of Annabell McPeak Gibson.)

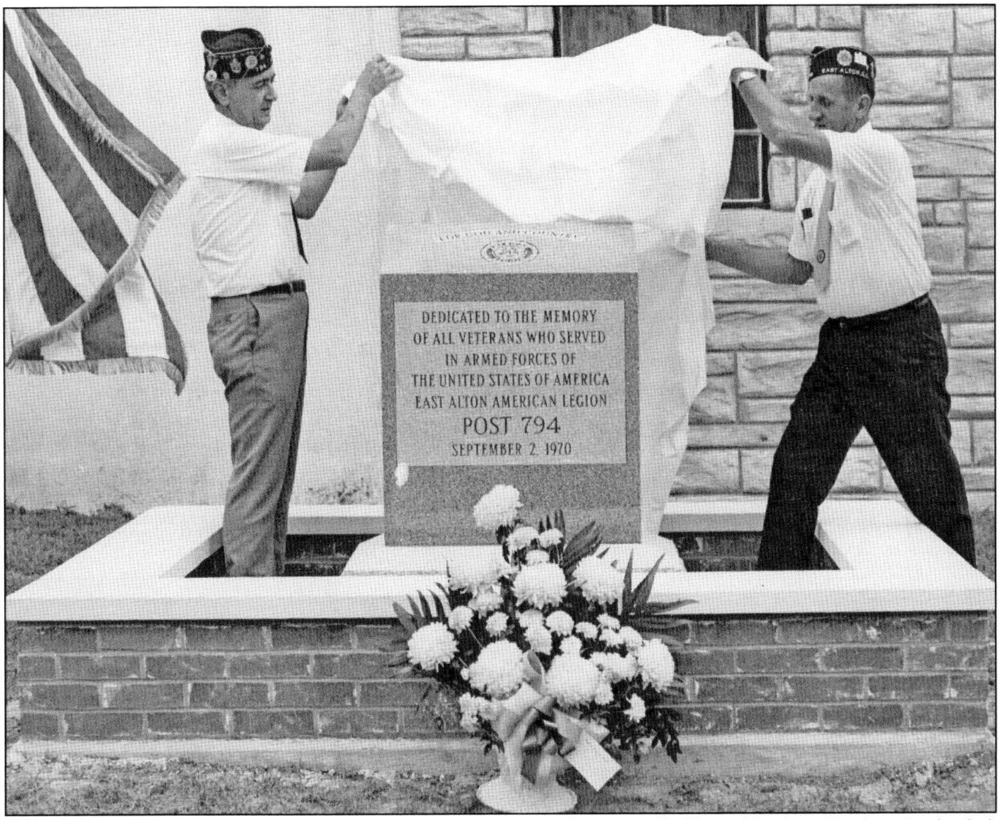

East Alton American Legion commander Henry (Hank) Watts (left) and Robert Richie Sr. (right) unveiled the Veterans War Memorial, dedicated by American Legion Post 794 of East Alton, on September 2, 1970. Commander Henry Watts was the master of ceremonies, and Mayor Frank Keasler gave the welcoming address on behalf of the city and all city officials. Ervin Bettman, past 5th Division commander of the American Legion, was the speaker. (Courtesy of Rosella Watts.)

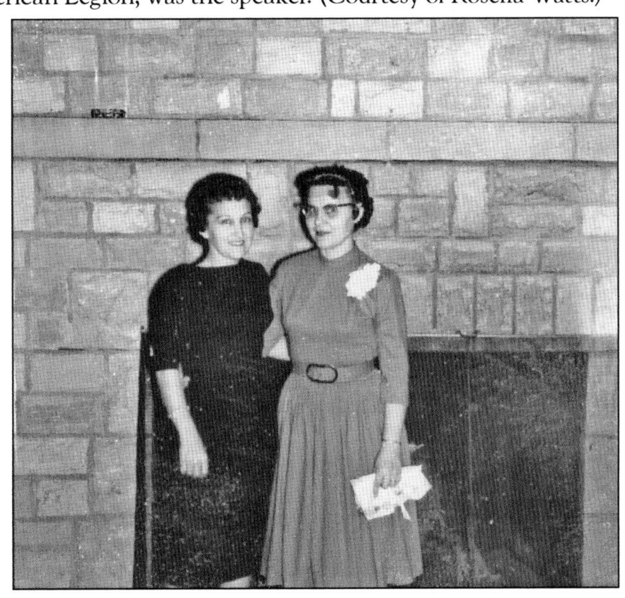

The Mothers' Club was organized in 1935 to help families struggling during the Depression. The club provided food for needy families and helped schools by providing supplies for the classes, sewing band uniforms, and other useful projects. The club was disbanded in 1977. Rosemary McCartney was president in 1959 and 1960. Pictured are McCartney (right) with an unidentified woman (left). (Courtesy of Pat Staley, daughter of Rosemary McCartney.)

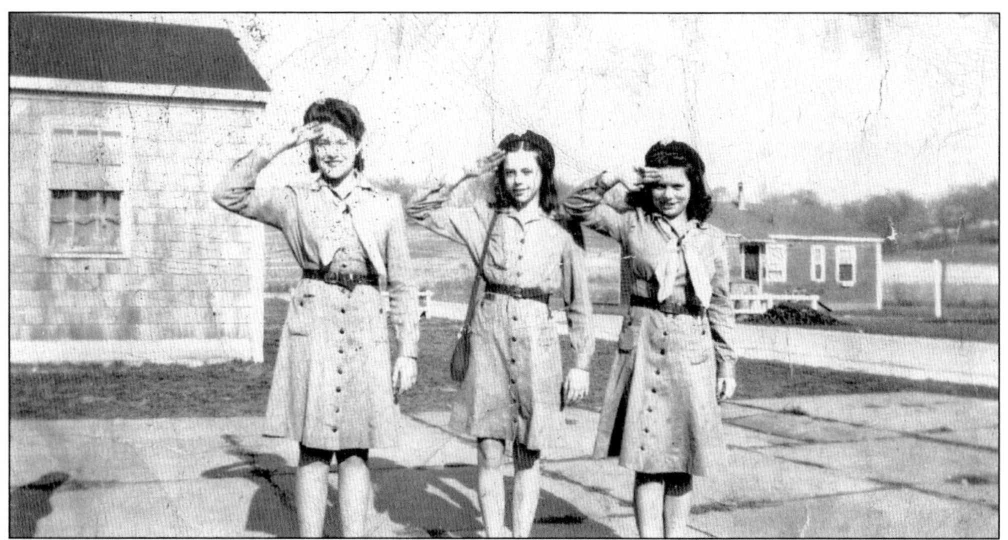

The Girl Scouts is a guiding organization that teaches girls to think of others before themselves and to do a good deed every day. Pictured from left to right are Donna Tillery, Dorothy Gibbs, and Wanda Downing at 679 Whitelaw Avenue in 1946. (Courtesy of Sharon Waggoner.)

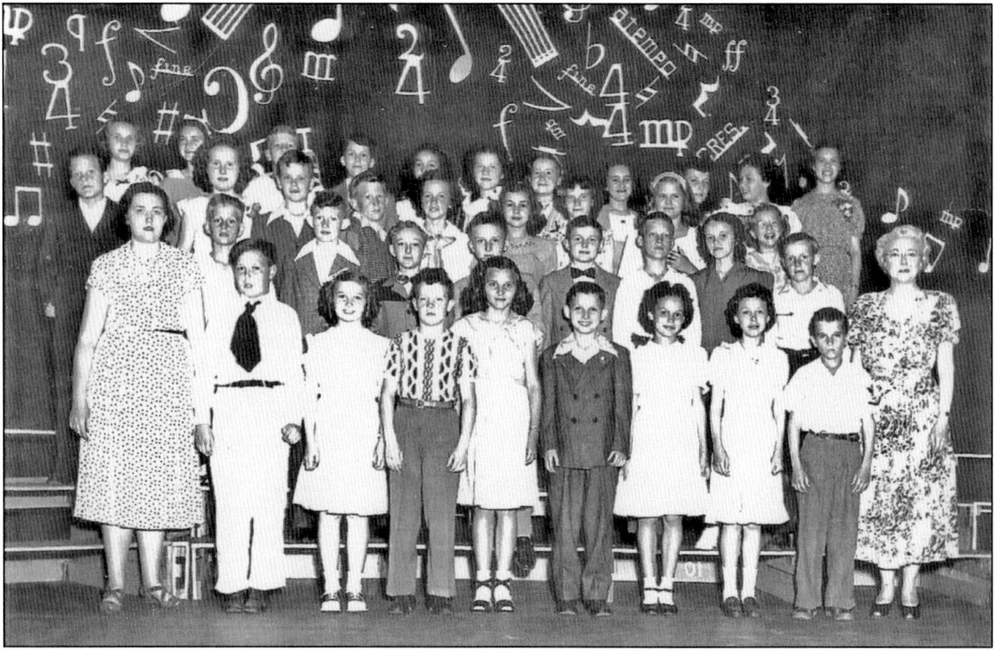

Pictured is the sixth-grade chorus of the Blair, Lincoln, and Washington Schools in 1949. From left to right are (first row) Olive Paddock (teacher), Gabriel Bourland, Joan Taylor, John Fry, Sondra Beckwith, Joe Ackerman, Loretta Haydon, unidentified, Bobby Ridenhauer, and Mildred Dunlope (teacher); (second row) unidentified, Bob Anthony, Ted Lotz, Tom Richardson, Lindell Walkington, Elgin Henson, Donna Ballard, and Bobby Abner; (third row) Gary Mowrey, unidentified, Jerry Autry, Ron Malley, Norma Jean Barnett, Janet Barnett, Sharon Blair, and two unidentified; (fourth row) Patricia Ledbetter, Patsey Plummer, Bobby Williams, Bobby Howard, Judy Terpening, Lorna Stone, unidentified, Janice Melvin, Judy Helm, Dixie Hall, and Janet Lee Brazier. (Courtesy of Ted Lotz.)

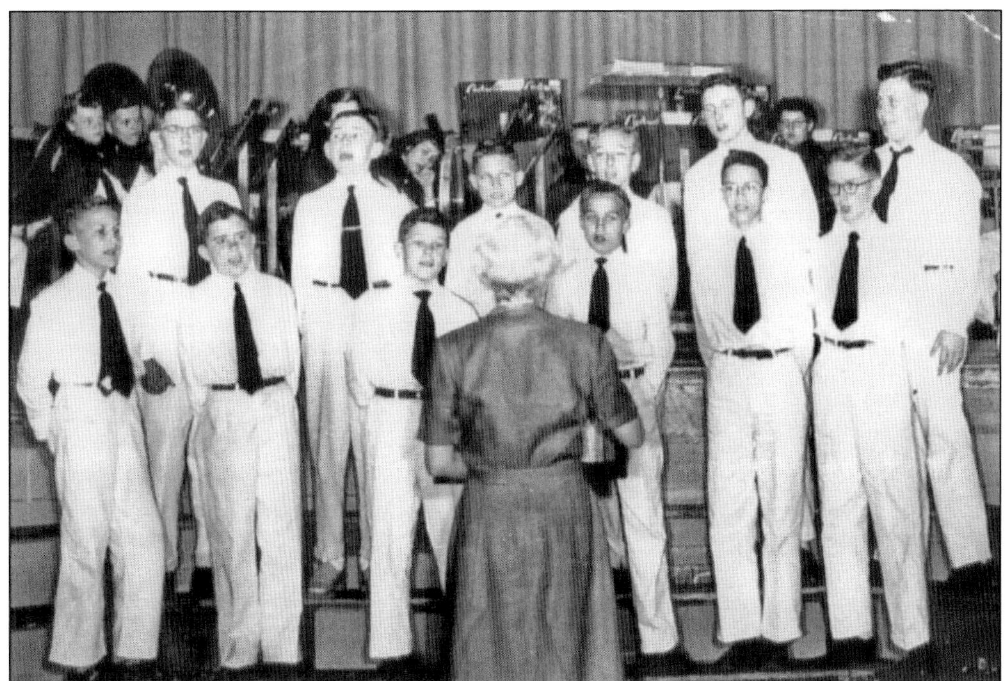

Members of the East Alton Junior High School seventh- and eighth-grade boys' ensemble are pictured in 1952. From left to right are (first row) Charles Hinson, Alfred Leavell, Bill Mathis, Mildred Dunlope (teacher), Charles Miller, Bob Howard, and Tom Richardson; (second row) George Probst, Jimmy Ray, Joe Ackerman, Ted Lotz, Lindall Walkington, and Gabe Bourland. (Courtesy of Ted Lotz.)

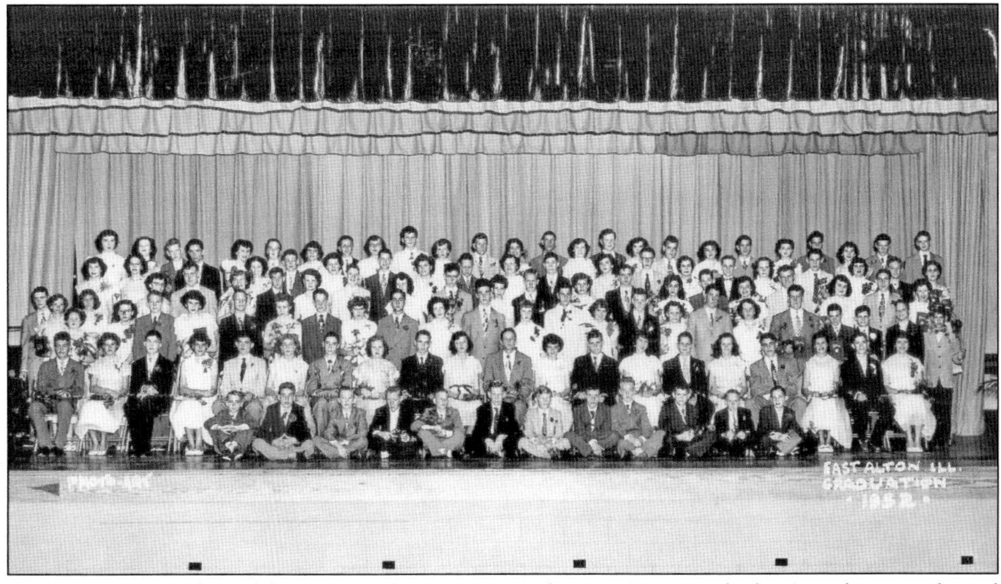

The first class graduated from East Alton Junior High in 1952. A total of 123 students graduated that year. (Courtesy of Ted Lotz.)

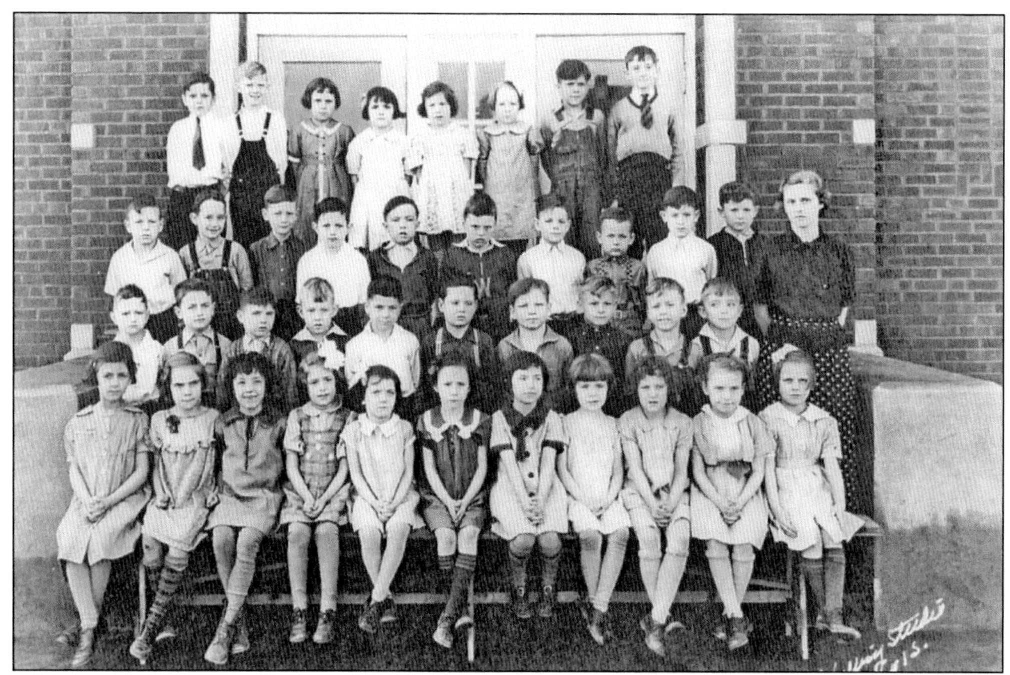

This picture is of the 1936–1937 second-grade class at the Blair School, the first after the addition was built in February 1936.

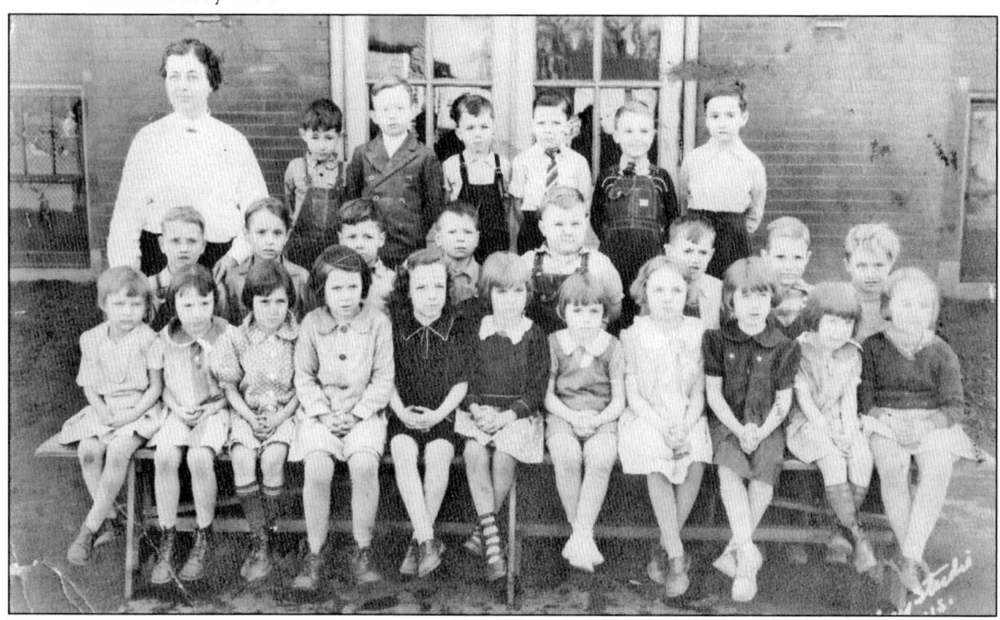

Lincoln School One B students are pictured in 1937. When school started, students began the grade number and letter B. In January, passing students went to their grade number and letter A. Some of the students identified, from left to right, are (first row) Esther Rhyne, Wilma Vannoy, Virginia Hanks, and eight unidentified; (second row) Jim Haycraft, Clarence Basham, Trenton Lyle, Raymond Fry, Clyde Hockett, Bill VanPreter, and two unidentified; (third row) ? Treece (teacher), Wayne Brady, unidentified, Quinton "Squeak" Booten, Dale Perry, unidentified, and Forest Taylor. (Courtesy of Quinton "Squeak" Booten.)

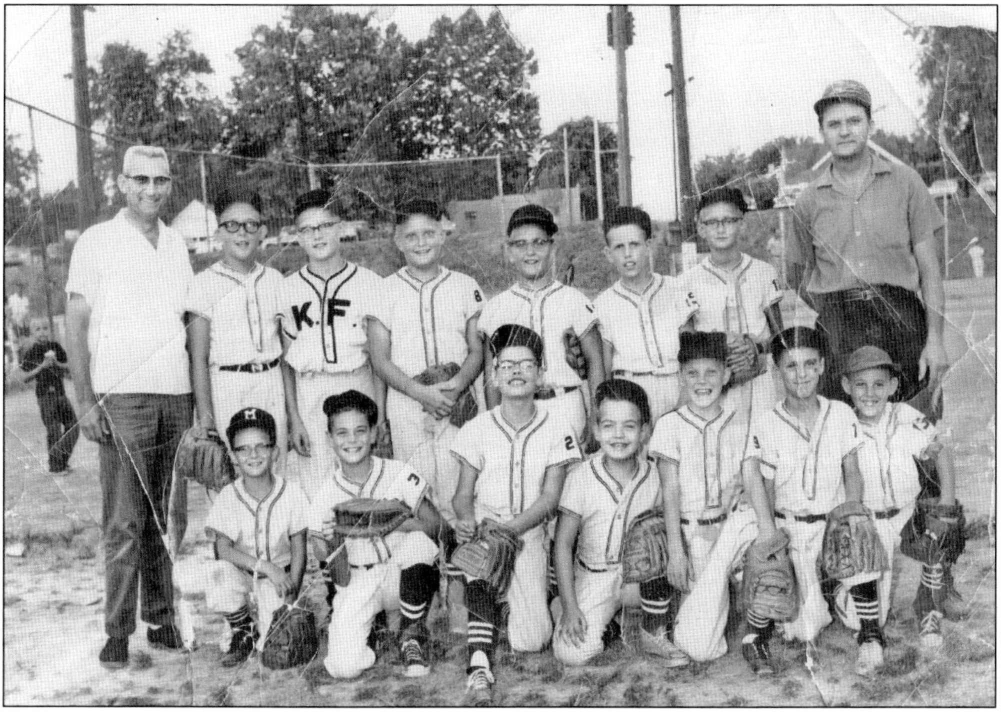

The recreation and park department sponsored Little League baseball at VanPreter Park. Pictured are members of one of the teams in 1964. From left to right are (first row) unidentified, Larry Dewese, unidentified, David Wieneke, Dickie Dawson, David Partridge, and unidentified; (second row) coach Jim Brenner, Scott Turnbaugh, Scott Arnold, Jim Kania, Phil Keasler, David Brenner, Rodney Boren, and manager Emil Kania.

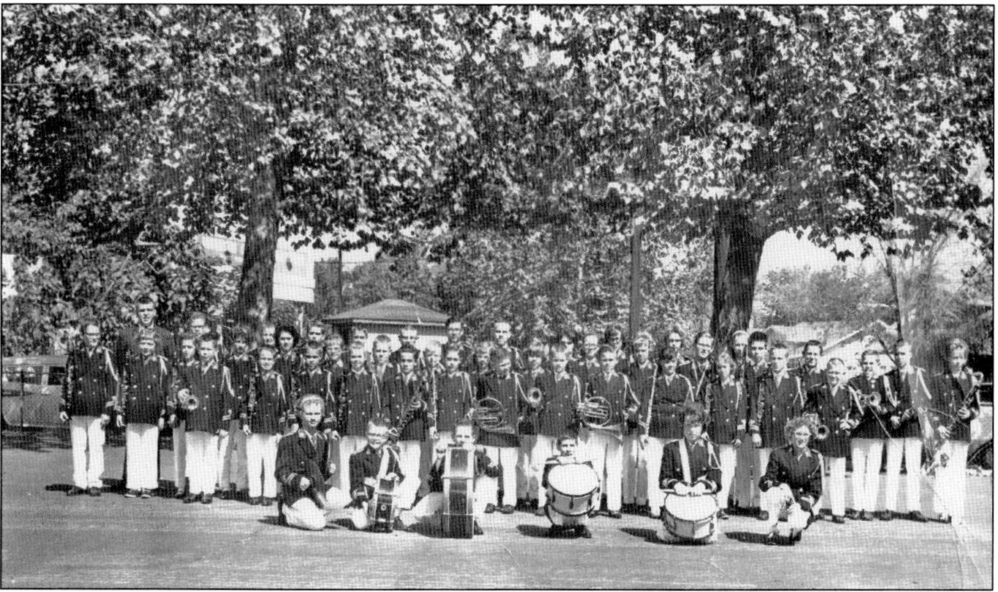

The East Alton Junior High band members posed for this photograph in the fall of 1963. The band was formed by Leroy Dalhaus in 1938. Dalhaus and the Parent-Teacher Association purchased material to make band uniforms. The Mothers' Club sewed the uniforms.

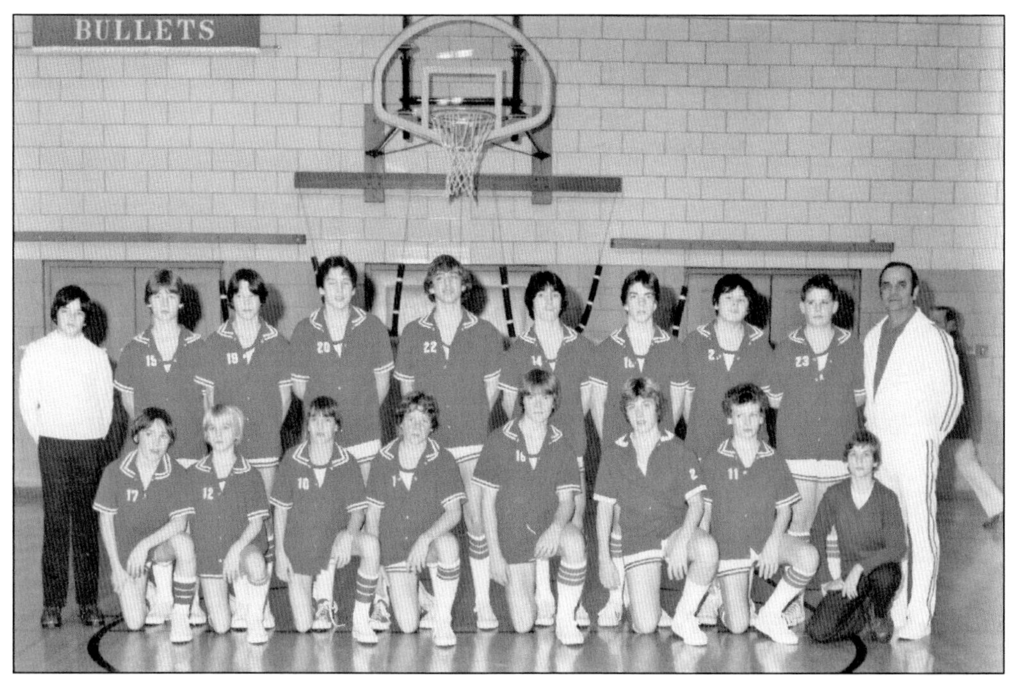

Pictured is the East Alton Bullets basketball team around 1978. From left to right are (first row) Darren Carlisle (17), Scott Richie (12), Shawn Barnard (10), Phil Tierney (1), Vince Opper (16), Brett McCory (2), Scott Knight (11), and Steve Stockton (manager); (second row) David Trujillo (manager), Dennis Krieb (15), Derek Estes (19), Michael Ringering (20), Scott Downing (22), Tony Lohagen (14), Steve Campbell (18), Tracy Roe (2?), John Smith (23), and coach Paul Palermo.

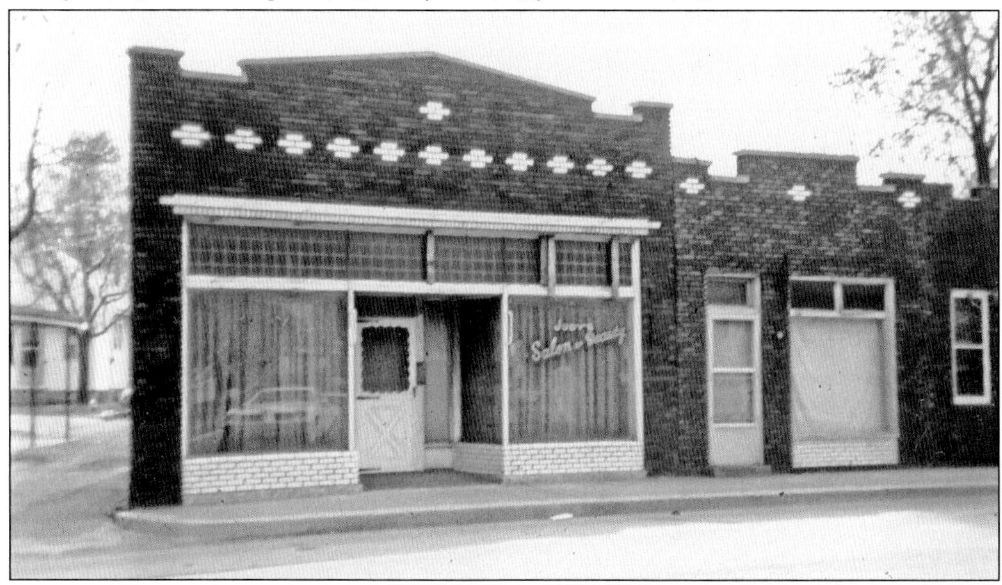

The public library was established in November 1935. On May 18, 1936, the library board leased the building on the right from Ben Hodges at 212 Edwardsville Road (now East St. Louis Avenue) for $400 per year. The first books were purchased in 1936 from Frances Mook. The library was open to the public three days a week in late 1936. In February 1954, the library served as a collection center for Truth Dollars, a campaign for Freedom Week, to finance Radio Free Europe.

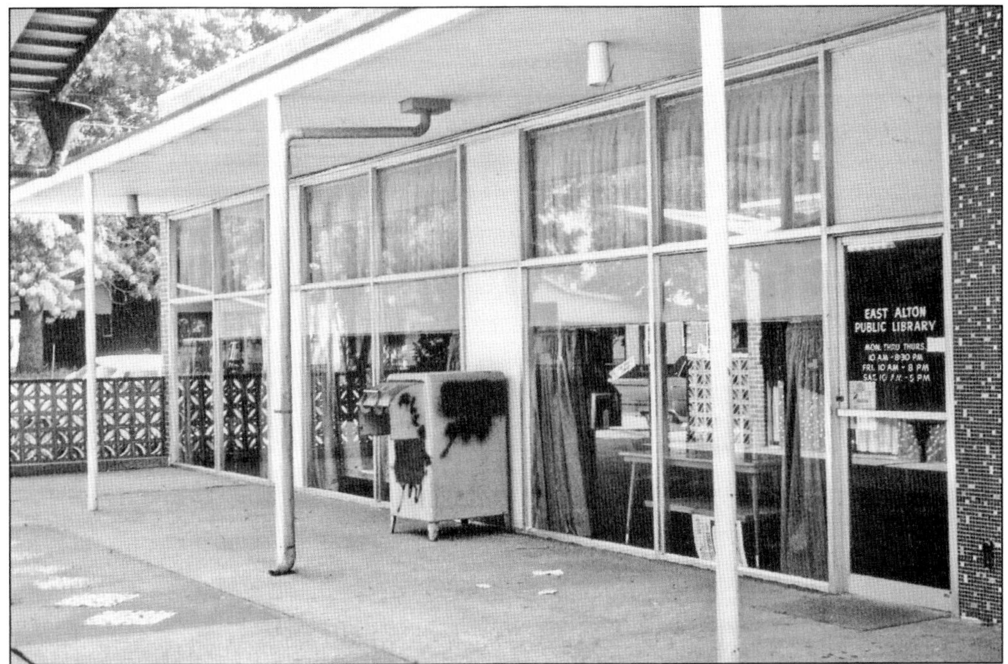

Requiring a larger space, the library moved to its second location in 1960. The library was housed in a store building in Wilshire Mall until November 1976, when it moved to the current location on Washington Avenue and Third Street.

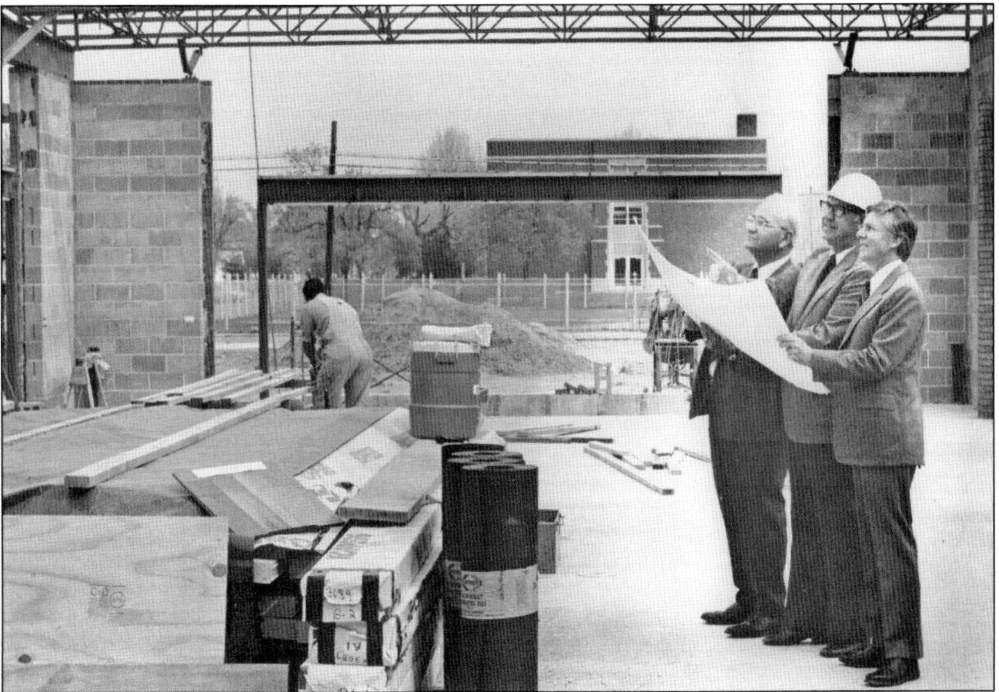

Ground breaking for the new library occurred on September 3, 1975. Overlooking the plans for the new library are board member Jerome Podesva (in the foreground), an unidentified contractor, and Mayor Frank Keasler. In the background is the Blair School, which was razed in 2001.

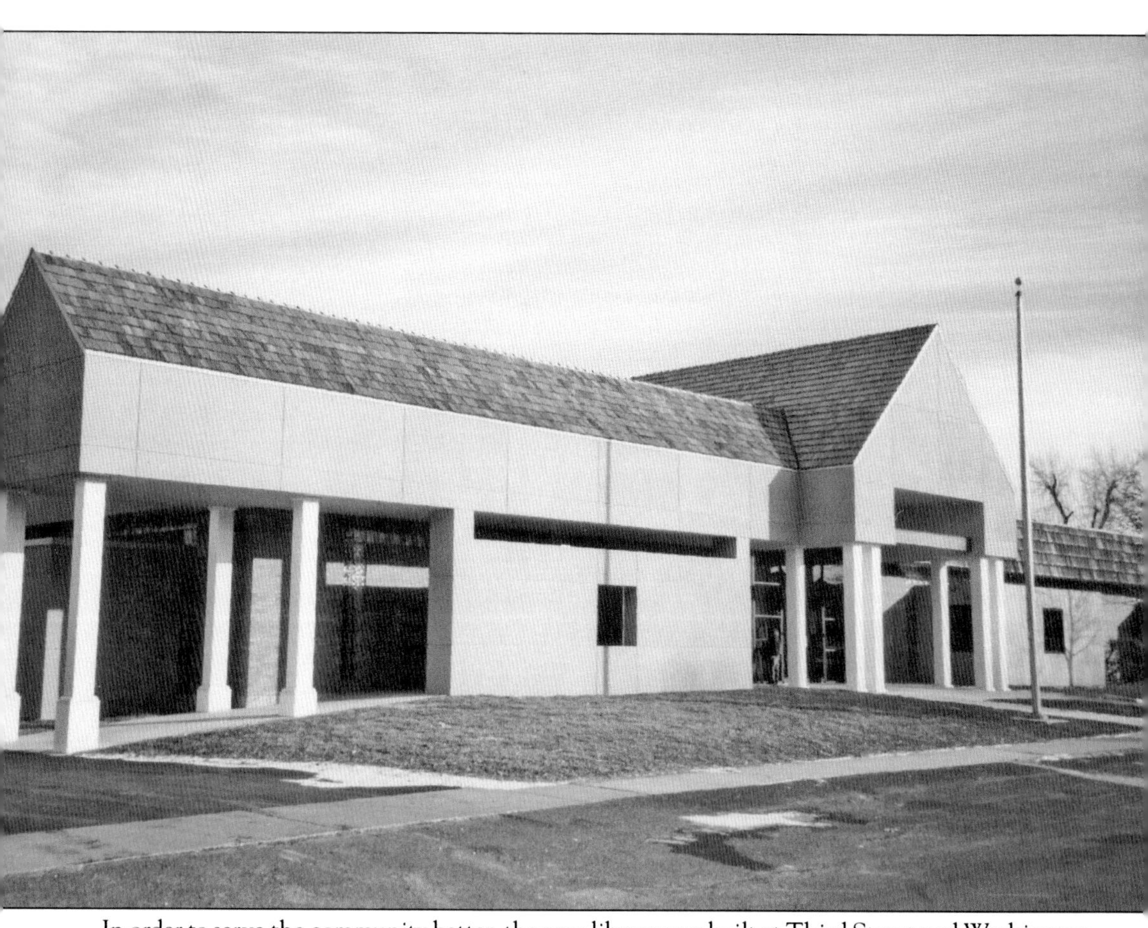

In order to serve the community better, the new library was built at Third Street and Washington Avenue. It opened in November 1976, and in 1995, an addition was built onto the current library to provide room for new technology and an area for young children.

Eight

Industrial Might

The railroads and the location of the Wood River were influential in East Alton's growth. The area was rich in clay and sand, which allowed the Stoneware Pipe Company to manufacture products made of clay. By 1907, Beall Brothers was the largest manufacturer of miner tools and heavy equipment in the United States.

The most beneficial business was the Equitable Powder Company, founded in 1892 by Franklin Olin. Equitable manufactured black powder for use in the coal mines of southern Illinois. In 1898, Olin formed the Western Cartridge Company, producing shotgun ammunition, as a sideline. In 1916, Western Cartridge started the brass division, producing brass for shells and firing caps used in the war. Because of the rapid growth of the brass division, in 1923, Western Cartridge built a cast shop containing 10 electric furnaces. In 1931, it purchased the Winchester Repeating Arms Company and controlled the largest plant producing firearms and sporting ammunition in the world. In 1935, Olin merged the two companies, forming Winchester-Western. Through the years, the company has expanded and merged with other companies, becoming the Olin Corporation. From 1897 through 2007, Olin has been the major employer in East Alton. In 2007, Olin Corporation sold the Brass Division to Global Brass and Copper Holdings Incorporation. Since 2004, the Olin Corporation has been moving some manufacturing of its Winchester products from East Alton to Oxford, Mississippi.

The Illinois Power Company built a power plant on the Mississippi River in the 1940s, providing much-needed power to East Alton and surrounding towns. Illinois Power sold the power plant, and over subsequent years, it has been sold several times. Dynegy Power purchased the plant in February 2000 but closed it in 2016.

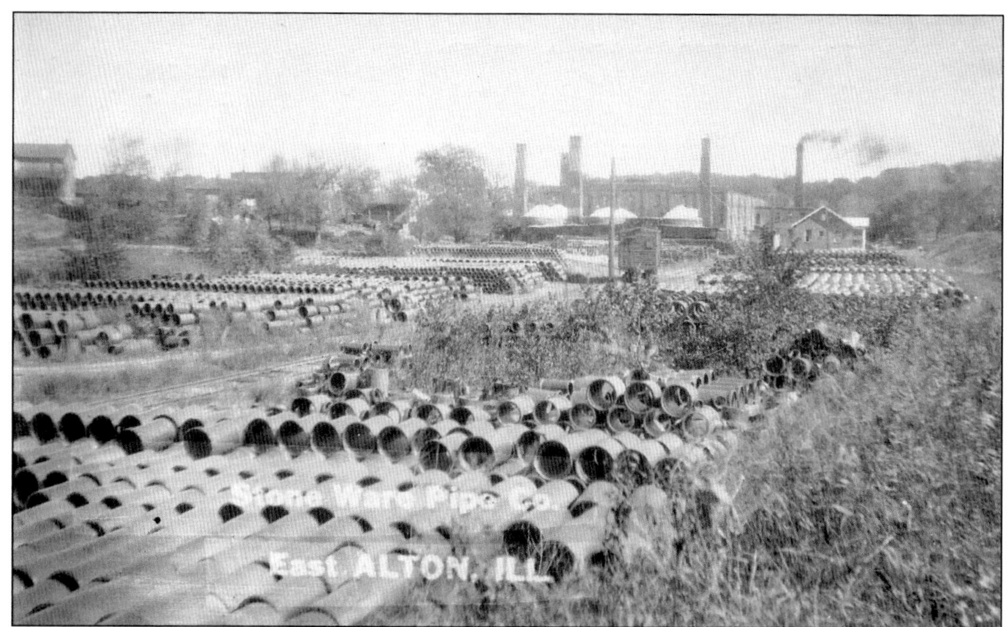

The area around the Wood River was rich in deposits of clay and sulfur, providing minerals necessary for Emerald's industries. The Western Fire Brick Company was built near the east edge of Emerald. In 1870, the company was purchased by Alfred F. Foster, M.H. Boals, and John W. Koch and renamed the Stoneware Pipe Company. It manufactured chimney pipe, tops, bricks, sewer pipe, drain tile, and flue linings. The plant was destroyed in the flood of 1902.

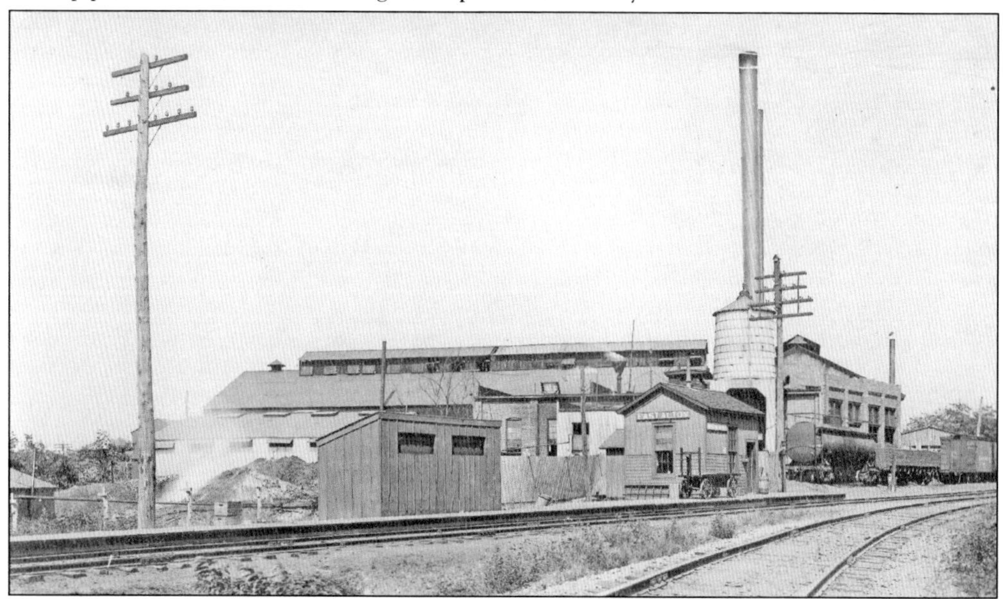

In 1904, Charles Beall started the C.L. Beall Manufacturing Company, producing a variety of tools. This company was sold in 1917. The Beall brothers continued to start and consolidate companies that manufactured shovels, mining and railroad tools, as well as automobile accessories. They closed the mining tool operation in 1928. Beall Tool Manufacturing is located on North Shamrock Street and produces replacement parts for farming implements. This picture was taken in the early 1900s.

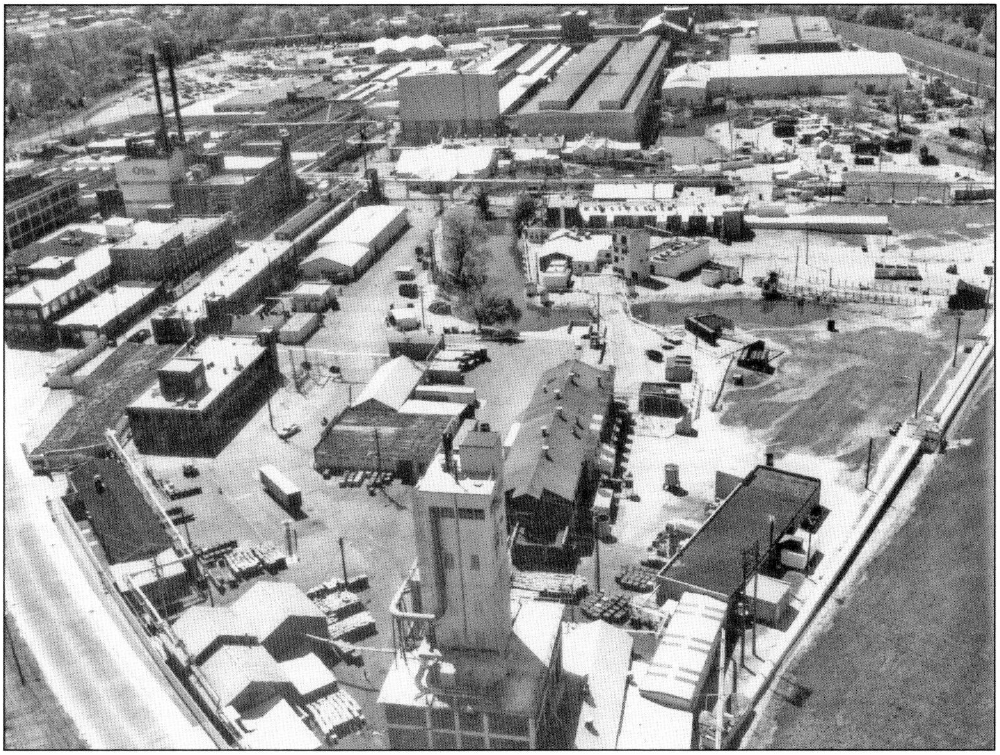

This is an aerial view of Winchester's operation in 1993. The Winchester plant in East Alton was the largest single plant location in the company and one of the largest employers in the area. It was the headquarters for two of the company's operating groups, Winchester and Olin Brass.

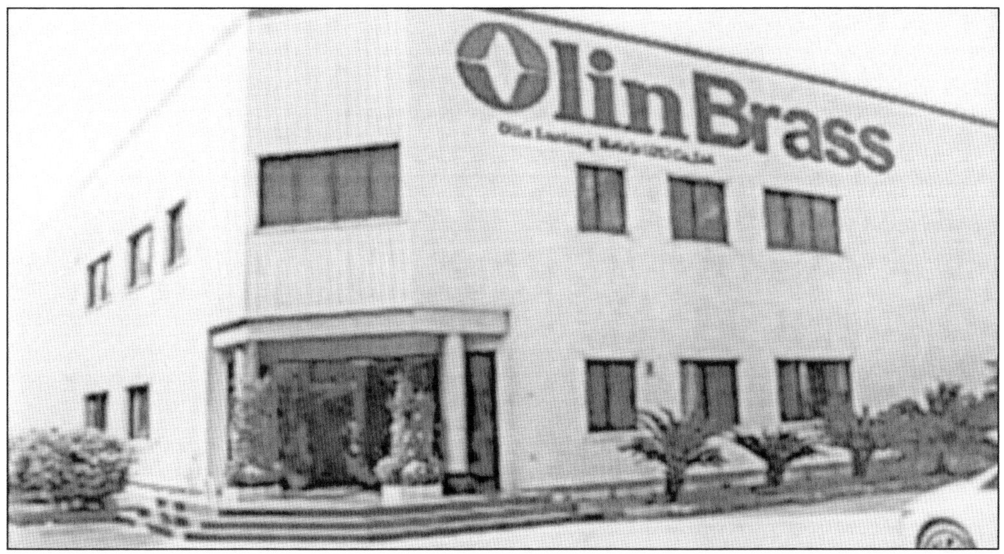

In 1916, the Western Cartridge Company built a brass mill and cast bars of copper alloy to supply munitions for World War I. In 1942, significant casting capacity was added to the Western Brass Mill in support of growing military demand for World War II. Olin Brass scientists have continued to developed copper alloys that have fueled technological breakthroughs and product innovation for companies in a wide range of industries.

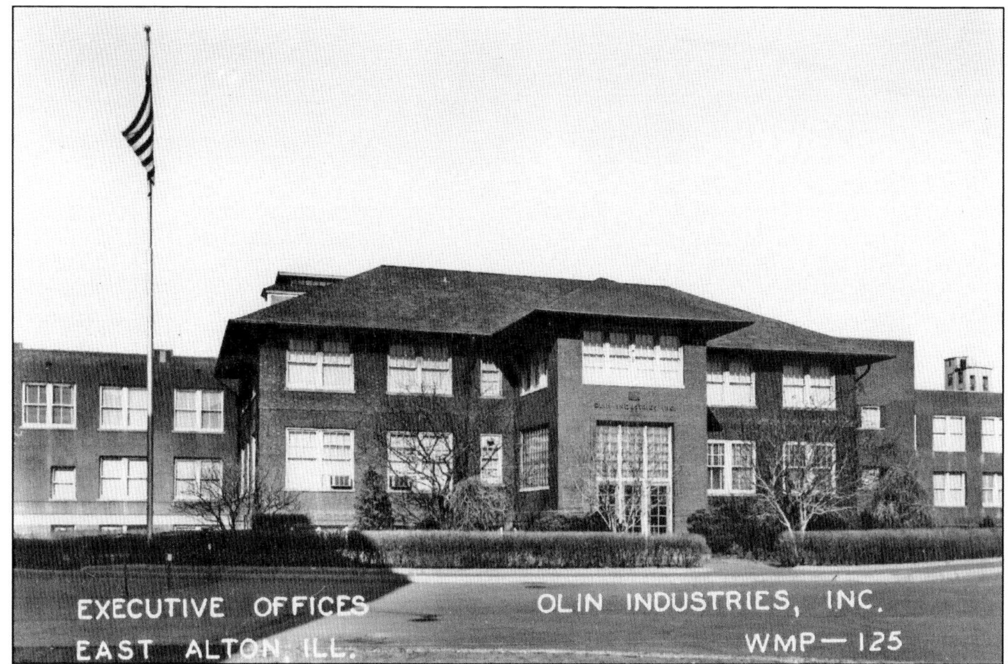

The second executive offices of Olin (Winchester Division) were located on North Shamrock Street at the main plant. This office complex was used until around 2007, when Global Brass and Copper Holding, Inc., purchased the Brass Division. Olin's corporate office is located in Clayton, Missouri.

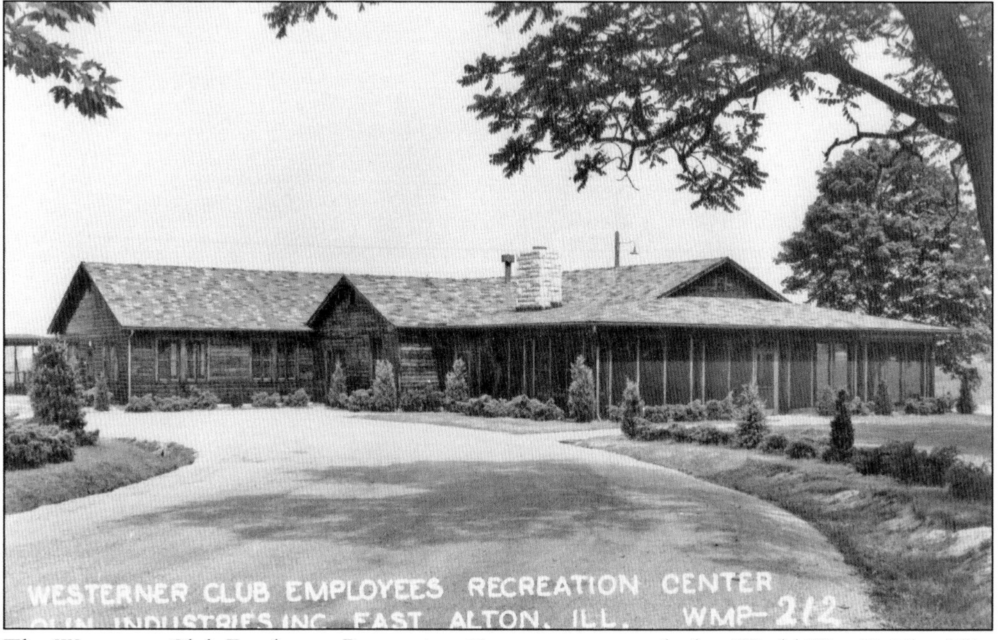

The Westerner Club Employees Recreation Center was created after World War II. The Olin Corporation held yearly employee picnics at the Westerner Club, providing food, drinks, games, and prizes for the employees and their families. The building was also rented to the general public. The Westerner Club was closed in 2007.

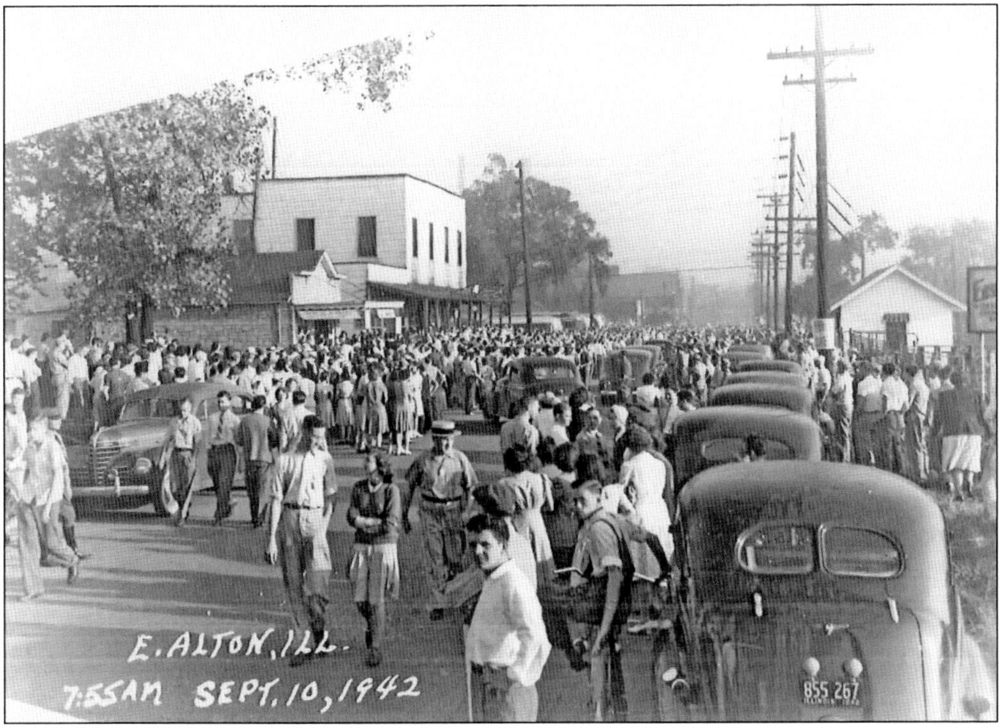

The Olin Corporation's Winchester Division played an important part in winning both World War I and II. Olin was the largest employer in the area, employing several thousand people. This photograph was taken on Shamrock Street during the strike in 1942. There were strikes in 1969 and 2000. (Courtesy of Martha Campbell.)

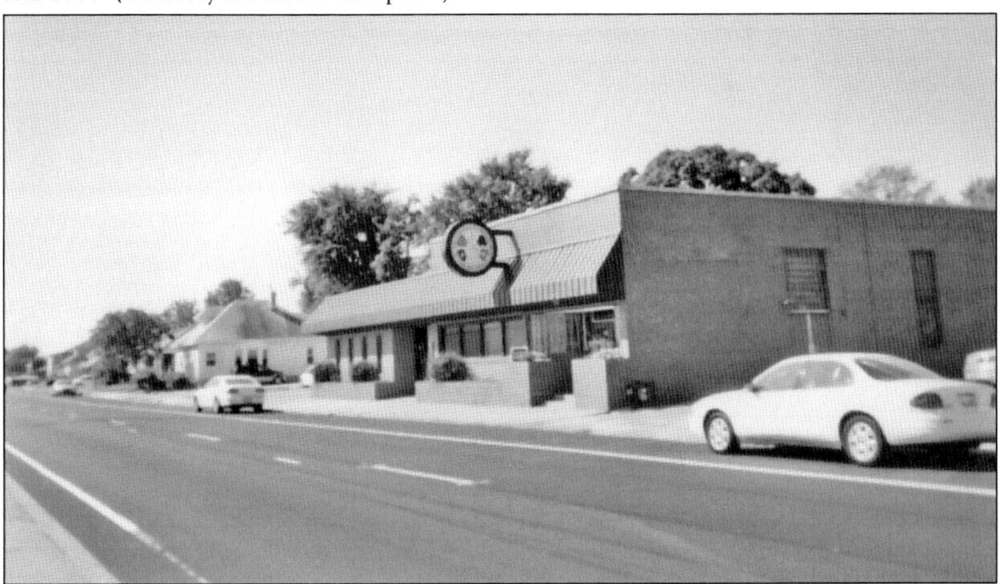

In 1948, the Machinist Union District Nine built a union hall on Shamrock Street. William Hambleton was the business agent for District Nine in 1939 to 1940. After 1940, he moved to the union hall in St. Louis. The business agent was responsible for helping to negotiate contracts. (Courtesy of Dorothy E. Hambleton Hartman.)

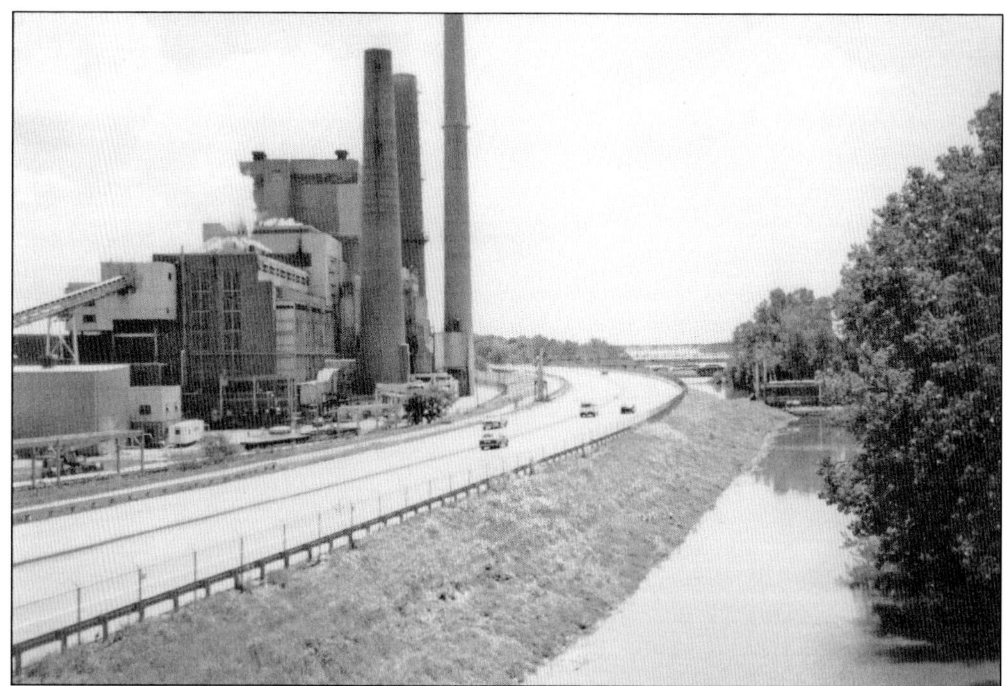
Illinois Power started building the power plant along the Mississippi River in 1947, with the first unit going online in 1949. Dynegy purchased the plant in February 2000 and continued to provide power for the locals. Dynegy closed the plant in July 2016. (Courtesy of Margaret Funke.)

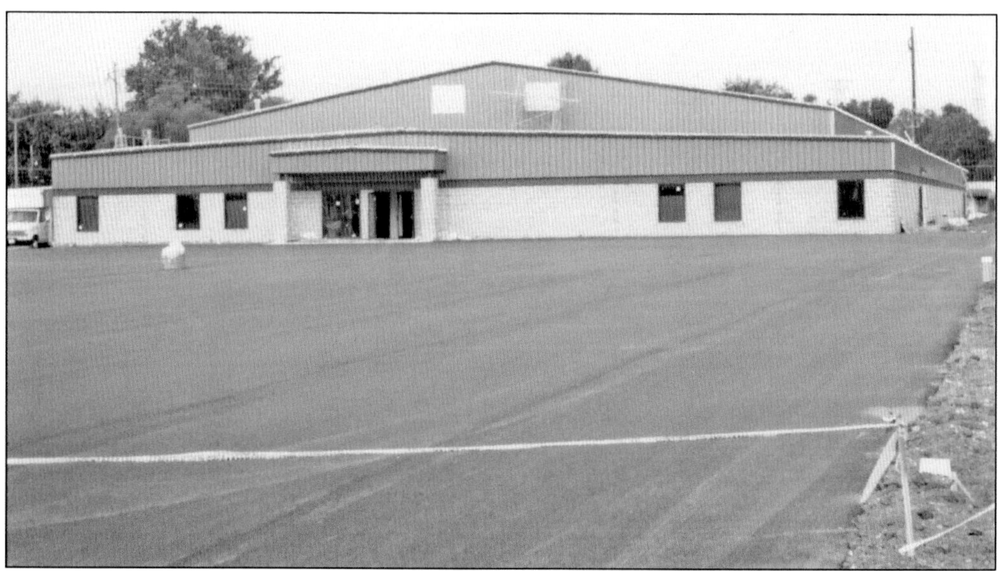
The East Alton Ice Rink was opened on November 18, 1995. It is a year-round indoor ice rink on the east side of the Mississippi River. It houses an NHL-size ice rink and features public skating as well as hockey programs for all age groups.

Nine

The Future Beckons

Pioneers saw the potential of what has been called the American Bottoms. With an abundance of natural resources and the railroad, East Alton flourished. The village is more than business and industry and has been built by strong people. From the pioneer to the spirited entrepreneur, East Alton citizens have served, taught, and led their community to a bright future.

With the changing times, the village has adapted to the needs of the citizens. Housing has been a priority for the past several years, with 90 new single-family homes being built throughout the village, 46 in the new Emerald Ridge subdivision. The water plant has been updated to accommodate a growing population. An ice rink was built to allow indoor winter sports all year round.

Through the years, churches and civic organizations and their members have responded to the needs of the community, promoting, supporting, and assisting in funding and volunteering in projects too numerous to name. Sometimes the efforts are easy to see, as with beautification and park projects, while others are behind the scenes and go unnoticed.

East Alton is centrally located within a few minutes of Southern Illinois University–Edwardsville, Lewis and Clark Community College, and St. Louis Regional Airport. The village is also within an hour's drive of entertainment and cultural venues in St. Louis as well as the St. Louis International Airport, which makes it a perfect place to live.

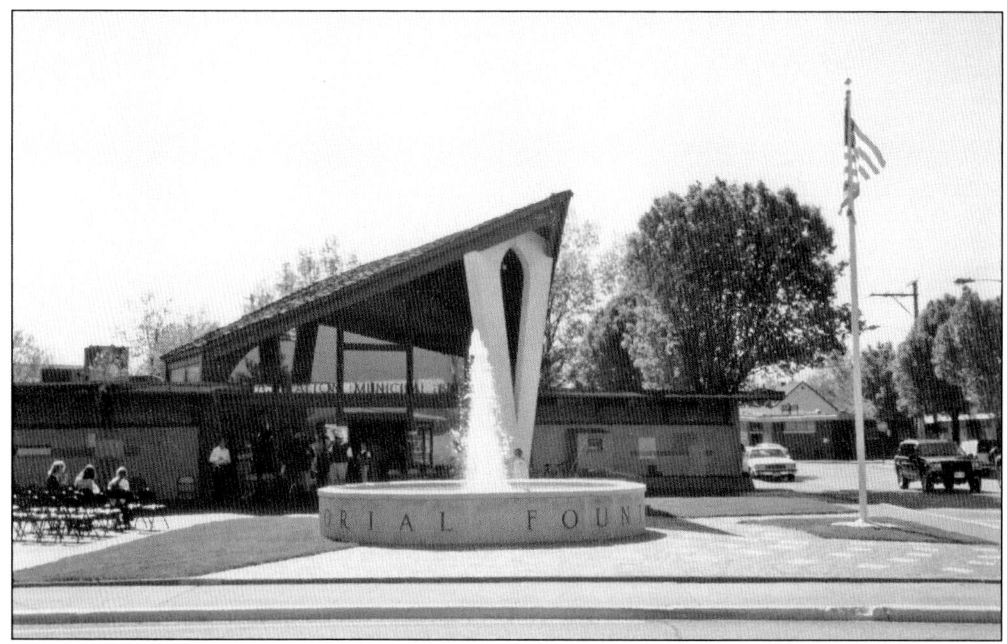

The municipal building was constructed in 1961 without issuing bonds. The bell of the first fire truck, the 1926 Reo, is in the council room at this building. The flagpole was donated by the Rotary Club. In 1998, a memorial fountain and memorial pavers were added near the flagpole. The Beautification Committee created a flowerbed at the hall in 1999.

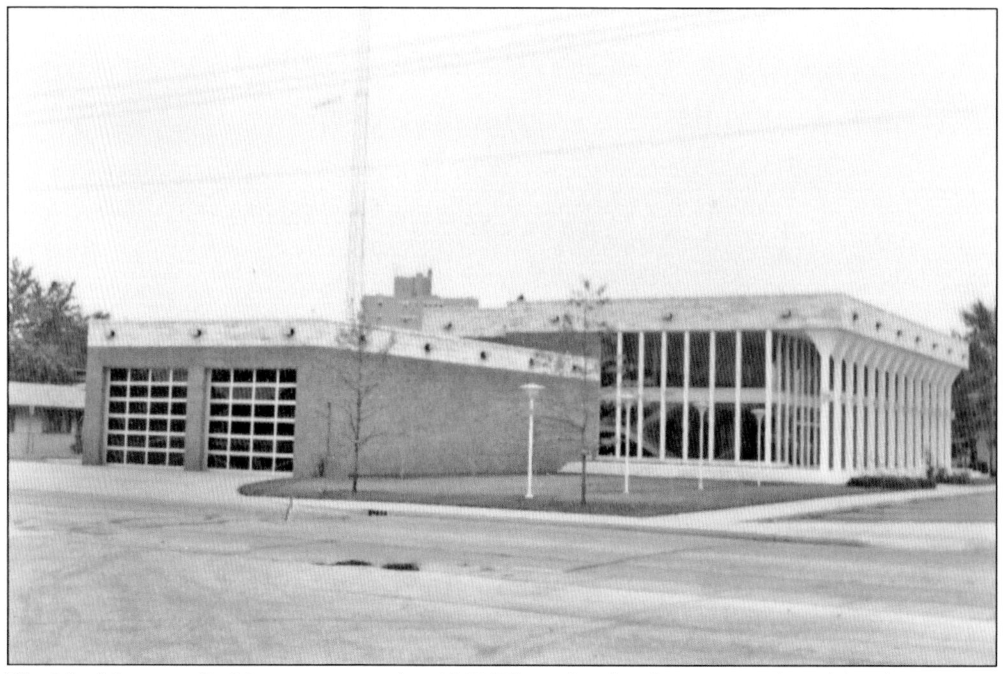

The Vital Services Building was erected in 1969. The police headquarters, jail, and fire department are located here. After the building was completed, Madison County District Court was held here. In the jury room is the first Olin Board of Directors table, which was presented to Mayor Charles VanPreter in 1932. The second floor now houses the East Alton Historical Museum.

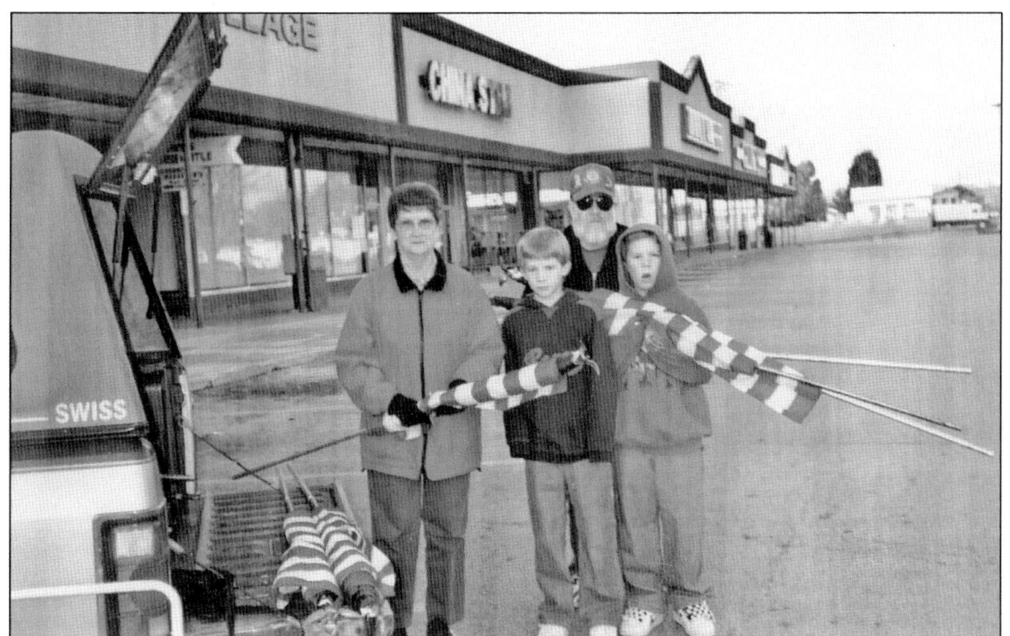

Volunteers from the Beautification Committee placed flags at Wilshire Shopping Center to celebrate Veterans' Day. From left to right are Rosella Watts, Brandon Lawrence, Jonathan Lawrence, and David Wiegand (in the back). (Courtesy of Charlotte Wiegand.)

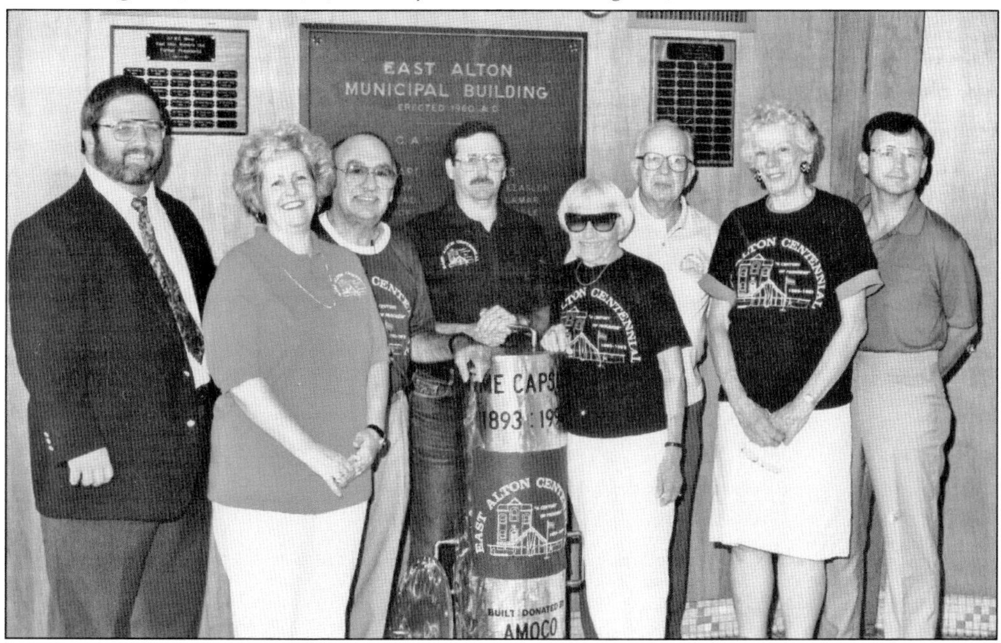

The East Alton Centennial Commission was appointed by Mayor Wayne Buttry. The members of the commission organized an activity for each month from 1992 through the final weekend Centennial Festival in August 1993. After the celebrations were over, a time capsule was buried at the village hall to be opened in 2093. Members of the commission, from left to right, are Phil Keasler, Charlotte Wiegand, Leo Pavish, Rick Newman, Marie Brazier, Lonnie Darr, Barb Nichols, and Mike Gray. Not shown is Debbie Angleton. (Courtesy of Charlotte Weigand.)

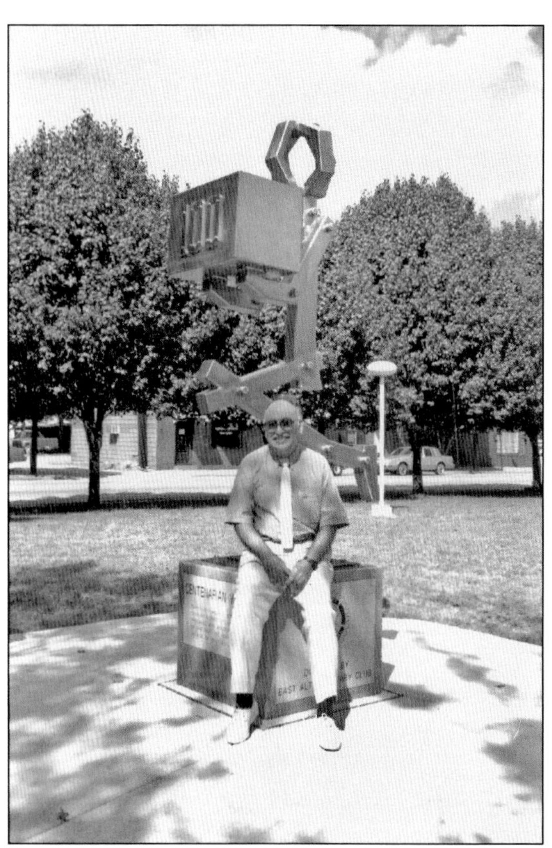

Leo Pavish, a self-taught sculptor, created the *Centenarian Worker*, a static figure that appears to be in motion, carrying into the 21st century the heavy chest filled with 100 years of progress and accomplishments of the village of East Alton. (Courtesy of Dolly Pavish Diaguid.)

The centennial parade kicked off a weekend-long celebration of the village's 100th birthday. The color guard from American Legion Post 794 marched in the parade, followed by vintage cars. (Courtesy of Charlotte Wiegand.)

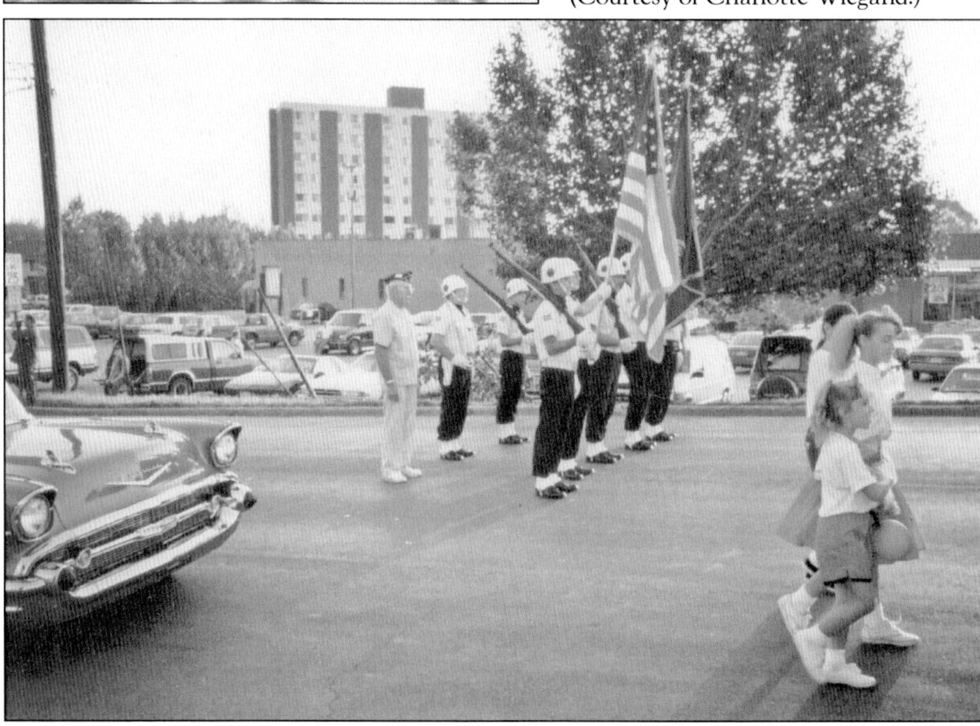

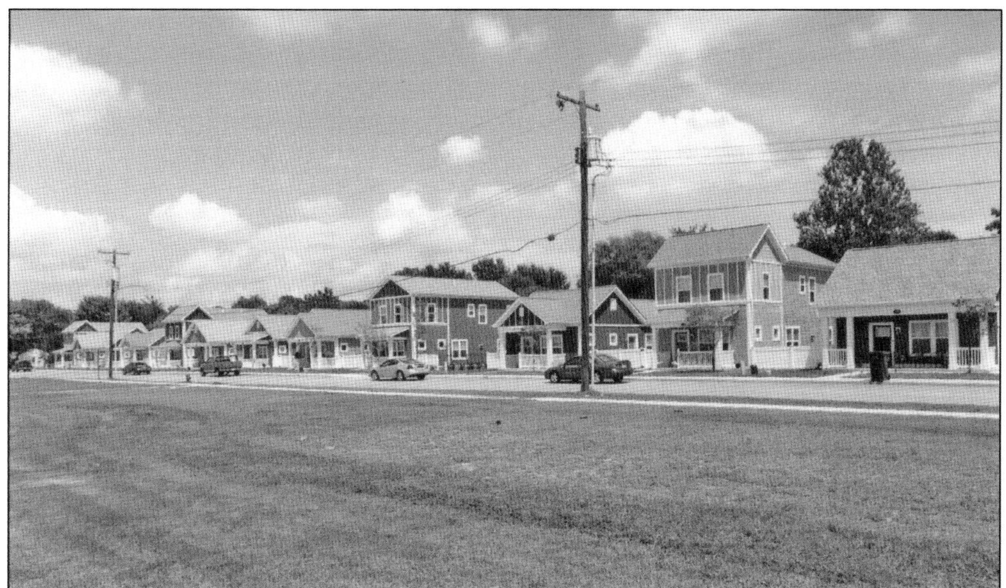

These houses were built in 2013 and 2014 to replace the "Defense Houses" built in 1940. The houses are starter homes for single families, the disabled, and low-income families. The subdivision was named Emerald Ridge after the name of the village before incorporation. (Courtesy of Village of East Alton.)

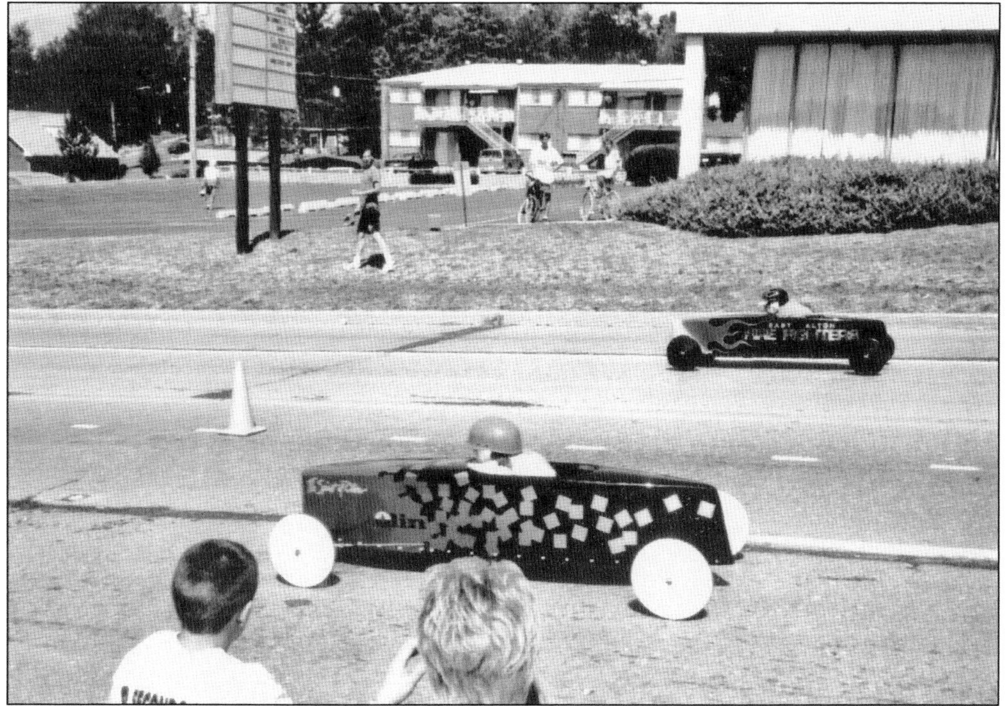

To celebrate the opening and dedication of the new Clark Bridge in Alton, officials requested cities in the area to host activities. The village held a soapbox derby in September 1994. The derby cars started at the top of Berkshire Hill, also known as Job's Hill, and raced down in front of cheering crowds at Wilshire Village. The derby has become a yearly event.

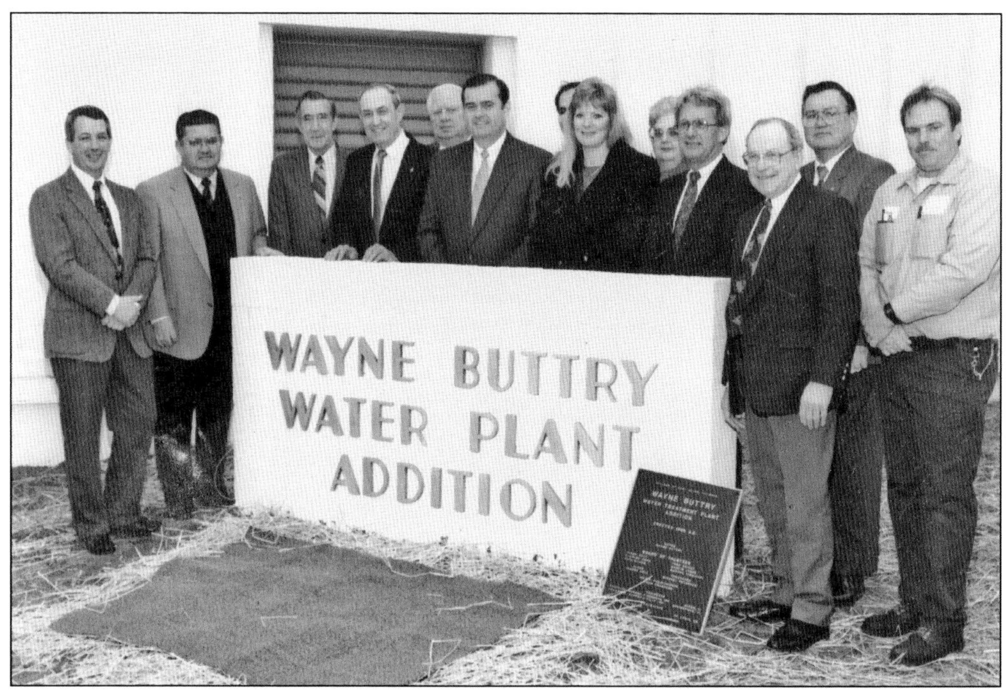

The dedication of the new water treatment plant took place in 1992. Attendees are, from left to right, are (first row) John Byron, Fred Bright, Charles Cope, Marvin Jones, Congressman Jerry Costello, unidentified, architect Charles Sheppard, Mayor Wayne Buttry, and Doug Chambers; (second row) unidentified, Jeanne Holt, and Jim Holt.

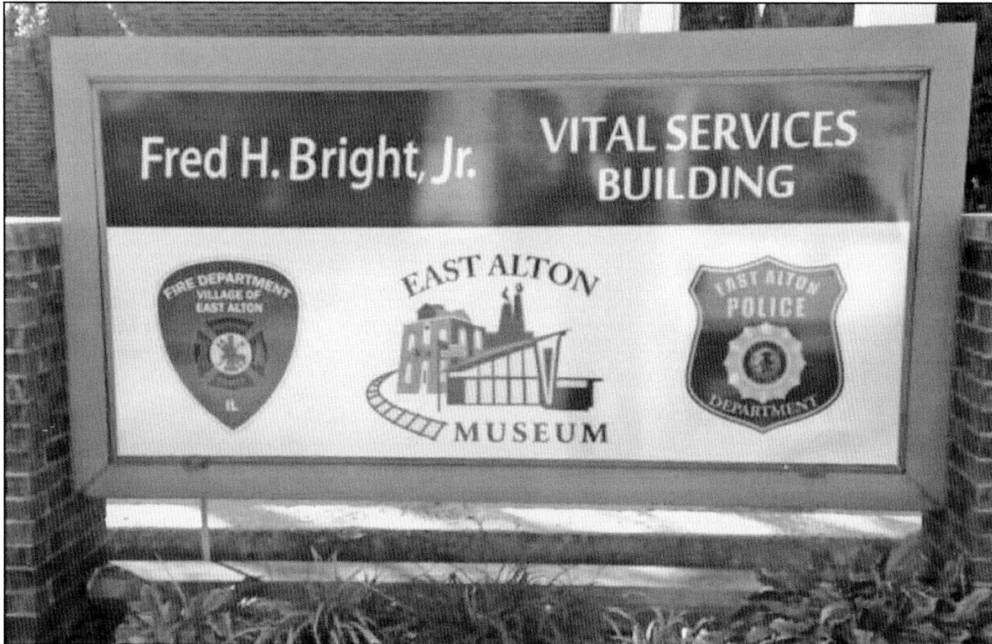

In 2016, the Vital Services Building, constructed in 1969, was dedicated to Mayor Fred Bright. The police and fire departments have operated from this building since it was erected in 1969. The newly formed East Alton Historical Museum was added to this location in 2016.

Ten

Mayors

Although it has taken all citizens to grow the village, from the time of incorporation in 1893, the mayors have led the village's growth from 50 in the early 1800s to around 7,000 today. The mayors and the city council realized the potential of the village and encouraged the residents to start businesses to meet its needs. The dreams of many men and women have been built and met in the lowlands of the American Bottoms.

When he died, Charles VanPreter had served as mayor for over 35 years. As far as is known, at the time of his death, he was the only man in the state to have held the office of mayor for that length of time. He led the village through its largest growth during World War II and beyond.

Serving the citizens of the village has always been paramount, with the mayors taking pride in serving the needs of the community.

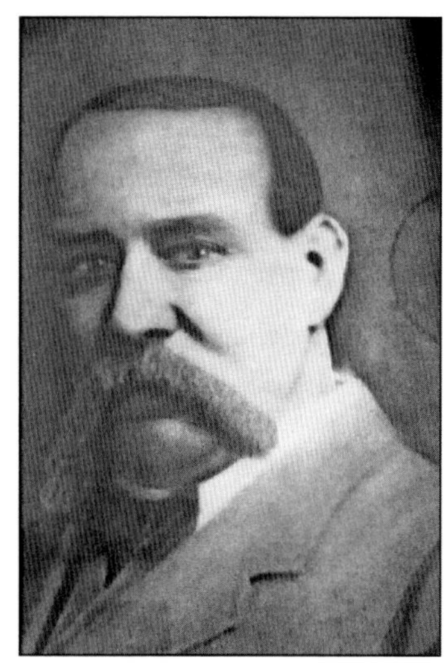
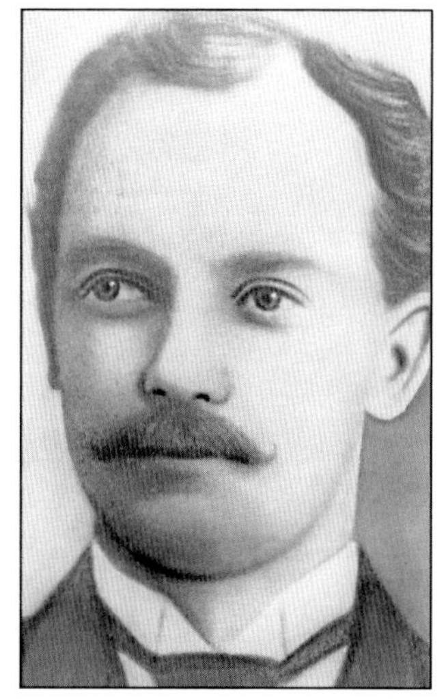
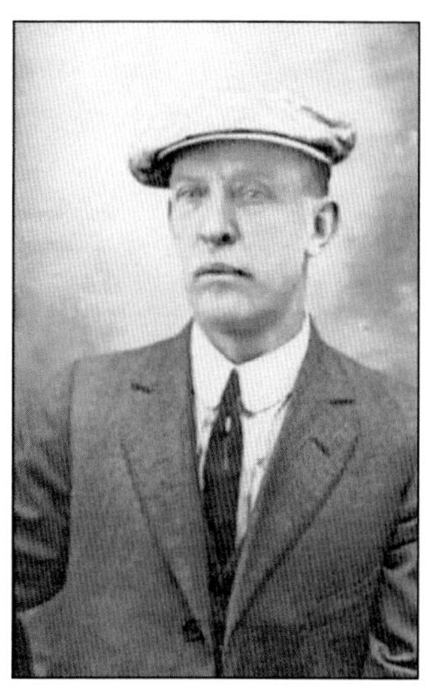
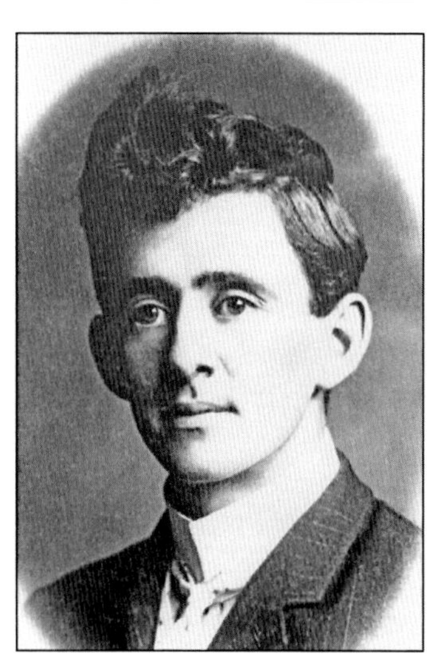
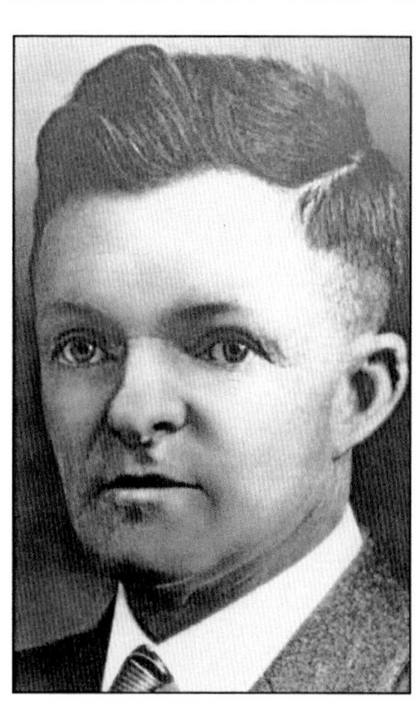
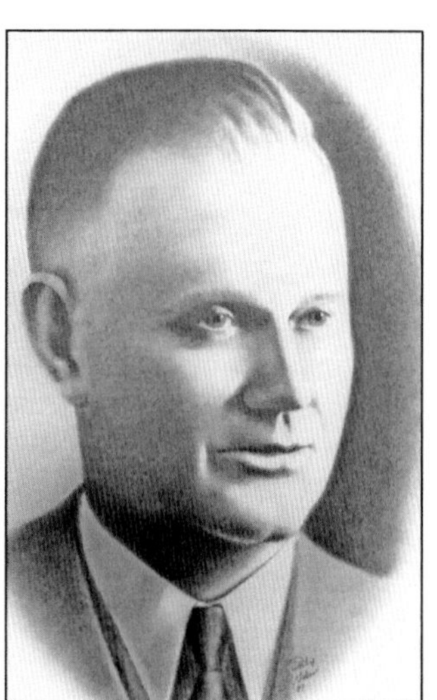
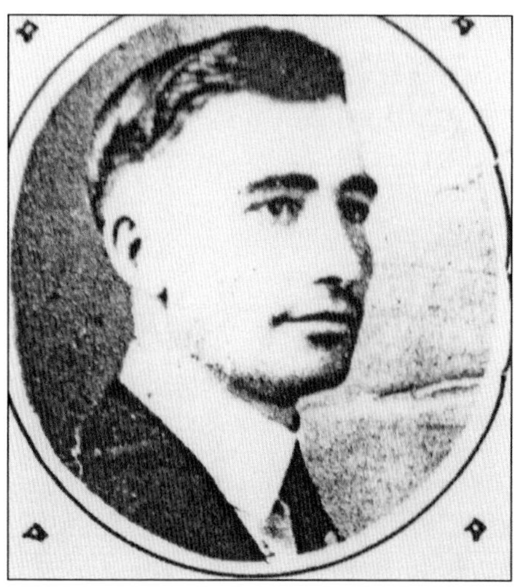

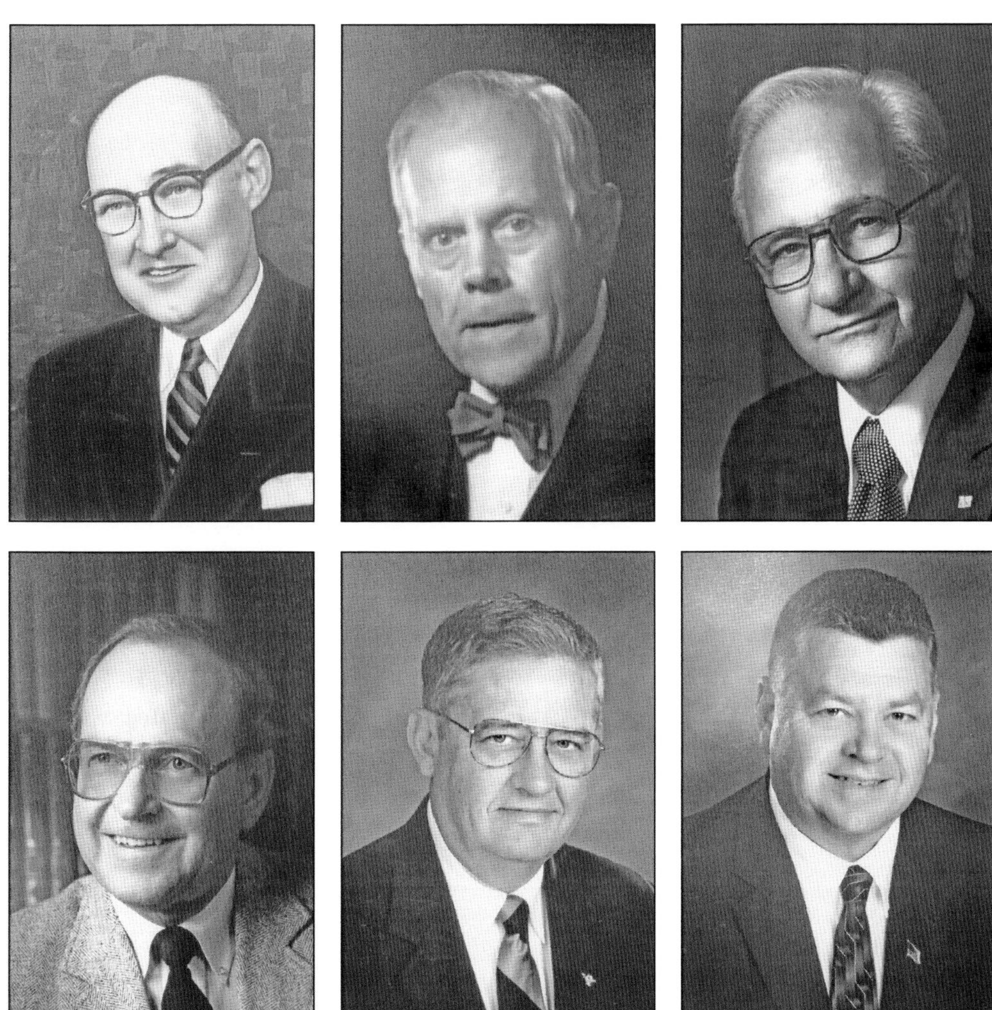

The mayors of East Alton, pictured from left to right and top to bottom, are as follows: (opposite page) David G. Tomlinson, 1893–1896; William Cobb, 1895–1896 and 1902–1905; Thomas L. VanPreter, 1917–1919 and 1923–1925; John F. Kruse, 1919–1921; H.W. Sanders, 1925–1927; Ben Hodges, 1927–1929; and George E. Luman, 1929–1931; Charles A. VanPreter, 1931–1949 and 1953–1970; Otto F. Brazier, 1949–1953; Frank Keasler, 1970–1986; Wayne Buttry, 1986–1997; Fred Bright, 1997–2015; and Joe Silkwood 2015–present. Mayors without photographs available are George F. Smitley, 1896–1897; William F. Henry, 1897–1898; Charles Newton Pence, 1898–1899 and 1901–1902; Frank Teipel, 1899–1900; George W. Wall, 1900–1901; George F. Smith, 1905–1907; R.E. Douglas, 1907–1909 and 1913–1915; R.W. Harper, 1909–1911; Ben Picker, 1911–1913; Henry Eckhardt, 1915–1917; and James Jameson, 1921–1923.

Consistent with our mission to preserve history on a local level, this book was printed in South Carolina on American-made paper and manufactured entirely in the United States. Products carrying the accredited Forest Stewardship Council (FSC) label are printed on 100 percent FSC-certified paper.

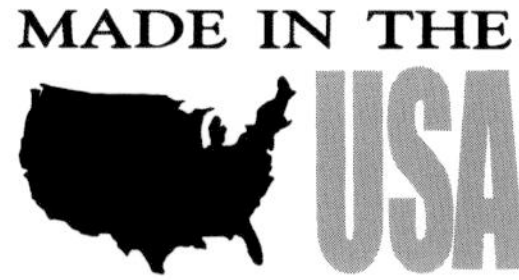